IMAGINING EDEN

BLACK LIVES IN THE DIASPORA:
PAST / PRESENT / FUTURE

BLACK LIVES IN THE DIASPORA:
PAST / PRESENT / FUTURE

EDITORIAL BOARD

HOWARD UNIVERSITY

CLARENCE LUSANE, RUBIN PATTERSON,
NIKKI TAYLOR, AMY YEBOAH QUARKUME

COLUMBIA UNIVERSITY

FARAH JASMINE GRIFFIN, FRANK GURIDY,
JOSEF SORETT

Black Lives in the Diaspora: Past / Present / Future is a book series that focuses on Black lives in a global diasporic context. Published in partnership with Howard University's College of Arts and Sciences and Columbia University's African American and African Diaspora Studies Department, it builds on Columbia University Press's publishing programs in history, sociology, religion, philosophy, and literature as well as African American and African Diaspora studies. The series showcases scholarship and writing that enriches our understanding of Black experiences in the past, present, and future with the goal of reaching beyond the academy to intervene in urgent national and international conversations about the experiences of people of African descent. The series anchors an exchange across two global educational institutions, both located in historical capitals of Black life and culture.

Wendell H. Marsh, *Textual Life: Islam, Africa, and the Fate of the Humanities*

Jarvis McInnis, *Afterlives of the Plantation: Plotting Agrarian Futures in the Global Black South*

Lauren Coyle Rosen and Hannibal Lokumbe, *Hannibal Lokumbe: Spiritual Soundscapes of Music, Life, and Liberation*

Laura E. Helton, *Scattered and Fugitive Things: How Black Collectors Created Archives and Remade History*

For a complete list of titles, please see the Columbia University Press website.

Holy Mountain III, Horace Pippin, 1945. Oil on canvas; 25 1/4 × 30 1/4 in. (64.6 × 76.8 cm). Gift of Joseph H. Hirshhorn, 1966

Cathy Carver, Hirshhorn Museum and Sculpture Garden

IMAGINING EDEN

BLACK THEOLOGY AND THE SEARCH FOR PARADISE

JAMALL A. CALLOWAY

Columbia University Press   *New York*

Columbia University Press
Publishers Since 1893
New York   Chichester, West Sussex

Copyright © 2026 Columbia University Press
All rights reserved

Library of Congress Cataloging-in-Publication Data
Names: Calloway, Jamall A. author
Title: Imagining Eden : Black theology and the search for paradise / Jamall A. Calloway.
Description: New York : Columbia University Press, [2025] | Series: Black lives in the diaspora : past / present / future | Includes bibliographical references and index.
Identifiers: LCCN 2025010791 (print) | LCCN 2025010792 (ebook) | ISBN 9780231209229 hardback | ISBN 9780231209236 paperback | ISBN 9780231557832 ebook
Subjects: LCSH: Eden | Black theology | Liberation theology | Literature—Black authors—History and criticism
Classification: LCC BT82.7 .C35 2025 (print) | LCC BT82.7 (ebook) | DDC 230/.0464—dc23/eng/20250723

Cover design: Milenda Nan Ok Lee
Cover art: Detail of *Holy Mountain III*, Horace Pippin, 1945. Oil on canvas; 25 1/4 × 30 1/4 in. (64.6 × 76.8 cm). Gift of Joseph H. Hirshhorn, 1966. Cathy Carver, Hirshhorn Museum and Sculpture Garden

GPSR Authorized Representative: Easy Access System Europe, Mustamäe tee 50, 10621 Tallinn, Estonia, gpsr.requests@easproject.com

This book is dedicated to Sabrina Robbson.

May her love, light, and memory rest forever in the subconscious of my daughter, Genevieve. So that when life gets a tad colder, as it often does, she will remember that she was loved deeply before she could say a word.

And God stepped out on space,
And he looked around and said:
I'm lonely—
I'll make me a world.

—JAMES WELDON JOHNSON

CONTENTS

Introduction 1

1 Giovanni's Eden 27

2 Eve's Paradise 71

3 Adam as the Outsider 127

4 The Serpent/Lilith's Liberation Theology 169

Coda 215

Acknowledgments 221
Notes 225
Works Cited 255
Index 267

IMAGINING EDEN

INTRODUCTION

The language of all the interpretations, the translations, of the Judaic Bible and the Christian Bible, is musical, just wonderful. I read the Bible to myself.
—Maya Angelou, "The Art of Fiction No. 119," interview by George Plimpton

For too long the Bible has been used to shut down eros and alienate human beings from our bodies.
—David M. Carr, *The Erotic Word: Sexuality, Spirituality, and the Bible*

I still remember the moment. It was around 1 a.m. I was in the basement of Yale University's Bass Library, poring over Zora Neale Hurston's *Their Eyes Were Watching God* (1937). I planned to read her novel quickly since it was my second time fully immersing myself in the story. My first time was in undergrad at Tougaloo College in Jackson, Mississippi. I needed to get through it quickly. Besides, I had my actual assignments to complete—but I never did. I was captured by the rhythm and lyricism of Hurston's prose. It was, in one word, mesmerizing. I was able to hear an older and yet unfamiliar Florida in her characters' voices. The eloquence of the narrator simply held me hostage. I had not known that a novel could sing. When I was on the verge of completing the text, pages away from being freed to focus on my course assignments, one passage completely seized me; it has held me in its grip until this very day. The poetry of the first sentence was so piercing it was almost unfair: "Somewhere up there beyond blue ether's bosom sat He." I remember sitting back, looking up, and repeating the sentence to myself in a whisper. I envisioned the cosmos above filled with some sort of indescribable blue fog—and saw a deity, a big guy with a silver beard, hiding "somewhere" in that fog, just watching. I saw him sitting on a chair with a face that bore no expression. Watching. But Hurston did not stop there. She continued: "Was He noticing what was going on around here? He must be because he knew everything. Did He mean to do this thing to Tea Cake and her? It was not anything she could fight. She could only ache and wait." And I saw Jamie on the ground holding her lover, wanting to scream for this deity *to do something other than watch*. "She looked hard for something up there to move for a sign. A star in the daytime, maybe, or the sun to shout, or even a mutter of thunder. Her arms went up in a desperate supplication for a minute. It wasn't exactly pleading, it was asking questions. *The sky stayed hard looking and quiet so she went inside the house. God would do less than He had in His heart*" (emphasis mine).

I didn't know what to do with myself. I don't remember what I did with myself. I believe I just sat back and breathed a bit after encountering a theological passage that felt true, that felt real. I thought about all the times I'd wondered the same. I read it repeatedly . . . I think. I don't know. But what is most important about reflecting on this moment many years ago on Bass's basement floor, I knew I needed to learn how to bring Hurston, her writings, and that feeling that felt true along with me to navigate the rest of my time in divinity school.

I knew I'd read *Their Eyes Were Watching God* before at Tougaloo College, but the truth is one does not truly comprehend all the contours of a book until they've read it more than once. This also was not the first time that a paragraph of literature—one that included profound and beautifully blasphemous passages—had arrested me. There were passages from Richard Wright's *Black Boy* (1945) and the piercing truths found in Toni Morrison's *Sula* (1973); I worked hard to memorize the first stanza of Countee Cullen's "Yet Do I Marvel" (1925), and will never forget the level of fulfillment I experienced when I turned the final page of Langton Hughes's *Not Without Laughter* (1930). And my affection for the literary was not something I cultivated on my own; I owe this obsession to so many others who inspired me to become bookish in 2007. I remember an old friend of mine, Mahlet, putting *Aesop's Fables* and *Frankenstein* (1818) in my hands at the Barnes & Noble in Evanston, Illinois, after I'd said something preposterous. I told her I was only interested in reading the Bible and doctrinal books on the church and she told me, in so many words, how ludicrous I sounded and that I needed to open my world to literature from across human civilization. She told me, in so many words, that if I wanted to be a theologian then I needed to open myself to the world, and it was in my best interest to read as widely and as much as possible.

Not only did she pick up *Aesop's Fables*, but she also handed me, in what felt like a cinematic moment, books by Jane Austen, Shakespeare, and Alice Walker, and anything else she could find to drive the point home that I'd been missing out on so much. That summer I heeded her advice. I blew all my summer internship money from Northwestern University and ordered everything that was on every list of important books. I locked myself in my dorm at Tougaloo and just read. I did not understand much at that time, but I tried. Also, the novels, plays, and poetry always took a backseat to my theology and philosophy books when the semester started . . . or at least that's what I thought.

I couldn't spend too much time with literature when there was so much James Cone, Paul Tillich, Jacquelyn Grant, and Anthony Pinn to read. I had to focus at Yale Divinity School. Plus, I was in Dr. John Hare's "Philosophy of Religion" course and really needed to impress him. That meant cutting my teeth on Plato and Immanuel Kant. And I did, every day. I struggled all the time and drowned in an unforgivable amount of insecurity. And to sustain my morale for not doing too well on my assignments, when I needed inspiration, or for educational pleasure that referenced my own heritage, background, and culture, I stole a couple of hours I didn't have and returned to some form of the black literature I'd been introduced to in undergrad and in my summer program.

That week, it was *Their Eyes Were Watching God*. And I am forever grateful because it was this precise passage—along with parts of Wright's *The Outsider* (1953)—that let me know I could do both, systematics and literature, at the same time. And I also didn't have to make a big distinction between the two regarding the questions I was pursuing. I could think earnestly about papers and projects where my theodicean questions could be investigated by placing Hurston in conversation with Kant or situating Plato in front of Wright. And that is not to elevate Hurston or Wright, but to set them across the table from each other as conversation partners on equal footing. Yes, there would be differences of centuries and audience, but they would be equals. Besides, this is not a monumental discovery. I realize this isn't a significant breakthrough, but at the time I had yet to come across the work of Nathan A. Scott, Leon Russell, or Katie Cannon. I hadn't been introduced to Benjamin Mays's *The Negro's God: As Reflected in His Literature* (1938). And most importantly, I had yet to have Professor Farah Griffin place *"A God of Justice?" The Problem of Evil in Twentieth-Century Black Literature*, by Qiana J. Whitted (2009), in my hand, a book that not only meant the world to me, that taught me so much about what was possible to accomplish by studying black literature, but also is the model for this very book you are reading. I was young and on the verge of putting the pieces together. And now, fifteen years later, here we are.

Imagining Eden: Black Theology and the Search for Paradise is my attempt to honor what I discovered in *Their Eyes* that day. It is my attempt to honor what Mahlet said to me in 2008. It is my attempt at treating some of the most talented, brilliant, and unique writers of the twentieth century *as theologians*. *Imagining Eden* is a textual meditation on the Edenic impulse in four canonical black American writers in the twentieth century: Richard Wright, James Baldwin, Alice Walker, and Toni Morrison. These writers were with me throughout divinity school and my PhD studies, and they are still with me to this day. This is because they use religious, biblical, and theological symbolism to create the worlds they are constructing or trying to take down. And for the purpose of this project, I will focus on one specific aspect that all of them have employed: the Garden of Eden in the book of Genesis. Each of these authors has in some way adopted the motifs found in the first three chapters of Genesis to produce undertheorized and overlooked literarily depicted constructive—and counter—theologies.

Imagining Eden: Black Theology and the Search for Paradise intervenes in the historical discourse among black liberation theology, religion, and literature. It sidesteps the repeatedly asked questions about the necessity of religious beliefs for black people or the usefulness of the God idea and asks the writers themselves—on their own terms—about their ideas surrounding the complexities of religious wonder, theological doctrines, social practices, and communal rituals. I take the mythological location of the "Garden of Eden" as a kind of common ground or a unifying center—a sort of common well of ideas from which all four writers drink—then place each black writer in conversation with a classical theologian who has offered a theological reading of Eden.

This comparison shows how my selected writers have employed and reimagined the theologians' arguments. Specifically, I place James Baldwin in conversation with Saint Paul to show how Baldwin's oeuvre—especially *Giovanni's Room* (1956)—is in many ways dedicated to countering Saint Paul's proclamation that one should "mortify the flesh." Next, I compare Toni Morrison's novel *Paradise* (1997) with Saint Augustine's reading of the Fall and, in particular, the way sexuality and its emergence is the principal cause for human banishment from Eden. Then I investigate how Richard Wright uses Søren Kierkegaard's reading of Adam in *Concept of Anxiety* (1844) to depict the fall of his character, Cross Damon, in *The Outsider*. Lastly, I place Alice Walker's *The Color Purple* (1982) in conversation with the writings of Catholic theologian Ivone Gebara, to show how both argue for a radical reinterpretation of the serpent in the Genesis myth to reconceptualize what it means to be a free-living person in a complicated world.

Ultimately, *Imagining Eden: Black Theology and the Search for Paradise* reveals that in these literary works an explicit liberation theology shows that a people marked by tragedy—marked by a loss of paradise—return to the Garden of Eden, as a kind of crucial metaphor for exploring that tragedy. This book asserts that these writers offer insight into spiritual and human qualities necessary to persist in the face of catastrophe, and this persistence is tied to what many consider a sacred time in ancient texts. Furthermore, placing these writers in conversations with theologians shows that they are not interested in reductively dismissing religion as much as in exploring the ways new conceptions of theology and the religious can bring about new life. For these writers, the Garden of Eden is a mythological site, singularly generative for thinking about black life and culture, romance and friendship, society and community.

This project is personal to me because as a black systematic theologian my own spiritual and religious consciousness was in no small part developed by studying scripture, and also reading African American literature like my life depended on it. And it did, because I come from a community, a people, who passionately love our literature and take it seriously as a supplement to scripture or a full alternative sacred composition, especially our poetry and novels. I come from a people who, for example, embrace the book of Exodus as a timeless abolitionist tale, even if we don't always use those words. Its liberating message is felt all the same; but that message, that declaration, and that imagery of Moses and Aaron brazenly confronting Pharaoh and his enslaving culture are augmented with books in our culture that contain a similar fervor and proclamation—like *The Autobiography of Malcolm X: As Told to Alex Haley*, *The Color Purple* by Alice Walker, *The Fire Next Time* by James Baldwin, *Narrative of the Life of Frederick Douglass*, and *The Souls of Black Folk* by W. E. B. Du Bois. These books of freedom are read through an implicit theological lens and function as what Farah Jasmine Griffin calls "black wisdom books" in their own right. In other words, it would not be peculiar to walk into a black Protestant church and witness little black girls reciting Maya Angelou's "Phenomenal Woman" or "Still I Rise" as a part of the liturgy. It would not be odd to hear little black boys read sections of James Weldon Johnson's *God's Trombone*. Since I was a child, I have known African American literature, and art more broadly, to exist alongside the Bible and its significance. And I believe, or hope, that this book will properly delve deeply into that reservoir.

In the first chapter, I turn to James Baldwin's second novel, *Giovanni's Room* (1956), to explore how it counters Saint Paul of Tarsus's command to mortify the flesh for the spirit. Saint Paul's reading of Eden is explicit; he understands the Genesis myth to outline how death entered time and space. And he explains to the ecclesia in Rome that all of us, as humans, are sinners because we are all offspring of the first human, Adam. Through Adam sin enters the world. It attempts to disrupt the order of creation. And the Gentiles are responsible because even though unaware of the Laws of Moses, they are accountable because they too are descendants of Adam. I argue that Adam becomes the subtle source of Saint Paul's theodicy. The flesh of Adam wreaks havoc, and therefore Paul's advice is to mortify the flesh, disassociate from the flesh, undo one's enslavement to the flesh to prepare for Christ—the Second Adam—to return. In Baldwin's novel, though, this habit of mortifying the flesh, of ascetic disassociation, practiced by the protagonist, David—along with his fidelity to white American masculinity—leads to the demise of his lover, Giovanni. This reinterpretation of *Giovanni's Room* as a private Garden of Eden exposes how Baldwin's text engages Saint Paul in an argument about loving someone, or anything, with one's whole flesh and body.

In chapter 2, I turn to Toni Morrison's *Paradise* (1997): If expulsion from paradise occurs because of the prideful disobedience of the first two humans, as the concept of Original Sin posits, then Morrison's novel is a tale of the consequences of trying to prevent people from entering the paradises of their own creation. *Paradise*—her most explicitly religious novel, by her own account—counters the implications of the Fall, following Baldwin, by ultimately reimagining the consequences of living in the flesh and thus reversing colonialism's effects on black and brown flesh. The theologian with whom I place her novel in conversation is the primary architect of Original Sin and perhaps the most significant theologian after Saint Paul in the East and West: Saint Augustine of Hippo.

For the great Saint Augustine, Adam's decision to disobey the Lord is proof of an *evil will* that existed within him before he succumbed to his desire. And his succumbing ultimately damaged the will completely, ruining it to the point that through concupiscence, the inclination to sin, or what Immanuel Kant called the "proclivity to evil," spread to every human being.[1] This affects not just individuals but entire human societies. Therefore, through sin, sinful human collectivities or cities developed. The sinful city, known as the city of man, is driven by greed, selfishness, pride, injustice, while the city of God is composed of people who have given their lives, their wills, their spirits over to God and live by God's grace.

My claim is that Ruby, an all-black town, was founded by nine black families traveling westward who were excluded from every black locale they found because their skin was too dark. Thus, the experience of colorism forced them to create their own city that protected itself from unknown outsiders. This was their paradise, their city of God, founded by darker-skinned African Americans who kept to themselves. However, the town's exclusivity is ruined by the actions of the local convent, a center where women who are fleeing some sort of trouble come and spend the night with the strange drunken woman named Connie. We eventually learn what happens when you try to exclude people from collective imagined paradises, and what is possible for the characters after Connie remembers her religious heritage from South America and develops a new perception of the divide between flesh and spirit. *Paradise* is a sort of love story. But more than that, it is a story that reveals the healing powers of African religions, when the dominant religion expels a person from its grace(s).

The third chapter centers around Richard Wright's second novel, *The Outsider* (1953), which reframes Adam and Eve as figures lost in a world of danger and self-deceit. The protagonist, Cross Damon, embarks upon a quest of dangerous existential self-fashioning. An intellectual who suffers from alcoholism, Cross pores over existentialist literature and encounters "freedom" after he survives a train crash but is mistakenly announced dead.

The theologian, or philosopher, whom I place in dialogue with Wright is Søren Kierkegaard. In *The Concept of Anxiety: A Simple Deliberation on the Dogmatic Issue of Hereditary Sin* (1844), through one of his many pseudonyms, Vigilius Haufniensis, the "Watchman of Copenhagen," questions when exactly freedom entered the psyche of Adam. For Haufniensis, it was when Adam learned that he could decide to do something other than what the deity wanted. Then freedom, along with the possibility of sin, entered the world. Wright takes this idea along with other elements of Kierkegaard and explores freedom through Cross's adventures and philosophical ruminations.

Cross Damon's newfound freedom allows him to leave behind all his troubles and family burdens for a different life under a different name (Lionel Lane). But as the story progresses, Cross finds himself killing to maintain his freedom from friends, fascists, and communists. Eventually he realizes that his trail of murders has also transformed him into one of the modern demigods—connecting him to one translation of his name (daemon)—he encounters on his journey.

The last chapter is an exploration of Celie's transformation in Alice Walker's epistolary novel, *The Color Purple* (1982). Celie, according to my reading, is the archetypal Eve who communes with God through letters to find purpose and succor. In the biblical text, however, Eve and the Hebraic deity share no communication. So Celie is in many ways lost until Shug Avery, who functions as the archetypal serpent, to follow the Edenic myth, helps her experience self-regard, self-love, and passion through a theological conversion where she gets the "white man off her eyeball," another way of saying she rids herself of white patriarchal Christian dogma. Ivone Gebara also finds the serpent to be the liberating character in the story. Both Walker and Gebara use the novel to identify what they conceive as the real and authentic moments of liberation for the women who are under the thumb of a God (and fellow liberators) who does not properly listen. Gebara helps me to show that Walker provides a sort of theopoetics, a spiritual rereading of the Garden of Eden that allows for a womanist theology to introduce new ways of being in the world.

I conclude the book with an exploration of Lucille Clifton's remarkable poem, "brothers," and try to remind us all of the power in African American hermeneutics.

THE BACKGROUND

Three prevailing misconceptions regarding the idea of Original Sin need to be addressed initially. The first, the most crucial for this text, is that theological discourse about Original Sin—in modern theology especially—tends to conflate the narratives of the Garden of Eden, the idea of a Fall, and the doctrine of Original Sin into a single, inseparable entity. Though these three concepts are interconnected historically, it is imperative to remember that in the history and development of the Edenic myth, they each possess their own unique and significant nuances.

The Garden of Eden is a cultural product of the ancient Near East, a myth from the cradle of civilization that bears traces of its diverse cultural climate and ancient Mesopotamian influence. The idea of a Fall is a theological interpretation of an ancient myth—regardless of religion—that speaks to a cataclysmic moment or event that ultimately severed, or at least altered, the relationship between humans and their deity and/or environment. The Original Sin doctrine refers to a terrible ontological transformation wrought by an inherited guilt theorized by ancient Christian theologians. While these concepts are historically interconnected, they are not identical or indistinguishable. And it is important to keep them separate to foster a more contextual understanding of the theological discussions surrounding them.

The second prevailing misconception regarding Original Sin is the assumption that it is a biblical claim, meaning the Hebrew writers of the Pentateuch, Saint Paul of Tarsus in the first century or the Pseudepigraphical writers in Paul's name, and the other New Testament authors are mistakenly thought to have forwarded, in unison, Original Sin as the primary explanation for the human condition. Though this error is understandable, it stems from an ahistorical, supersessionist interpretation that erases all prior Mesopotamian origins, influences, and context. Plus, it overlooks that the Fall as a concept was not always synonymous with Eden—literature on the ancient Jewish book of Enoch locates a Fall elsewhere—and that Eden's event seemed to grow in importance at the turn of the millennium, essentially existing without note until its prominence in the first century. Before the story of Adam and Eve's insubordination altered the course of Judeo-Christian metaphysical history, the Watchers stories about fallen angels (as well as Cain and Abel) were also important for trying to understand not only the human and divine severance but the very appearance of evil itself.

The third prevailing misconception regarding the idea of Original Sin is the opposite of the prior one. It states erroneously that Original Sin was entirely conceived by Saint Augustine of Hippo, through his solitary efforts and genius, with no previous foundation or predecessors. While Saint Augustine is accurately credited with *theorizing the Fall into what would develop into a church doctrine*, the history of the idea far precedes his pen. Between Paul and Augustine were several Greek, Latin, and Jewish theologians debating how to understand the consequences of the bitten fruit.

There are many misconceptions about Original Sin, but the point of highlighting these few major ones is to show that the idea developed in history through dialogue and arguments and was considered in numerous social and historical contexts. It is not a doctrine that fell from the sky. It is an idea still going through the various processes of interpretation. This book is centered on how black writers *outside of traditional theological arenas* have contributed to and challenged that discourse, either by invoking aspects of it in their literature or by offering counter "heretical" theologies conceived as liberating.

Before turning to the creative and insightful black writers of the twenty-first century, I want to continue exploring the religious complexity of the ancient Near East and the various readings provided by ancient Hellenist insight. In other words, I begin with investigating how the Edenic myth became important to the man James Baldwin calls "the architect of Christianity" himself, Saint Paul of Tarsus, and Saint Augustine of Hippo.

Saint Paul interpreted the Fall *as a theodicy* that established the salvific significance of Jesus the Messiah, who nullifies the consequence of death that subverted the initial Edenic harmony between Creator and created. Saint Augustine of Hippo, on the other hand, elevated the Fall to the status of theory. A theory, known as "Original Sin," argues that consuming the forbidden fruit was proof of some preexistent human awfulness that requires the grace of God to heal. Due to human pride, a sinful source of irrevocable vileness, Adam singlehandedly demolished the divine purpose of creation, subsequently corrupting the will of every human after him.

For Paul, the story of our lost Paradise points to Jesus's divine rescue, a proof that God kept a promise he made at the beginning of time. For Augustine, the myth of our destroyed harmony reveals a human condition that can only be corrected by accepting our own defects and praying that God's mercy invites us back into the fold, despite our stench. I will return to Saint Augustine in the third chapter but begin with Saint Paul and the history of the Fall as a concept in the postexilic apocalyptic literature.[2]

Before Adam and Eve became the dominant Fall legend in early Christianity, another story, revealed by Second Temple Jewish literature (produced and disseminated between 516 BCE and 70 CE), was widespread in explaining the origin of evil. One such myth is the Watchers-Fallen Angels story about fallen angels, insatiable giants, and cosmic warfare that was only eradicated by a divinely orchestrated deluge. The seeds of this myth are spread throughout the New Testament Christian scriptures, and the Yahwist (or "J") writer of the Pentateuch placed aspects of it at the beginning of the Noah's Ark legend (Genesis 6). Some aspects remained in circulation all the way up to the beginning of the second century, but by then the Garden of Eden story surpassed it in importance.

THE GARDEN OF EDEN

Though biblical tradition typically depicts Moses as the sole author of the Pentateuch, we must understand through biblical scholarship that the Torah is a historically interwoven series of stories and codes edited into a cosmic linear narrative by the Yahwist (J), Elohist (E), Deuteronomist (D), and Priestly (P) sources.[3] This version of creation that includes Adam and Eve is from what is considered the earliest source by most scholars, the Yahwist (J) source. The book of Genesis begins with the Priestly creation account, Genesis 1:1–2:4, while the Yahwist creation account begins at Genesis 2:4b.[4]

I will briefly explain some of the crucial distinctions between the two narratives. In the Priestly account, the creation of the cosmos takes center stage and culminates with the creation of humans, developed through broadly construed aspects of human sexes, "male" (*zakar*) and "female" (*neqevah*).[5] This creation account is clearly structured. Its organization is intentional and outlines, in a more systematic way than the Yahwist source, the indisputable grandeur of the deity. The God of the Priestly account, referred to as Elohim, is a sovereign deity, a transcendent god-king often credited for creating the universe either ex nihilo or through overpowering cosmic chaos, showcasing celestial power with no equals. The text showcases power and grandeur but in a way that reveals this God as far superior to the other gods of creation in the region. There is no God like Elohim. And though the language describing Elohim's creation of the world bears traces of Babylonian influence, mostly Tiamat from *Enuma Elish*, the editors and compilers of the Priestly narrative produced a text with absolute clarity about the sheer sovereignty of Elohim.

The conflation of the Garden of Eden with the symbolism of Paradise creates the visual image of an actual garden, a lush orchard surrounded by beautiful foliage and diverse flora. Though an ethereal space dedicated to innocent humans inspires a uniquely alluring botanical venue, the language may betray us by revealing something much more aristocratic. Giorgio Agamben explains:

> The history of the word "paradise," which sounds so familiar to us, is a succession of loans from one language to another, as if the foreign term were for some reason always held to be untranslatable or else one wanted at every cost to avoid its obvious equivalent. The Greek term *paradeisos*, which Latin transcribes as *paradisus* and which appears for the first time in Xenophon, is in fact, according to the lexicons, a calque of the Avestic *pairidaeza*, which designates a spacious walled garden (pairi means "around" and daeza "wall"). It is possible that, in recalquing the Iranian term instead of using the Greek word for "garden," kepos, Xenophon... could not imagine that his Greek-Iranian neologism was destined to furnish to Christian theology one of its essential technical terms and to the imagination of the West one of its most persistent fantasies.[6]

Agamben helps us understand that the garden was a walled enclosure, like a temple court. And highlighting it is necessary because the image of the cherub guarding the Tree of Life bears the traces of the Temple's influence after its reconstruction. David Carr writes:

> The myth ends with God expelling the humans from the garden and setting cherubim guards at its eastern end to guard it (Gen. 3:24). Such mythical creatures often guarded temple entrances, and this eastern entrance to the garden probably corresponds to the major eastern entrance to the temple sanctuary. These and other associations would have been obvious to ancient readers. Ancient Israelites reading the garden of Eden story would have heard it telling them that the world was created in a setting much like the temple they knew well. But as in most such creation stories, the main point of the tale was to tell them about who they were and how they fit into the broader cosmos.[7]

In other words, and following Agamben, Carr, and some of the claims of reformed biblical scholar Gregory K. Beale, the garden was presented as resembling the Temple intentionally.[8]

In Genesis 2:4b, the Yahwist creation narrative does share some similarities with the Priestly account, considering that it more than likely served as a source, but the differences between the two are striking. In the Yahwist account, this deity called Yahweh (YHWH) is presented as corporeal, fleshly, and physically among creation in space and time. This is more of a narrative than an explanation, bearing traces of an artist (or an ensemble of artists and editors) invested in portraying a story of hope and loss. According to Carr, "We do not know exactly when either text was written or when they were joined, but what is important at this point is this: whatever the differences between Genesis 1:1–2:3 and Genesis 2:4–3:24, the authors of Genesis apparently did not wish to give up either. So they put one after the other, and these creation stories now stand together as complementary visions of the deepest nature of reality."[9]

Thus, in this timeless second creation narrative, Yahweh is described intimately; he feels emotions, has desires, and knows his way around the garden. He created man, later known as Adam, out of dust, and through trial and error tries to find a living being who could accompany him as a partner throughout life. Yahweh fails, until he creates a being called out of him. We know the first human, whom we will associate with the name "Adam," which Carol Meyers teaches that we do not learn officially until Genesis 4 and 5.[10] The literal translation suggests that the human is an androgynous being not categorized as a "man" until there is a creation of another human being we associate with "woman." Then we learn in verse 23 that the other human is *designated* "Woman." The tale is not necessarily cosmic in scope, but personal and almost romantic. The intimacy of the Yahwist account is crafted to register the disappointment of the next chapter.

The notorious third chapter introduces an added character not in the Priestly account: the serpent. This is a Mesopotamian talking animal that holds a conversation with "Woman" about the lay of the land. Woman explains to the serpent the prohibition we assume Adam explained to her. She should not *and cannot* eat the fruit gently hanging from the Forbidden Tree. If she does so, she will die. The serpent listens but disagrees. After the serpent provokes sudden suspicion with his retorts, Woman eventually eats the fruit. Nothing happens. She hands the bitten fruit (we assume) to Adam. He also bites it. Their "eyes were opened." They saw that they were *naked*. They felt *ashamed*. And at some point while Yahweh is walking in the garden, he realizes something is awry when Adam refers to his own nudity. Immediately Yahweh is aware of what has transpired and punishes the serpent, Woman, and Adam. Adam names the woman "Eve," alluding to her current or future pregnancy. Yahweh then banishes them from the garden and places a cherub at the entrance with a flaming sword to guard the Tree of Life.

Though the significance of this myth is beyond measure, the ancient Mesopotamian world had no shortage of epics and religious lore, sagas that comprised various creation stories, innumerable deities, and pivotal events that occurred inside or outside time that either influenced humanity's relationship with their gods and the environment or, at worst, completely severed a prior harmony between them. The Edenic myth, the Deluge, great cosmic battles, and appearances from Tiamat found subtly in the biblical narratives may be regarded as stories that resemble motifs, plots, and characteristics of the *Epic of Gilgamesh*, *Enuma Elish*, *Atrahasis*, and a host of others.

The book of Genesis is unique. But its uniqueness stems from the fact that the stories survived the test of time and the broken debris of rubble and stone. The narrative lasted throughout the ages, appearing in the world as the product of vast amounts of intellectual and artistic labor by the hands of freed Hebrews during the Persian Empire.[11] Not only were they focused on rebuilding the temple and inaugurating what we call Second Temple Judaism, they also sought to create historical and ethnic distance from the Babylonian cultural matrix by compiling all their stories, legends, myths, and practices. Slowly, the genius and wisdom of exiles who had a newfound appreciation of their ancestry—under the leadership of Ezra—collected myths about Elohim, Yahweh, and a host of angels; they assembled local legends about figures named Abraham and Sarah, Isaac and Rebecca, Jacob and Leah, Joseph, Moses, Aaron, Miriam, and Rachel. They used their myths to craft stories of defeating the deities they wanted eradicated from their collective consciousness, like Marduk, Tiamat, Baal, and Asherah. Their

God crushed Ra and the Egyptian pantheon, marking its territory in time, asserting its heritage as consisting of slaves and glory, justice, and hard-won triumphs. The Hebrew scriptures are not documents isolated from their cultural context but records and manuscripts that tell how they survived their cultural context, rose from ashes, and persisted and endured the constant threat of always being vulnerable to larger kingdoms.

One story necessary for properly comprehending the background of the early church theologians' view of Eden is lodged in between the words of the tale known as Noah's Ark, Genesis 6, a significant Mesopotamian legend on its own that bears traces of the *Epic of Gilgamesh*. In the editing it was placed after Genesis 3 and 4 to create the illusion of a linear narrative.[12] This is important because before we can interrogate how Saint Paul of Tarsus uses Genesis 3 for his theodicy, we must first see how Genesis 6's Deluge legend and Ethiopian Enochic literature reveal the popularity of the other Fall narrative, the Watchers.

THE WATCHERS

The earliest written record of aspects of the Watchers story is found between Genesis 5 and Genesis 6:1–8. The Watchers story is used as the justification of the great Flood. N. P. Williams notes that the first eight verses of Genesis 6 are placed as an introduction to the Deluge story despite how the first four verses seem different and distinct from the possible oral tradition. In the fourth verse the writer states: "The *Nephilim* were on the earth in those days—and also afterward—when the sons of God went to the daughters of humans and had children by them. They were the heroes of old, men of renown" (emphasis mine). Though there is wide disagreement on the proper translation of

"Nephilism," the Septuagint translates it to "giants." Which means that the presumption, according to Williams, is that the Nephalim were possibly giant demigods or "giants [who] were sprung from the union between divine and human partners."[13]

Yahweh was disturbed by the angels' actions to the point that he grieved and regretted creating the humans with whom they procreated. His rage rose, culminating in a decision to wipe the humans from the face of the earth, enacting divine vengeance by storm and flood. Yet Williams writes, "But vv. 1–4, containing the legend of the angels, seem to come from a cycle of tradition which knows nothing of the Deluge."[14] The editing, according to Williams, is pronounced. Yet the cycle of tradition from where the story of the Nephilim and the "Sons of gods" originates is explored more fully much later, before the turn of the millennium, in the book of Enoch. There the angels—also called the Watchers—were attracted to the human women and made an oath together to descend to Mount Hermon and marry them, procreate with them, and live among them, thus creating the Nephilim. Human resources were not able to fully accommodate the needs of the giants. Therefore, some betrayed the humans by eating them and the animals, and drinking their blood—ultimately wreaking indescribable havoc across the land. Yahweh was not only disturbed by the heinous activity of the giants but also angry that the fallen Watchers—led by Azazel in one tradition—taught the humans various skills that the Creator did not intend for them to learn. Enoch 6 says that Azazel "taught men to make swords, and knives, and shields, and breastplates, and made known to them the metals [of the earth] and the art of working them, and bracelets, and ornaments, and the use of antimony, and the beautifying of the eyelids, and all kinds of costly stones, and all colouring tinctures."[15] This is significant because it contributes to the ancient idea and literary motif of the Creator's jealousy, thus becoming another source that expresses how the Deity possesses knowledge that is prohibited from the created. According to Williams, this ancient motif parallels the Adam and Eve story as well as the Greek Prometheus legend.[16]

Another example of the Watchers-Fallen Angels' presence is found in the first half of 2nd Enoch, a first-century text dominated by a cosmic drama involving the angels of Satanail. This story includes both the Watchers and the characters from Eden. The tale narrates in an alternative account that *the angels* seduced Eve into partaking of the forbidden fruit. Again, this is evidence that in some Mediterranean circles both theories of the Fall—Eden and Watchers—were vital in Jewish popular literature.

Moreover, despite the elevation of the Garden of Eden narrative, the Watchers story, or aspects of it, did not completely vanish. Long after Saint Paul, there was the *Greek Apocalypse of Ezra*, a thought-provoking theodicean interrogation that occurs between Ezra and God, where the mysterious author refuses to blame humanity for the presence of evil, instead attributing all malevolence to God. The author argues that God, as the creator of Eve and the serpent, bears responsibility for creating the conditions that allowed evil, both natural and moral, to emerge. After Ezra ridicules God for his corrupt perspective on responsibility and justice, God not only reveals his redemptive plans for humanity but also expounds upon his desire to eliminate death as an experience from the world of the living.

The debate among historians and biblical scholars concerning the Watchers story's decline in centrality compared to the Eden tale after the first century is endless. Mark S. Smith writes, "The Fall of the angels in Second Temple literature was woven out of several older threads. The basic idea can be traced back to an old tradition of gods competing for authority and power in heaven."[17] Apocalyptic literature across the board reveals the decline of the Watchers story's significance in Hellenistic Jewish culture. On the other hand, these texts expose the slow dissemination of the Edenic myth, allowing for widespread reengagement with Adam and Eve's act of defiance. Both narratives, and at least allusions to them, are spread across different sections within early Jewish writings. For example, references to Eden and the fallen angels are also found throughout *The Testaments of the Twelve Patriarchs*.

RETURNING TO THE GARDEN OF EDEN

When it comes to canonized biblical scriptures, there is little engagement with Adam, Eve, Eden, or Paradise, in the Tanakh or the Gospels. James Barr says,

> The typology of Adam and Christ is absent from the teaching of Jesus, from the Gospels in general, from the other Johannine literature, from Hebrews, Peter and James, from everything. Jesus himself, though he noted some features of the early Genesis story in other respects, shows no interest in Adam or Eve as the persons who brought sin and death into the world. Apart from Paul, Adam is mentioned little in the entire New Testament and only incidentally.[18]

John J. Collins writes on this peculiar detail, "They are entirely absent from the Hebrew Bible. However important the story later became, it does not serve as a substantive point of reference for the later biblical writers."[19] And the combination of the Gospels' glaring silence on the bitten forbidden fruit with Jesus quoting aspects of the Yahwist account's creation narrative reveals its early insignificance.[20] The only reference in the Hebrew Bible to some of the aspects of Genesis 3—as in the Garden of God—is from the book of Ezekiel, which, according to biblical scholars, served as the *inspiration from the Edenic myth*.[21] This shows that the Garden of Eden's cataclysmic consequence as a theory for declaring the origin of evil, or the cause of human or natural malevolence, did not gain widespread prominence in Greek or Jewish literature until the middle of the first century, around the same time that Saint Paul was writing his letters to various assemblies.

Yet when we do find the early mentioning of Adam in Second Temple Jewish literature, it is first in the wisdom book of Sirach and the Aramaic book of Jubilees. The story of the Watchers does not vanish, but the Eden myth begins to expand in prominence. These two books were composed around the same time, and each offers a somewhat different portrayal of the Adam character, yet both interpretations reveal their anti-Hellenistic perspective and desire for freedom from any aspect of control. In the book of Sirach/Ecclesiasticus, written by Ben Sira, Adam is referred to not as the clumsy offender who sinned and ruined creation but as valiant patriarch of Israel. He failed, but he is redeemed by wisdom. Yet there is no mention of a serpent. There is no forbidden fruit that caused death and destruction; in fact, death is configured as a natural outcome of life, an aspect of creation that God orchestrated. Death is not a punishment. Death is not a consequence of disobedience. Death is simply a part of life, not counter to it. And what's more, God's fear about humans gaining wisdom is uniquely absent.

Most scholars have assumed that Ben Sira was referring to Eve when he wrote, "From a woman sin had its beginning, and because of her we all die (v 25.24)." However, Teresa Ellis argues that this text was in reference to Pandora.[22] In other words, though Eve is insignificant to Ben Sira and his father, she is also not liable for undoing creation.

The book of Jubilees echoes the canonical motifs while also exhibiting influence from the Watchers legend. In this version, Adam and Eve worked and toiled together for precisely seven years and *were receiving instructions from the angels* until they sinned against God and disobeyed the rules of the garden by partaking of the forbidden fruit. Their sin consequently ruined the common language that was spoken among the living. Yet another unique distinction about what transpires after Adam and Eve are punished is that the writers portray Adam as turning into a priest-like figure in chapter 3, verse 27: "[Adam] offered as a sweet savior an offering, frankincense, galbanum, and stacte, and spices in the morning with the rising of the sun from the day when he covered his shame."

This reveals, with just the two examples of the book of Sirach and the book of Jubilees, that there was a diverse range of interpretations and understandings regarding the story of Adam and Eve within Hellenistic Judaism in the period before the first century. The Jewish community, influenced by Greek culture and revolutionary ideas, had varying perspectives on biblical myths that often speak as much about their context as the content of the story itself. In other words, Eden and the Watchers story, along with multiple other myths and traditions, were constantly reevaluated based on whatever was unfolding within the community that was interpreting them. Engagement with the Edenic story contributed to the growth of various interpretations. And Saint Paul was intricately a part of making the Garden of Eden central to theological history, even if he only mentioned it in writing *a few times*.

Hermeneutics broadly construed keeps the Bible alive, and the discourse and discussions on interpretations, conclusions, practical applications that one can glean from the text is a historical enterprise, but also a living and thriving practice. In other words, the practices of the councils who determined which scriptures were sacred and why were not limited to the councils themselves. Across black diasporic letters, there is a rich underexplored oeuvre, a treasure of novelists, poets, playwrights, and artists from every genre, who have contributed in their own unique way to the arguments concerning what's sacred, significant, life giving, or soul stirring about the text. Black writers across time and space, continent and ocean, have provided different ways to not only read the text but engage it, wrestle with it, and offered insight into how to find a life within the grappling. Their work has let us know it is okay to fight with it, to think against it, even if there is little life useful in the biblical ink on the page.

Most of the writers engaging the text and the Edenic motifs have opened and expanded different horizons, providing us with a language to imagine other ways of living, of existing, of being what Nietzsche said: all too human. I find what they have produced fascinating, and for the sake of hyperbole: life giving. Therefore, we return to the scene of the crime: the deserted garden. On the floor of a garden that resembles a temple, there are half-eaten fruit, sinuous tracks, fig leaves, and an angel with the face of one with a broken heart, seemingly upset but tasked with drawing their sword at the first hint of sound. Have we taken from here enough? Is there anything left to turn over? Does this scene still offer us points and lessons to discuss? The writers I am studying here believe so. Therefore, we begin with one of the most celebrated writers to ever quote and fight with the Bible: James Arthur Baldwin.

1

GIOVANNI'S EDEN

I address you as one of those creatures, one of God's creatures, whom the Christian church has most betrayed.
—James Baldwin

Therefore, just as sin entered the world through one man, and death through sin, and in this way death came to all people, because all sinned.
—Saint Paul of Tarsus

In our exploration of how black writers in the twentieth century engaged with the afterlife of Original Sin and its Edenic interpretations, one literary figure most consistently grappled with Saint Paul's theological interventions: James Baldwin. While all four of the primary writers of this project invoke Paradise, Edenic motifs, and several facets of Original Sin, he most consistently kept his finger on the theological implications of Paul's unparalleled triumph. What's more, we have yet to scratch the surface of his theological insight. When it comes to Baldwin and his well-known preoccupation with the "religious," most scholars turn to his most popular writings, like *Go Tell It on the Mountain* (1952), *Notes of a Native Son* (1955), and *The Fire Next Time* (1963), as well as his less popular but important play, *Amen Corner* (1954). Studying these works is understandable, considering that they most overtly express Baldwin's religious tenor. And though I will engage with them as well, my singular focus is to uncover Baldwin's theological contribution to Edenic discourse with unique attention on his second novel, *Giovanni's Room* (1956).

My central argument is that *Giovanni's Room* is an Edenic novel that explores the human condition, love, flesh, sexuality, and America. The tale follows David, the protagonist, who, to invoke Jack Halberstam's *The Queer Art of Failure* (2011), is a failed "American Adam." He enters Giovanni's room, where the two lovers privately express their passion, until that Paradise is lost through David's "innocent" self-deception (he believes he is a successful American Adam).[1] David's troubled self-perception requires a form of Pauline asceticism that tells him to "deny his flesh" in order to conform to the image of a successful American man who practices heterosexual norms. Overall, this novel is Baldwin's apocalyptic warning. It is his theological reinterpretation of not just Eden, but *particularly Saint Paul's reading of Eden*, which states that Adam's defiance stems from his embracing the flesh and causing death to enter the world. Yet for Baldwin, it is refusing the flesh that is the origin of evil, the exact opposite argument. Said differently, for Baldwin, *refusing to love with and through the flesh* leads to various series of events that leave all of us in a world of ruin. That is what happens to Giovanni, as recounted through David's narrative confession.

Thus, Baldwin—much like certain historical black religious intellectuals—adopted what Lisa M. Bowens calls a distinct African American Pauline hermeneutic. According to Bowens, there is a particular Pauline *Wirkungsgeschichte* in black American history.[2] Some people of African descent from across the continent and diaspora have considered Saint Paul the singular source for slavery's biblical justification because of the letters that scholars agree stem from his pen, like Romans and Philemon, or the pseudepigraphic writings like Timothy and Ephesians—each reveals the insight or at least the influence of this Jewish Roman intellectual who consecrated empire and was thus comfortable with any form of domination.[3]

Other black people have sought to instead rescue or reclaim Saint Paul from this interpretation by heeding his other words for the betterment of their spiritual lives. For this group, according to Bowens, Paul's canonized words help them live, endure, and he is therefore held in high regard for his theological prose and candor. Baldwin is far from the latter group but not completely in the former. He finds some value in Saint Paul's compositions, but overall, he sees Paul as a large culprit in ruining human relations. To be clear, Saint Paul's eschatology requires an asceticism that Baldwin finds repulsive. And this conflict, this ascetism—which is tethered to every doctrine Saint Paul inspired—is what undoes the Eden in David and Giovanni's tragic story.

THE CONFESSIONAL

The fact that this novel is communicated through confession is an important point for registering the theological theme that exists underneath the text. According to Foucault, not until Tertullian's writing in the second century did "confession"—the *confessio peccatorum*—become a central rite for converts preparing for baptism. The idea was that one needed a deliberate "truth act," a moment of intense self-revelation, to prepare for the journey of purification. This form of penance not only assisted with the oncoming metanoia but also became necessary for the overall mind and heart of the catechumen. Foucault writes:

> In a general way, from the end of the second century onward one sees the growing place occupied, in the economy of every soul's salvation, by the manifestation of one's own truth: in the form of an "investigation" where the individual is the respondent of a questionnaire or the object of testimony; in the form of a purificatory trial where he is the target of an exorcism; in the form, finally, of a "confession," where he is both the subject who speaks and the object of which he speaks, but where it's a matter of attesting that one knows oneself to be a sinner rather than drawing up an exact list of sins to be forgiven.[4]

The confession enabled the catechumen to comprehend their place within the faith's salvific history. It not only highlighted the sinful actions they had committed and regretted but also emphasized that they themselves were especially flawed and helplessly prone to sin. It was the act of embracing the truth: they were subjects who desperately needed to attach themselves to the symbolic death and resurrection of the baptism. *Giovanni's Room* is first and foremost an act of confession. David—one of Baldwin's "stock names" for characters, according to Herb Boyd—is the voice of the story who tries to confess but fails.[5] What specifically he tries to confess we do not know; neither does he, yet he makes the attempt. And the reader is listening, sitting in his presence, as he struggles with his reflection in the mirror, trying to confess his own inhumanity to himself.

In this fable, guilt drips from every page. Shame and remorse leak from between words. The story's atmosphere assumes the presence of a listener who is listening to David but also watching

Giovanni head to his execution. And though David was not around when Giovanni murdered Guillaume, we are compelled to believe that David holds himself responsible for all of it. Therefore, this novel not only is a confession but also *beckons the image of the confessional.* And the act of confession is what first ties *Giovanni's Room* to theology. It is subtly as theological, or concerned with the religious, as *Go Tell It on the Mountain* (1952).

In *Go Tell It*, Gabriel Grimes's suffering over what he cannot confess to himself is the source of his torture, and in *Giovanni's Room* this motif is also present in David's internal torment. Gabriel disowned his son, his flesh and blood, which he believes led to his unfortunate demise. David disowned his lover, disavowed his own flesh, which he believes also led to his lover's execution. Ultimately, he bares his soul about all the consequences of his actions, desperately hoping to be seen and forgiven.

David is a run-of-the-mill, white American Protestant in Paris trying to "find himself" while his partner, Hella, travels across Spain doing the same. In an essay entitled, "A Question of Identity," Baldwin writes: "For Paris is, according to its legend, the city where everyone loses his head, and his morals, lives through at least one *histoire d'amour,* ceases, quite, to arrive anywhere on time, and thumbs his nose at the Puritans—the city, in brief, where all become drunken on the fine old air of freedom."[6] David loses his head when he meets an Italian bartender named Giovanni and involves him in a queer subculture where he manipulates the possibilities inherent in queer temporality for his own deceptive hidden appetite. What is temporal for him becomes the road to destruction for Giovanni. Yet in the beginning their eye contact alters the trajectory of both of their lives. What does David see in Giovanni's eyes? It seems he is enraptured in his beauty, a beauty he remarks upon to Hella toward the end of the story. And what does Giovanni see in David's eyes? Perhaps the innocence that leads to his demise.

In their mutual eye contact I find a resonance with the subtle interactions between A and Moth in Ashon Crawley's *The Lonely Letters* (2020). In A's first letter to Moth, he writes:

> It happened again and I don't know what to make of it. Not staring but the sorta moment you feel someone looking at you from across the room and you look up from the convo you'd been engaging and, sure enough, there he is, looking. You make brief eye contact, he takes a deep breath and looks away. It's almost as if his looking—the very fact of his doing it—stunned him, and that stunning took place in the space and pause between inhale and exhale, so he also was not immediately able to look away. You're the trainwreck. You're the fire to which the moth is attracted.[7]

The "stunning" reflects what I see as the mood between David and Giovanni. And the imagery of a train wreck is highlighted in the story, while the fire is noted explicitly by other characters.

Moreover, A writes to Moth that "Declarations of heterosexuality are cool but then the people long for something otherwise and see and really really *sense* me, and act as if whatever that otherwise might be is somewhere hidden in me, is something familiar."[8] Perhaps David senses in Giovanni "something otherwise or inexplicably possible." This is not something that he senses in Jacques, which causes in Jacques both suspicion and resentment. The question is what does David sense in Giovanni that makes him fail at his own self-deception? Perhaps some concealed familiarity? We do not know. What we do know is they fall madly in love.

The two men, to David's chagrin, are smitten.[9] For a short period of time, David moves into Giovanni's small room, where the heart of the story takes place. I consider *the room to function as the Eden or the Paradise* of the story. "The room itself," says Marc Dudley, "is a squalid, smallish space on the outskirts of town, hidden away from prying, knowing eyes."[10] It is their place of privacy, their space of romance, a designated area of sexual pleasure and self-discovery, until it transmogrifies into the singular site of contention between them.

Hella eventually returns to Paris to meet David and declare her love and wish to marry. Then David leaves the room, escaping the relationship—without telling Giovanni about Hella's return—leaving Giovanni to wither in cold despondence. Desperate and humiliated, he discovers the truth about David's departure, tries to find life despite the abandonment, but ultimately kills Guillaume, his corrupt employer, who wields his power whenever and however he sees fit after knowingly falsely accusing Giovanni of stealing. The Police Nationale capture Giovanni and incarcerate him, until the judge sentences him to death by the guillotine. The news sends David spiraling until Hella finds him at a queer bar in the south of France, discovering the secret he kept from not only her but also, in a way, himself.

My argument is that a deeper look into this novel, with Saint Paul's reading of Eden and asceticism in mind, reveals an argument occurring between the text and Paul's epistles. Though David does not reveal any Christian or evangelical fervor, for Baldwin, white Americans' religious sentiments exist at a lower frequency than his Black Pentecostal upbringing. White Americans do not need religion as much as the poor black people, so the influence of Christian doctrine is more subtle in their lives. In other words, David's lack of religious expression conveys more than conceals Saint Paul's influence. To prove my argument, I will explore Paul's interpretation of Eden and the Fall, then return to Giovanni's room to make connections.

SAINT PAUL OF TARSUS

Saint Paul is a figure who emerged out of thin air in the first century.[11] He was not a member of Jesus's circle, and he had no prior relationship with any of the Jews from Galilee prior to Jesus's execution. Yet he penned multiple letters Alain Badiou calls "speeches of rupture" to diverse assemblies in Corinth between 52 and 57 CE.[12] His intention was to answer their complicated theological and ethical questions that arose from their varying ethnic, religious, and socioeconomic backgrounds.[13] However, writings meant for small locales resulted in the alteration of a religion that then expanded across the globe. Letters sent to specific assemblies became ageless teachings to people across time and space. And although we may lack a substantial amount of the materials Saint Paul produced, we do possess some specific letters regarding Eden.

We have a letter known as "First Epistle to the Corinthians" and a possible compilation of letters, or simply one letter edited out of its order, to the Corinthians known as the "Second Epistle."[14] Saint Paul expounds upon some of the central theological ideas he penned to the Corinthian assemblies in a letter to a church he did not establish in Rome entitled, "The Epistle to the Romans."[15] All three early documents are significant regarding the creation theories because Saint Paul alludes to the Watchers story, but he mostly elaborates upon the ramifications of the Edenic myth and what occurred as a result of Adam partaking of the forbidden fruit.[16]

This rhetorical choice to focus on Eden as opposed to the Watchers is ultimately what elevates the Garden of Eden myth to greater importance for the church theologians who wrote and studied after Paul. In other words, the Edenic myth gained traction alongside Saint Paul's growing significance in the second century and afterward.[17] By the second century, the pseudepigraphic Pauline writers were not only reinterpreting the Eden myth but also refusing to blame Adam and placing all of it on Eve's shoulders. 1 Timothy 2:13–14 says, "For Adam was formed first, then Eve; and Adam was not deceived, but the woman was deceived and became a transgressor." This is fascinating, considering that N. P. Williams states that much of Paul's commentary on Adam and Eve was just rhetorical allusions. They were not fully fleshed ideas that he conceptualized and put forward. The concept of Original Sin as a doctrine would not receive serious treatment until the following century, but the seeds and foundation of that change were in Saint Paul's possible side remarks.[18]

Felipe de Jesús Legarreta-Castillo, however, does not see the Adam typology as mere fodder in Paul's writings. For Legarreta-Castillo, there is direct, intentional thought and creativity put into this dichotomy between the first Adam, in Genesis, and the last Adam, Jesus:

> Paul uses the Adam Christology to explain the event of the resurrection as the new creation and the last aeon already inaugurated by Christ, which for the believer still lies in the future. With the Adam typology Paul challenges the believer to participate in the present in the resurrection of Christ through a new lifestyle, that of Christ. Although to rise with Christ is a future event, it can be anticipated in the present through ethical behavior.[19]

According to Legarreta-Castillo, Adam and Eve are constantly alluded to for the sake of moral arguments and examples. Also, Eden is not reducible to the few times it is referenced in Corinthians and Romans. In fact, it is present and alluded to throughout the entirety of both books, and that truth is only revealed through conducting exegesis and following the literary patterns of both letters. All in all, whether as a side remark or with clear intentions, these specific letters convey Saint Paul's interpretation of the Garden of Eden, and I will read them in succession before showing how Baldwin's novel engages with their ideas.

Saint Paul wrote to the Corinthian assemblies from Ephesus to correct a considerable number of misunderstandings and differences between his theology and that of some contemporaries. Dale B. Martin argues that a group was present in Corinth known as the "Strong," comprising people of a higher socioeconomic status. The Strong maintained a common but upper-class ideology about the body and its inferior status in the cosmic grand scheme of existence.[20] Paul, Martin argues, tried through his letter to invert their logic of hierarchy for just about everything (other than women), because it was so determined by status. Saint Paul was committed to presenting the gospel in paradoxical terms that would elevate those considered low and humble above those who deemed themselves noble.

Questions surrounding rituals and etiquette were also important. The Corinthians, we assume, inquired about the proper protocol for the Eucharist, asked Saint Paul for his thoughts on sexual practices, and wanted him to mediate in ecclesial rivalries. The notion of splits and factions dominates the letter. Paul was disappointed in what he had heard from them, especially the cynical "slogans" that the elite were asserting. Nevertheless, the Corinthians had questions, and Saint Paul needed to address them.[21]

The Corinthians held various other opinions concerning not just the death and resurrection of Jesus specifically but the very possibility of resurrection for a human body. Considering how difficult it was, or is, for anyone to believe in the rise of a dead organism, they wondered why accepting the resurrection of the human body was the ultimate sine qua non for identifying as a believer in Saint Paul's sect of Judaism. All throughout the first century there were debates about the afterlife and what body entered such a place, whether physical or astral. Martin states that because of a misunderstanding of specific Greek words, the Corinthians thought that Paul was arguing not just for resurrection but for the crude resuscitation of corpses. And Saint Paul thought the Corinthians were against the resurrection of the body entirely.[22]

To Saint Paul, if Jesus was not resurrected, then the faith itself is pointless, without purpose, and the Fall's consequences are still in order. He writes, "And if Christ has not been raised, your faith is futile; you are still in your sins."[23] And if the faith is false, then all of us are unjustified, guilty of the crimes we have committed, and condemned to death. Then we are imprisoned in the ground whence we came. This theology against death is why I interpret Saint Paul as a Jewish apocalyptic theologian.[24] His theology—which we can only glean and piece together from the disparate sections of the various letters he sent—shares significant resonance with other contemporary apocalyptic literature and prophets, which all argue through numerous political theologies that God, in some mysterious capacity, is breaking into time and space and ultimately changing reality as we know it from an evil, deathly eon to an eon that is yet to come.

The synoptic gospels refer to this with different language, oscillating between the "Kingdom of God" and the "Kingdom of Heaven." Yet Saint Paul, whose letters preceded the gospels, envisions the oncoming eon as the dawn of a new cosmos, a new creation. Paula Fredriksen writes,

> The Jesus who is the focus of Paul's fierce commitment is the divine and pre-existent Son of God, the agent of creation "through whom all things are" (1 Cor 8:6), who came to earth, died by crucifixion, was raised and exalted, and is about to return. This pattern of descent, ascent, and approaching return is the essential content of Paul's gospel—or, as he sees it, of the Gospel, the secret and hidden wisdom of God decreed before the *aiones* (ages) for the glorification of the believer.[25]

To be sure, Paul's perspective is distinct from the purely apocalyptic viewpoint of other Jewish theologians. For Saint Paul, the "age to come," or God's invitation, is not simply an event brought about by God but is *identical with Jesus's resurrection*.[26] Therefore, it has already commenced and will not be fulfilled until Jesus's return. In other words, the resurrection is a cosmic invitation to continue with life, with existence. And Paul's mission, in his heart of hearts, is to rescue as many people as possible from the inevitable cosmic destruction by informing them about what is ahead for this world.[27]

While Saint Paul speaks of the resurrection as the beginning of a new creation, where believers will experience the fullness of sharing in God's community, he invokes Adam in describing the current order of existence *as the age of death and decay*. For Paul, the Edenic narrative symbolizes the destructive onset of sin's appearance within our slowly declining epoch. Adam stands as an emblem of disobedience, of the wretchedness that is pervasive in the here and now. In Paul's analysis, *Adam is the figure of undoing*, the culprit who caused the cosmic corruption of our reality. Death and destruction were not part of God's original plan for the world. The Hellenistic Jewish author of Wisdom of Solomon, writing around the same time as Saint Paul, makes an identical claim: "God did not make death, and he does not delight in the death of the living. For he created all things so that they might exist; the generative forces of the world are wholesome, and there is no destructive poison in them, and the dominion of Hades is not on earth."[28] These words overlap with Saint Paul's claim that Adam's disobedience altered how God intended to fulfill his desire for creation. Herman Ridderbos writes, "One man has given sin access into the world; he has, as it were, opened the gate of the world to sin. So sin has entered in, here represented as a personified power (cf., e.g., v. 21); through and with sin death has come in as the inseparable follower and companion of sin."[29] With that in mind, Tatha Wiley says, "The whole of creation is in bondage to sin."[30] Therefore, Adam represents flesh, the source of nature's wounds. And flesh is trapped in time, crumbling, and feeding on itself until it withers and perishes. Jesus Christ, the savior, or corrector, of our eon, is known as the "Last Adam," the figure of our remaking.

Jesus, the Messiah, represents eternity, timelessness, and the persistence of life outside of the world we know. If we want to be saved from this evil age, if we yearn to be rescued from time, space, and ourselves, we must link our spirit to Jesus's spirit; but how? Saint Paul says baptism, the ritual of death's defeat. Fredriksen says the believer "participates in the triumph" over death by way of baptism, offering themselves up for adoption by the spirit of God, ultimately attaching their fate and destiny to the resurrection of Christ.[31] John E. Toews writes:

The context is concerned with corporate entities and realities—
Adam as a representative figure, Sin, old man, body of sin, slaves
of sin, versus Christ as a representative figure, Grace, living in
God, slaves of righteousness, slaves of God. The burden of this
text unit is the relationship of Christians to two kingdoms and
two lords—both kingdoms and lords by definition involve a community of people. In baptism into Christ believers have been
transferred from one kingdom into another.[32]

In other words, one must—and here is a connection to *Giovanni's Room*—remove their Adamic flesh and adopt Jesus's spiritual flesh to gain entrance to or continuance with the oncoming
eon. This baptism and resurrection ultimately signal the correction to the first Adam's transgression.[33] Yet there is more. Paul's
letters to the assemblies in Corinth are not the only times he gave
an Edenic interpretation.

LETTER TO THE ROMAN ASSEMBLY

While Paul was in Corinth, near Cenchreae, he wrote a letter to
the church in Rome that was drastically different in tone and
structure from his Corinthian letters. He highlighted essential
points of his theology and expounded upon his complicated
notions of the human body. Wayne A. Meeks and N. T. Wright
agree that the letter is not a "systematic summary of Pauline
theology" or a "summary of Paul's lifework" but in many ways
a theological treatise, an outline of his central theological
arguments.[34] Paul did not plant the Roman church; but, following Meeks again, I believe this letter is not an introduction
to his overall theology as much as a defense against whatever

controversial image of him the Roman church held in their minds, given his reputation and interventions.

In this letter, which clearly reveals Saint Paul's cultural prejudices regarding the lifestyles and cultures of non-Jewish peoples (most noticeably in chapter 1), Paul emphasizes the "priestly" notion of Christ dying for the wicked and ungodly, highlighting the significance of God reconciling with Gentiles and Jews. For Paul, this is essential: *justification is a kind of reconciliation*, and *reconciliation means life*, a life that bypasses death and starts the process of sanctification. Furthering the thoughts in his first letter to the Corinthians, Paul writes:

> Therefore, just as sin entered the world through one man, and death through sin, and in this way death came to all people, because all sinned; To be sure, sin was in the world before the law was given, but sin is not charged against anyone's account where there is no law. Nevertheless, death reigned from the time of Adam to the time of Moses, even over those who did not sin by breaking a command, as did Adam, who is a pattern of the one to come.[35]

Paul uses the Hebraic myth to emphasize to the Roman church that sin—and its consequence, death—was a powerful cosmic force wreaking havoc on the living before Moses issued the law, thanks to Adam's disobedience. And even though Gentiles did not know the law and so cannot be held completely accountable for breaking it, they still experienced death because of Adam. Here is the key: Adam becomes the source of Saint Paul's theodicy. Adam helps Paul understand human sin and death on a cosmic level without saying that God is the reason for or source of it.

Albert Schweitzer thinks the first and last component should be inverted: "As a pre-existent Being, Christ should really be designated in Paul's argument as the First Adam. But it is by His coming in the flesh and His dying and rising again that He first becomes man, from whom new humanity can go forth."[36] Karl Barth goes further than Paul with an Edenic interpretation on this point and offers this reading of Adam and the law:

> The people of Israel are brought to ruin by their law and by their peculiar election and vocation; and they must suffer and decay in a manner unknown to the Philistines and the Moabites. So was it originally with Adam. Only because, having been warned concerning the tree of knowledge, Adam actually possesses the law, could sin enter into the world; and Adam became a sinner, because he was so nearly related to God. Is there any place, any epoch in history, any single human life, in which law plays no part?[37]

To Barth, Adam possessed the law. That was the one rule in the Garden of Eden, where he was prohibited from eating from the forbidden tree. And through his disobedience, sin entered the world.

Adam, however, is not analyzed in Saint Paul's letter as much as he is leveraged to convey the reconciling work of Jesus's death and resurrection. Once again, Adam is humanity, the cause of nature's sufferings, and spiritual imprisonment within a body makes it cumbersome to keep the law, which means he is inherently *a symbol of the punishment of death*. In proselytizing fashion, Saint Paul states that God's grace and forgiveness abound, even greater than Adam's trespass. "For if, while we were God's enemies," he proudly writes, "we were reconciled to him through the death of his Son, how much more, having been reconciled, shall we be saved through his life! Not only is this so, but we also boast in God through our Lord Jesus Christ, through whom we have now received reconciliation."[38]

For Saint Paul, Adam's fall and embracing of his own desires, his own urges, his own flesh explained the severance in the relationship between God and humanity. That separation engendered a world of evil, of heinous activity, of oppression and domination between creatures. Christ's work centers around reconciling humanity to God, to life, and restoring them from the ravages of separation by offering grace, erasing the consequences of embracing the flesh. Saint Paul reads the Edenic myth like a Jewish apocalyptic theologian: he perceives the narrative as a tale of the quintessential opportunity for continuing with life after the destruction. Adam disrupted the original harmony, the original goodness, but we do not have to fret because Jesus has already established the road to recovery. But the invitation comes with moral requirements, a request to live with an ascetic impulse that refuses to allow the flesh to dictate one's actions.

Now I return to *Giovanni's Room* with Saint Paul's essential points in the background to show how Baldwin argues with him through his apocalyptic tale.

THE WARNING

In the Garden of Eden, Yahweh warns Adam that he is prohibited from partaking of the forbidden fruit lest he experience the punishment of nonexistence—the undoing of existence, otherwise known as death. This punishment is the revoking of life. The serpent, however, challenges the veracity of the threat and asks Eve if she is confident that the deity was being honest. In *Giovanni's Room*, the character Jacques, an older gay male acquaintance, occupies both the deity's and the serpent's position. Jacques warns David about how terribly things could end for Giovanni (like the deity). He also warns David about the consequences of *not engaging* in what has been forbidden (like the serpent). Jacques tells David that Giovanni has no idea that he is "putting himself in the lion's mouth," a frightening allusion to the threat of Persian punishment in the book of Daniel.[39] Yet he also tells David that he is fortunate to experience what is transpiring with Giovanni while he is young, as opposed to experiencing the loneliness that he endures in his older life, because then, like him, David would "simply be destroyed."[40]

Instead of offering compassion or understanding, David reveals to Jacques that he is aware of his lifestyle and finds it despicable.[41] The frequent sexual escapades in which Jacques engages around Paris are not as clandestine as he thinks; they are well known, and David judges him harshly. Jacques says in response: "There are so many ways of being despicable it quite makes one's head spin. But the way to be really despicable is to be contemptuous of other people's pain. You ought to have some apprehension that the man you see before you was once even younger than you are now and arrived at his present wretchedness by imperceptible degrees."[42]

Though David asserts an insulting assessment of Jacques, Jacques requests compassion and understanding. And he uses his life as a warning for David. In one of the most moving passages of the text, Jacques, already described as shameful, counters the great apostle's portrayal of the flesh and its perceived impurity. While Saint Paul describes the flesh to the churches across the ancient Mediterranean as a destructive barrier to achieving holiness, essentially labeling it as unclean, Jacques offers a Baldwinian perspective and response by admonishing David to:

"Love him . . . love him and let him love you. Do you think anything else under heaven really matters? And how long, at the best, can it last? since you are both men and still have everywhere to go? Only five minutes, I assure you, only five minutes, and most of that, *hélas!* in the dark. And if you think of them as dirty, then they will be dirty—they will be dirty because you will be giving nothing, you will be despising your flesh and his. But you can make your time together anything but dirty; you can give each other something which will make both of you better—forever—if you will not be ashamed, if you will only not play it safe . . . You play it safe long enough . . . you'll end up trapped in your own dirty body, forever and forever and forever—like me."

Jacques's use of the word "safe" not only mirrors how Baldwin defines religion but also invokes what Baldwin calls in his essay "Here Be Dragons" a "dependence on a formula for safety."[43] For him, religion and its imposed heteronormativity are nothing more than an adherence to a Western cultural protocol that instructs humans on how to live without trouble, passion, or risk.

Jacques warns David about his American precautions and doctrines. He reveals to David what could happen if he views his time with Giovanni as dirty, and he probably also means as sacrilege. David has a chance to allow himself to love and be loved without corrupting it with theology, a theology corrupted with American masculinity and with, in so many words, the voice and presence of Saint Paul.

It is Jacques's words that offer the inspiration for this chapter. When David tells Jacques that he wishes Giovanni had remained in Italy planting olive gardens and singing until he died in his slumber, Jacques responds, "Nobody can stay in the garden of Eden . . . I wonder why."[44] Yet when we forget Saint Paul's analysis of why we can't or keep such a theology at bay, according to Baldwin, we have the chance to experience a fullness, a vulnerability, an openness to love and an Eden that was always ours. However, when we remember Saint Paul and hold on to him, according to Baldwin, we encounter the consequences that come with a theology that transforms his insight into an imposing, self-judging force.

This insight is an inherited punishment that we must remember to live under lest we mistakenly believe ourselves too worthy of anything worthwhile. In other words, Baldwin's world is dominated by a Pauline influence that causes all of us to believe that "mortifying our flesh" is the divine prerequisite for our mere existence. David says again, "Perhaps everybody has a garden of Eden, I don't know; but they have scarcely seen their garden before they see the flaming sword."[45] To Baldwin, it is the cherubim's swords that threaten us with death if we dare try to reenter the Garden and declare to the deity that we did nothing wrong.

After Jacques's words, however, the flaming sword and the fear of the inferno and its tormenting death appears. David sees out of nowhere a figure resembling a zombie or a mummy gliding toward him. He does not quite know how to describe the experience. In fact, we understand David's fear in the moment better this way than through an actual description of the person. He says: "*It seemed* to make no sound, this was due to the roar of the bar, which was like the roaring of the sea, heard at night, from far away. *It* glittered in the dim light; the thin, black hair was violent with oil, combed forward, hanging in bangs; the eyelids gleamed with mascara, the mouth raged with lipstick" (emphasis mine).[46]

David continues: "The face was white and thoroughly bloodless with some kind of foundation cream; it stank of powder and a gardenia-like perfume."⁴⁷ It asked David if he liked Giovanni. David eventually told it to go to hell. And it responded in a way that caused David to yearn to flee.

> "Oh, no," he said—and I looked at him again. He was laughing, showing all his teeth—there were not many. "Oh, no," he said, "I go not to hell," and he clutched his crucifix with one large hand. "But you, my dear friend, I fear that you shall burn in a very hot fire." He laughed again. "Oh, such fire!" He touched his head. "Here." And he writhed, as though in torment. "Everywhere." And he touched his heart. "And here."⁴⁸

Here the novel reflects an encounter with Saint Paul's words again. Paul writes: "But if they are not practicing self-control, they should marry. For it is better to marry than to be aflame with passion."⁴⁹ Perhaps this burning passion is what causes David to see the image of a zombie, because Baldwin also writes: "Freaks are called freaks and are treated as they are treated—in the main, abominably—because they are human beings who cause to echo, deep within us, our most profound terrors and desires."⁵⁰ The description of the person who approached him reflects what David imposes on them. What David sees terrifies him because what he is experiencing with Giovanni is terrifying. Yet Saint Paul is there to suggest marriage, but not out of love or desire. This suggestion stems from what Foucault calls the aphrodisia regime for self-mastery.⁵¹

David's encounter with Giovanni functions like a definitive theologically momentous event. Their first conversation is followed by divine imagery, warnings, fires, and zombies. It is an *apocalyptic event* that requires the imagery of Daniel and Revelations to capture it. David's world is undone. His vision is skewed. He is lost in the moment thereafter until he finds himself in

Giovanni's room. The room is the Eden of the text, the Paradise that he flees, which causes the crumbling of their world.

THE FALL

Before David meets Giovanni and finds himself inside an Edenic Paradise, he is despondent and reflecting on his life and past, trying to confess what happened. In these reflections David's thoughts reveals the fingerprints of early creation stories and the subsequent Judeo-Christian debates about their implications. First, David thinks about an earlier sexual encounter with a friend named Joey. What connects this memory to the Judeo-Christian debates is that Baldwin frames the story for David as an initial "Fall" where David and Joey's passionate lovemaking was a terrible awakening, engendered by partaking of something forbidden. Afterward, David looks at Joey's body, his nakedness, and feels tainted. He feels guilty. He feels ruined. And in David's mind this is an awakening where "something" inside him emerged and decomposed.

Second, relating to issues of creation (and divine punishments), David's nameless father functions in the novel as an allusion to Noah and his "drunkenness" in Genesis 9. His father's alcoholism—according to his aunt—serves as an omen or a curse to David, to the point that he ends up in a hospital after drunk driving. I will explain further how Joey emerges as an "object" who causes David's fall and inaugurates his Original Sin, then draw the connection between David's father and Noah in the book of Genesis.

While gazing out the window, deep in contemplation of the unfortunate ripple effect of his actions that ultimately led to Giovanni's death sentence, David's mind drifts back to Joey. Joey and their sexual encounter, in David's mind, caused "something" to *happen within him*. This "something" was so terrible to David that the mere thought of having a friendship with Joey in his childhood was proof of a unique inner depravity. David reflects, "For a while he was my best friend. Later, the idea that such a person could have been my best friend was proof of some *horrifying taint in me*. So, I forgot him. But I see him very well tonight" (emphasis mine).[52] As he reflects upon the circumstances that led him and Joey to share an erotic moment, he acknowledges to himself that during their playful interaction, they touched and "something happened in him and in me which made this touch different from any touch either of us had ever known."[53] The touch brought an unfamiliar joy. Baldwin writes,

> And he did not resist, as he usually did, but lay where I had pulled him, against my chest. And I realized that my heart was beating in an awful way and that Joey was trembling against me and the light in the room was very bright and hot. I started to move and to make some kind of joke but Joey mumbled something and I put my head down to hear. Joey raised his head as I lowered mine and we kissed, as it were, by accident.[54]

They felt pleasure. They felt a mutual love that seemed to be fulfilling and transformative. However, it was not the type of transformation with which David was comfortable. I interpret, in the early section of the novel, that Baldwin frames Joey's body as *David's forbidden fruit*. And enjoying Joey's body awakened the "something" inside David that had lain dormant, but once it was awakened, he felt fear like that Adam and Eve felt after Yahweh noticed that they had eaten the fruit. Clarence E. Hardy III argues: "For Baldwin, sexual intimacy holds a sacramental quality as a vehicle for love and truth. In this world, love's emotional territory of human sexual connection replaces the institutional church and reveals risky truths that no one can afford to deny if they want to stay vibrant and alive."[55]

Yet this encounter and its repercussions remains David's own secret. He says, "I could not discuss what happened to me with anyone, I could not even admit it to myself; and, while I never thought about it, it remained, nevertheless, at the bottom of my mind, as still and as awful as a decomposing corpse. And it changed, it thickened, it soured the atmosphere of my mind."[56] For Saint Paul, Adam's bite of fruit brought the reality of death. It undid creation and introduced decay. For David, his erotic moment with Joey polluted his psyche with *the presence of decay*. And he ignored this decay with the Pauline asceticism that denies any feelings or information from his flesh.

The other Genesis story that subtly appears in David's reflection is the image of Noah after the demiurge. In Genesis 9, Noah plants a vineyard in the wake of God's destruction of everyone on the planet besides his family, and drinks until he's drunk. Ham, Noah's youngest son, looks at his father lying naked in his tent and has a different reaction from that of Shem and Japheth. When Noah awakens and hears from his two elder sons what Ham did, he curses not only Ham but also Ham's son and future generations.

David's Aunt Ella disapproves of the drinking habits of David's father. She warns him that his behavior will have a negative effect on David. And in David's reflections, he sees the impact of his father's actions. Using the Genesis language, Baldwin writes: "Fathers ought to avoid utter nakedness before their sons. I did not want to know—not, anyway, from his mouth—that his flesh was as unregenerate as my own."[57] His father's drunkenness is connected to David's conception of his own Original Sin because of his Aunt Ella's warning. In so many words, she believes that David will one day be responsible for his own freedom and his poor decisions will reflect the drunkenness, or overall nakedness, of his father. David connects that warning to not only his moment with Joey but also the "something" inside him that *compelled him into* that moment with Joey.

DAVID, THE AMERICAN ADAM

My following argument, which establishes another connection between *Giovanni's Room* and the Garden of Eden, illustrates how Baldwin skillfully writes within, and critiques, a specific American literary tradition. Baldwin uses David to embody the characteristics of what literary scholars and historians call the "American Adam." According to R. W. B. Lewis, this archetypal character presents "the image of a radically new personality, the hero of the new adventure: an individual emancipated from history, happily bereft of ancestry, untouched and undefiled by the usual inheritances of family and race; an individual standing alone, self-reliant and self-propelling, ready to confront whatever awaited him with the aid of his own unique and inherent resources."[58]

Although this symbolic man is normally lauded for his heroic sense of adventure, his desire to instantiate new ideals in his environment, and his complete disavowal of history and ancestry, Baldwin's novel takes a significantly critical stance on the self-deception and immaturity this character and overall consciousness portrays.[59] Therefore, Baldwin is writing in the tradition of Herman Melville, Ralph Waldo Emerson, Walt Whitman, and his beloved Henry James. Yet Baldwin is distinct in that by casting David as a bland "American Adam," he unveils not only the flaws and limitations of this idealized figure but also how shattering it is for American men who deceive themselves into believing they personify it. David fails this archetype in every way. This overwhelming failure causes me to read *Giovanni's Room* through the lens of Halberstam's *The Queer Art of Failure*.

On one hand, David's failed rugged masculine individualism brought him to Paris, but on the other hand, his projected Emersonian self-reliance is completely nonexistent. He relies on everyone around him, yet behaves as if he is an island unto himself. This failed prototype is also a significant contribution to the American ideals of sexuality, which rely on such failures to exist in contrast. In "Here Be Dragons," Baldwin writes: "The American ideal, then, of sexuality appears to be rooted in the American ideal of masculinity. This ideal has created cowboys and Indians, good guys and bad guys, punks and studs, tough guys and softies, butch and f*****, black and white. It is an ideal so paralytically infantile that it is virtually forbidden as an unpatriotic act that the American boy evolve into the complexity of manhood."[60] The failed Adams serve as the foundation for the American Adams to exist theoretically.

Moreover, Robert Armour states, "The Adam must face an adventure which will test his heroic abilities and also jeopardize his innocence."[61] Baldwin's character, David, is an American Adam in flight. I read his escape as a decision based on his desire to evade—or work to accept—the heteronormative pressure to wed and live. He feels the "death drive," as Lee Edelman theorizes, being thrust upon him by the community, his father, and eventually Hella; as a result, Paris functions as a massive testing ground or place to confront his asceticism, positioning himself to fight against his flesh while also attempting to maintain his own theoretical and theological innocence.[62] I am not saying that David is fully consciously aware of his reasons for traversing around the city; he is for all intents and purposes oblivious to what I am outlining, and to much else. Yet he does know and understand that he has a life already premade for him. And it is always available. He can rely on the "safety" described earlier. In Paris, there is something about that life that he is not only refusing but also in denial about refusing. David's own Adamic "ignorance" about who and how he is with other people is also connected to his own self-projected—and, quite frankly, very American—innocence.

For David, there is a mysterious erotic force pursuing him, akin to a sinful taint (though he does not employ that language), that seeks to *dirty him*, soil him, and place him in community with the filth by which he is disgusted and surrounded. His concession to this mysterious erotic force causes him, in the most unexpected moments, to feel the need to confess a guilt that he does not fully comprehend or investigate. This obliviousness and innocence are also connected to how Lewis sees the Adamic characters and consciousness emerge throughout early American literature: "It was not surprising, in a Bible-reading generation, that the new hero (in praise or disapproval) was most easily identified with Adam *before the Fall*. Adam was the first, the archetypal, man. His moral position was prior to experience, and in his very newness he was fundamentally innocent. The world and history lay all before him."[63]

David may not understand what makes him an archetypal American figure to the other characters, but he takes offense when his own American disposition is lodged as an accusation of some wrongdoing, and he is terribly confused when he is not associated with its new historical grandeur. Ernest L. Gibson, III, is correct that Baldwin "does not simply use America as a metaphor for a certain type of sexuality but also shows how the history of it as a geographical and colonial space also informs the limits of sexual expression."[64] All the main characters focus on David's Americanness, not only the ways it appears in the story but also the distance it creates between himself and them.

In Matt Brim's reading, several American Adams surround David.[65] These include the sailors and David's father. Brim brilliantly argues that the image of "Mr. Clean" is the ultimate Adamic figure but is also an impossible heteronormative ideal that David strives for but can never imitate.[66] Baldwin writes about these various American Adams elsewhere.[67] I, however, will isolate the archetype to David and counter it with Giovanni.

Giovanni is, quite significantly, the opposite of David but, most importantly, the *challenge* to the Adamic archetype. He is not only confident, unlike David; he is also, in a Tillichian sense, *self-accepting*.[68] He is not only self-aware, unlike David; he is also attentive to the historical forces that have contributed to *who he is*. The messiness of his room is a result of the life he lives and has lived. As an Italian in Paris, he is also aware of what it means for David to be an American (Leeming argues that Giovanni is a "metaphorical or symbolic vehicle for [Baldwin] and black America's confrontation with the white world"[69]). That distinction serves as the foundation of their first conversation but also of all their differences. David struggles with his commitment and/or failure to meet the demands of "America." There is a heteronormative life awaiting him if he will accept it by marrying Hella and heading home. Each letter from David's father is filled with reminders about his Americanness, his nationalist inheritance—which is the drive Edelman warns about. In a letter pleading for David to return home and marry a woman, any woman, his father tells him that there is nothing for him in Europe and that he is "as American as pork and beans."[70] Returning home would consequently provide David with everything he should want and need. Giovanni, in contrast, is both the vocal critique of and the existential challenge to that inheritance.

In *Giovanni's Room*, David grapples or compromises with all the unrealistically high societal expectations of his manhood, and he struggles to conform to the prescribed mold of the

American Adam, although that ideal was initially easily his. And he attempts to suppress his true desires and emotions, following a path that ultimately leads to a deadly self-betrayal. Through David's journey, Baldwin unveils the destructive consequences of adhering to this rigid notion of masculinity, showcasing the toll it takes on what it means to be a human, to be a creature on this planet. Furthermore, by critiquing the American literary tradition through David's characterization, Baldwin challenges the larger cultural norms of his time. He dares to question the societal pressure to conform to certain ideals of manhood and explores the ramifications of this conformity for personal relationships and emotional well-being. Through this critique, Baldwin redefines the concept of masculinity and offers a more nuanced portrayal of human identity. Calling into question the narrow definition of the American Adam, he advocates for a more compassionate and accepting understanding of human complexity and vulnerability.

In David and Giovanni's first conversation, Giovanni is a skeptical critic of "America" and what it means, what it excuses, and how it operates in the world. Bill V. Mullen writes that "Baldwin's invocation here of American 'manifest destiny'—westward expansion via Indian genocide—implicates David from the first in the demise of Giovanni."[71] America as a mythical concept is the source of David's self-projected innocence and the foundation of his yearning to be clean. All the critiques of America are explicit critiques of the source of David's behavior. However, Giovanni never offers a comprehensive critique of America. His criticism exists in between the lines of his responses to David, as does the attitude of the other characters.

In one of their first conversations, Giovanni alludes to the Adamic archetype consciousness by stating that Americans have become a different species from the Europeans. Giovanni is approaching a theory of whiteness, but it is suggested, not fully developed. America, to Giovanni, is a new empire in the world that carelessly exercises its will across time and space and lives without any responsibility to the rest of the world. In other words, Americans are powerful children with little knowledge of contextual history regarding who they are or *why they are the way they are*.[72] Mullen writes that Baldwin thus "combined an open account of gay life with a ringing critique of American racial history, settler-colonialism, and white supremacy."[73] But the pain that David causes Giovanni creates a desire to flee within him. Giovanni too, before his death, wants to escape from his own flesh. His love for an American Adam in flight, and failure, succeeds at making him despise himself in the end.

David and Giovanni represent a battle between Saint Paul's theology and Baldwin's counter to it. David, as the Adamic character, concedes to a philosophy that states that the body is a barrier to a proper life. Ignoring the body, suppressing the impulses, and mortifying or denying the flesh is the key to achieving the good. For Giovanni, the flesh informs. The flesh does not lie. And to love someone requires one's whole entire body to participate. That David flees, sends Giovanni spiraling, and causes Giovanni to say, "je veux m'evader—this dirty world, this dirty body. I never wish to make love again with anything more than the body" is Baldwin's way of conveying how pervasive, powerful, and triumphant is Paul's perspective.[74]

THE ROOM

After a nightcap with friends, David finally enters Giovanni's room. This is, at first, their Eden, their Paradise, their privacy away from the world. David Leeming sees the room as a metaphorical place of freedom for the characters, "a symbol of the paradoxical gift offered, the enveloping and overpowering gift of freedom that is so hard to accept."⁷⁵ They stare at each other through the gloom, trembling, ignoring the clutter and items in their way, then descend onto the bed to create a forbidden moment of love. Christopher V. Hobson writes: "Beyond experiential responses, Baldwin presents sexual union as able to create a partial, temporary break from oppressive reality into a zone of freedom, and this experience, at least by implication, offers a foretaste of a future freedom that will be available to all."⁷⁶

In David's reflection after the dust settles and Giovanni heads toward the guillotine, he tries to capture the meaning of the room but cannot. He remembers that life there "seemed to be occurring beneath the sea."⁷⁷ David is trying to discover the proper words for erotic immanence, attempting vigorously to give language to the experience of Paradise. He wants to honor the life inside that room. He needs to, but without erasing the flesh paramount for the pleasure. Let us, as the readers and interpreters of this tale, ask him ourselves:

What was it like there, David? What feelings or moments of truth and enjoyment did the space not only allow but compel? What was time like?
"Time flowed past indifferently above us; hours and days had no meaning."

In the beginning, were you happy?
"In the beginning, our life together held a joy and amazement which was newborn every day."

Was it Paradise? What was it like?
"Beneath the joy, of course, was anguish and beneath the amazement was fear; but they did not work themselves to the beginning until our high beginning was aloe on our tongues."

We know it didn't last. Perhaps Paradise never does. But when did it all begin to fall apart?

"By then anguish and fear had become the surface on which we slipped and slid, losing balance, dignity, and pride. Giovanni's face, which I had memorized so many mornings, noons, and nights, hardened before my eyes, began to give in secret places, began to crack. The light in the eyes became a glitter; the wide and beautiful brow began to suggest the skull beneath. The sensual lips turned inward, busy with the sorrow overflowing from his heart. It became a stranger's face, or it made me so guilty to look upon him that I wished it were a stranger's face."[78]

Giovanni has plans for remodeling his space and is in the process when he meets David. David recalls Giovanni's wallpaper, paint brushes, and tools all over the floor. He recalls the windows painted white to prevent outsiders from seeing in. He recalls the bottles of oil and turpentine, along with the laundry spread everywhere. The mess, to David, reflects the disarray of Giovanni's life. All around the room, cardboard, leather, and various other objects are bursting out of boxes. He notices a violin as well; "lying on the table in its warped, cracked case, it was impossible to guess from looking at it whether it had been laid to rest there yesterday or a hundred years before."[79] David believes the disorganization of Giovanni's room is an external representation of grief. He then concludes: "I understood why Giovanni had wanted me and had brought me to his last retreat. I was to destroy this room and give Giovanni a new and better life. This life could only be my own, which, to transform Giovanni's, must first become a part of Giovanni's room."[80]

David believes that Giovanni brought him to the room to undo his life, redo his room, simply by becoming a part of it. What I see is that the room, the space—from Giovanni's perspective—is only an instrument, a vehicle through which David can grow and create a life with Giovanni. Marc Dudley's interpretation is that "Like David, the room is a keeper of secrets, seemingly shut off from the rest of the world. Also, like David, it is itself sequestered, scattered, scarred. Way too small, cluttered and disorganized, and in a perpetual state of disrepair, the room stands as a testament to and reflection of David's spiritual torment."[81] Mullen notes that "Baldwin uses mirror imagery and claustrophobic rooms throughout the novel to suggest how both David and Giovanni are trapped in a heteronormative social matrix that destroys their love."[82]

The Edenic nature of the room, for Giovanni, seems closer to Jose Muñoz's description of a queer utopia: queerness "is a warm illumination of a horizon imbued with potentiality."[83] They have discovered a possibility, together, that could alter their realities, propel them to a *there* that will be better than the imprisoning *now*. In fact, the *now* is only a glimpse, a taste of what could be. And what could be is neither abstract nor theoretical— they experience it in the *now* that they seek to escape.

According to Muñoz, "queerness as utopian formation is a formation based on an economy of desire and desiring. This desire is always directed at that thing that is not yet here, objects and moments that burn with anticipation and promise."[84] This perfectly encapsulates what Giovanni feels. He allows himself to experience something utopian with David, only for David to sabotage it in accepting the promises given to normativity.

According to my reading, from what David says before he searches for the meaning of the room, he does not know how to describe the room at all. All he can truly interpret is that it is the place where a transformation has occurred, "beneath the sea." This change is so overwhelming for David that he feigns contentment in his flesh to mentally disassociate from their intimacy: "I was in a terrible confusion. Sometimes I thought, but this is your life. Stop fighting it. Stop fighting. Or I thought, but I am happy. And he loves me. I am safe. Sometimes, when he was not near me, I thought, I will never let him touch me again. Then, when he touched me, I thought, it doesn't matter, it is only the body, it will soon be over."[85]

David cannot heed Jacques's warning. Perhaps Jacques knew David would not be able to and clearly saw the trouble toward which Giovanni was heading. And that foreboding comes to fruition after Hella arrives in Paris. Giovanni senses that David is itching to leave the room, which means leaving him, and tries to find ways to prevent his inevitable departure. David, however, is tormented by both his self-devouring love and his passionate desire to flee. He lives with that tension, trying to find ways to hide it, conceal it, until one morning when he cannot help referring to the room as "hideous" and asking Giovanni why he buries himself in it.

Yet for Giovanni, the room is not a hiding place as much as it is a haven. He does not see what David sees or experience what David experiences inside it. Both men are in Paris trying to escape something. David is trying to escape his inheritance, his masculinity, *his nakedness from his time with Joey,* while Giovanni is trying to escape his grief. Perhaps that is not the best way of putting it. Maybe grief is what caused Giovanni's arrival, carried his feet to the Seine. Not too long before the story begins Giovanni and an unnamed woman were in love. They lived in a vineyard in Italy and were expecting a baby until an unfortunate intrauterine death. This crushed Giovanni. He was in such despair that he went inside his home, took his crucifix off the wall, and spat on it, ultimately blaming Christ for the heartbreaking misfortune. After that he fled to Paris, never seeing his family again.

In the last moments of Giovanni's life, David wrestles with Saint Paul most explicitly, in front of a mirror. Giovanni, in David's imagining, is saying—perhaps silently—his Hail Mary. Returning to the moment when Giovanni revealed his actions after the death of his child, David imagines that he kisses the cross around his neck and again needs to spit, but this time he can't. His mouth is dry. As Giovanni faces the door to the guillotine, David reflects, "That door is the gateway he has sought so long out of this dirty world, this dirty body."[86] Back to the mirror, David then invokes Saint Paul's teaching directly and thinks: "The body in the mirror forces me to turn and face it. And I look at my body, *which is under the sentence of death*. It is lean, hard, and cold, the incarnation of a mystery. And I do not know what moves in this body, what this body is searching for. It is trapped in my mirror as *it is trapped in time* and it hurries toward revelation (emphasis mine)."[87]

Josiah Ulysses Young, III, draws a compelling connection between Baldwin's use of the mirror and Saint Paul's assertion that having various God-given skills and gifts amounts to nothing if love is absent.[88] The body is the problem of the text. Life, in the flesh, is the curse that will not let go. David believes himself to be convicted, practically ill fated, and trapped in a world that is counting down to his demise. He returns to Paul and quotes his Corinthian letter verbatim: "When I was a child, I spake as a child, I understood as a child, I thought as a child: but when I became a man, I put away childish things." This moment in the story displays a collaboration between Baldwin and Saint Paul. What Baldwin sees as childish—in the Pauline sense—in David's actions is his Adamic Americanness, his inability to be an adult, which means to accept himself on his own terms and in front of his own reflection. For Baldwin, Americans are children precisely because they are ignorant of not just history but their own behavior and practices in the world. Yet David wishes he could make the Corinthian scripture true for his own life. "I long to crack that mirror and be free. I look at my sex, my troubling sex, and wonder how it can be redeemed, how I can save it from the knife. The journey to the grave is already begun, the journey to corruption is, always, already, half over. Yet, the key to my salvation, which cannot save my body, is hidden in my flesh."[89]

He does not know exactly *where* this key is. He does not seem to know *what* the key is, either. All he knows, or believes, is that his flesh is the stumbling block that obstructs his access. And his inability to know where and what that key is, is one of the primary factors that leads Giovanni to his demise. However, I believe that, for Baldwin, *David's flesh is the key*. And the constant flight from it guarantees its destruction.

I am not alone in seeing a connection, or at least an encounter, between James Baldwin and Saint Paul. Hobson's main argument is that in Baldwin's novels, particularly the less-explored later ones, there is a recurring theme: an endeavor to lead us toward a concept he terms the "New Jerusalem."[90] This represents an earthly city to which admission hinges on a fervent acceptance of the sacred nature of the human body. To put it differently, Hobson perceives Baldwin as, like Saint Paul, an apocalyptic writer with a distinct, albeit somewhat postsecular, eschatology that revolves around coming to grips with revelations that can only come from accepting the enigmatic, corporeal human body and all its immense potential and splendor:

> The central biblical ideas for [Baldwin] are those of apocalypse and prophecy. Though these terms are rare in his fiction, he repeatedly suggests the ideas themselves in the way just described. The first—variously denoting the revelation or "unveiling" (Greek

apokalypsis) of God's purposes; the sense of an approaching eschaton or end-time when those purposes are realized and a renovated world is born; and frequently both suggests for Baldwin two linked ideas. One is an apocalypse, or revelation, of the holiness of the body and sexuality, especially homosexuality, a shift in awareness and action that anticipates but also differs from recent ideas of sexual-homosexual liberation and queer sexuality, yet, for Baldwin, cannot by itself achieve liberation within an inimical society. The second is a potential transformation in society, or advent of a new life, in which earth's outcast and dishonored carve out a path to dignity, power, and the end of oppression.[91]

Baldwin's characters rarely reach the transformation Hobson outlines. In fact, David is an example of the possibility but ultimate failure.

Furthermore, Hobson offers the idea that both Baldwin and Saint Paul were apocalyptic writers, though what he means is distinct from the ways we understand Paul as an apocalyptic writer, as I will explain in the following sections.

Hobson is using the literal translation of "apocalypse" as revelation or *unveiling*. Therefore, for Hobson, Baldwin seeks to unveil sacred truths through pushing us to accept our bodies. Yet Saint Paul—my reading of him is influenced by J. Christiaan Beker—was a Jewish apocalyptic writer because he declared that God was *breaking into* time and space and altering reality from an evil, deathly aeon to an aeon *yet to come*. For Saint Paul, the evil eon of which we are all a part is because of the flesh. And for Baldwin, the terrible and loveless world we all inhabit and contribute to exists because humanity *disavows the flesh*.

James Campbell considers *Giovanni's Room* pioneering because it was one of the first "novels to treat the subject of homosexuality with the same frankness permitted for discussions of heterosexual love . . . likely causes of its continuing popularity are its neat, fable-like structure and congruously neat moral warnings."[92] Yet the flaws that he finds with the text are the strengths found in Baldwin's essays. Baldwin, to Campbell, struggles to maintain a distinct voice for his characters as his own voice inadvertently permeates their consciousness throughout the entire narrative. This is more evident because the entire ensemble of characters in the novel is white.[93]

For David Leeming, *Giovanni's Room* is one of Baldwin's "modern parables" where the protagonist is either a guilty enforcer or an unfortunate victim of the larger society's norms. All of Baldwin's protagonists throughout his career, to Leeming, encounter a wall, a world, that they are constantly striving against or fleeing. These characters represent a mixture of the best and worst of us, always consumed by a pressure and a force that refuses to allow our individual yearnings and wishes to be granted. Instead of taking on the world and assuming the responsibility of declaring distinctiveness against the pressure, David becomes the prime example of the one who chooses safety and innocence over and above love and freedom. According to James Campbell, "Baldwin's book is trim and neat; in a way it resembles the kind of antiquated morality tale in which the heroine is tempted away from the path of virtue, risking doom. In this case, the heroine is called David, and the virtue he/she is blind to is the life-affirming honesty of Giovanni. Virtue in this modern moralizing fable involves the acceptance of physical love between two men. Denial of it is a sin."[94]

Hobson says, "In the broadest context, Baldwin's emphasis on the fleshly body's holiness rejects the traditional Western dualism of soul or spirit and body, as well as the specific Pauline view of the flesh as source of corruption for the body."[95] According to my reading, when Saint Paul references Adam and the forbidden fruit in his letters to the various assemblies, he uses it as an allegory, a warning, to illustrate the current age as the "age of decay" and the "age of death." In contrast, Baldwin looks to the innocent American Adam's image and behavior to exemplify a particular way of living that leads to the destruction and ruin Paul believes he's avoiding.

The first Adam's disobedience is the source of Paul's theodicy, to which he attributes all the subsequent ruin. However, Baldwin views the first Adam's transgression as heroic, necessary for this current age to experience love. The requirements for meeting Saint Paul's "Last Adam" are the source of his theodicy. Hardy writes,

> Baldwin's understanding of the body and sex goes beyond his denunciations of a Christian tradition that engages in sexual repression. His understanding of human creativity and sex as deeply revelatory of the human personality cannot help but be, in part, derived from his evangelical heritage. The very language Baldwin uses to describe sexual intimacy—as an "act of confession"—suggests a deep connection between his understanding of sex and religion.[96]

Giovanni says to David in an argument, "Ne me laisse pas tomber, je t'en prie." And David does not tell him the truth. He says, "I smiled and I really felt at that moment that Judas and the Savior had met in me."[97]

However, I do not want to posit that everything Baldwin says is right and everything Saint Paul says is wrong. Is it possible that in Baldwin's theological world, Saint Paul has been taken out of context to a uniquely significant degree?[98] Is Paul, with all his fervor, quite unjustly vulnerable to Baldwin's most passionate and consistent criticism? Is his epistolary work, as well as the writings attributed to him, unjustly held accountable for a measure of catastrophe for which he bears no ultimate responsibility? Although Baldwin openly admits that he is not a theologian in any way, shape, or form and does not identify as a Christian or belong to any Christian church, he does seem to possess, across all his writings, a modest view of Christ's divinity, in other words a low Christology—in stark contrast to what he perceives as the all-encompassing sway of the Christian architect, Saint Paul.

Baldwin writes in "An Open Letter to the Born Again" that "the people who call themselves 'born again' today have simply become members of the richest, most exclusive private club in the world, a club that the man from Galilee could not possibly hope—or wish—to enter."[99] For Baldwin, Saint Paul's teaching on the Last Adam, the divine Christ, is unrelated to the impoverished Jesus he finds across the synoptic gospels. And the process of sanctification, the Christian practice of making one worthy of rescue, is the actual cause of the decay he sees. Yet for St. Paul, Adam is the symbol of time's consequence. But God is on God's way. And there is a second chance at existence, which requires bypassing a curse we were never meant to experience. Is there no value in ignoring your flesh? Is there no way of seeing some truth in Saint Paul's declaration that one's flesh should not dictate or overdetermine their actions? Paul sees the flesh as responsible for so many wrongs, for sin itself, and as a curse thrust upon us.

But for Baldwin, there is nothing wrong with experiencing love, pleasure, tenderness, and community while we await the end. What makes eternity with a deity, from either the Priestly or the Yahwist account, whose love demands obedience, better or more fulfilling than the touch of the prohibited? What's divine about avoiding hell for the sake of a heaven that feels like living eternally as kneeling supplicant? Is a private Eden with compassion and care and intimacy not worth the end of time? Can I have my own heaven after the eschaton where someone sings my praises too?

Moreover, it might appear more logical for Baldwin to direct his attention and his pen toward figures—like Martin Luther, John Calvin, or, within the American context, Jonathan Edwards—responsible for how the doctrine has persisted in the modern world. In other words, Original Sin and its repercussions within American Protestantism have played a substantial role in shaping the cultural challenges Baldwin is directly confronting. Yet he sets his sights on Saint Paul because he deems him the mastermind behind all the ruin. To put it differently: for Baldwin, Paul is the "first Adam," *the cause of the fall of humanity*. Baldwin writes: "It's got to be admitted that if you are born under the circumstances in which most black people in the West are born, that means really black people over the entire world, when you look around you, having attained something resembling adulthood, it is perfectly true that you see that the destruction of the Christian Church as it is presently constituted may not only be desirable but necessary."[100]

Baldwin is not against religion or the figure of Jesus from Nazareth. However, Baldwin sees the Christian church across the globe as the corruptive—perhaps even heretical—force that wreaks havoc in the world. The church has wreaked havoc politically through colonization, enslavement, and all sorts of violence that its professed savior seemed to be against, but its savior is distinct from its mastermind. Saint Paul invented a religion that has undone the world politically; it also, and perhaps firstly, ruins the human from the inside. Baldwin writes: "One of the things that happened, it seems to me, with the rise of the

Christian Church, was precisely the denial of a certain kind of spontaneity, a certain kind of joy, a certain kind of freedom, which a man can only have when he is in touch with himself, his surroundings, his women, and his children."[101]

For Baldwin, David is the prime example of a man completely disconnected from his own interiority. He is unable to truly feel, inside of him, the people who have made him, who love him, who surround him, who reach out for him. His American asceticism is complete by the end of the story. That is why Baldwin says to be a follower of St. Paul, or a Christian, means that "one's concept of human freedom is in a sense frozen or strangled at the root."[102]

Freedom for Baldwin carries a different meaning, though. He argues repeatedly that embracing oneself is the key. Ironically, it is the one thing people can do that is not only remarkable but also like the Jesus he invokes:

> [Jesus] claimed to be the son of God. That claim was a revelation and a revolution because it means that we are all the sons of God. That is a challenge, that's the hope. It is only by attempting to face that challenge that one can begin to expand and transform God's nature which has to be forever an act of creation on the part of every human being. It is important to bear in mind that we are responsible for our soul's salvation, not the bishop, not the priest, not my mother, ultimately it is each man's responsibility alone in his own chamber before his own gods to deal with his health and his sickness, to deal with his life and his death.[103]

For Baldwin, God did not create humans. Humans create gods. And the ethics of their creation reveal the doctrines that either cause life or revoke it. This means we all have an opportunity to write our own creation tales that either give us hope and freedom or predict an inevitable apocalypse. No matter what, death is coming. So why not enjoy our own Edens, our own Paradises, our own rooms with our own Giovannis, because we haven't got much time. And imagining love, the flesh, or freedom as a sinful and dirty entity only causes the hells we are passionately told to avoid.

2

EVE'S PARADISE

The whole point is to get paradise off its pedestal, as a place for anyone, to open it up for passengers and crew. I want all the readers to put a lowercase mark on that "p."[1]

—Toni Morrison

Yet, this evil itself took its rise from the evil will of the first man; so that there is no other origin of sin but an evil will.

—Saint Augustine of Hippo

If the Fall of Man or Original Sin—developed first through Saint Paul's elevation of Eden and then through Saint Augustine of Hippo's conviction—is understood as the havoc wrought by creation's unfortunate plunge, then Toni Morrison's understudied *Paradise* (1997) is a cautionary tale of the personal and communal ramifications of internalizing and perpetuating the Garden of Eden's raison d'être, a theme that resembles Baldwin's objective in *Giovanni's Room* (1956). In other words, if James Baldwin was trying to steer us away from Pauline asceticism by illustrating the downfall of an aspiring American Adam and by preaching through his pen that we needed private gardens away from the world's cruelty, then Morrison's novel is a completely different project that argues the opposite conclusion but bears overlapping intentions.

Morrison's *Paradise* drives an alternative theology that includes a reevaluation of what is necessary for Catholic salvation, and centers a black diasporic theopoetics that—in contrast to Baldwin—*cautions against* inhabiting private heavens designed to classify other people and forms of life as "other," as intruder, or what Richard Wright calls "outsiders."[2] My central claim is that Morrison, like Baldwin, is invested in the theological, in restructuring belief, by exposing the repercussions of living in the aftermath of Original Sin. Yet, instead of addressing Saint Paul or his reception history like Baldwin's novel, Morrison's story approaches the architect of Original Sin, Saint Augustine of Hippo, himself.

If *Giovanni's Room* argues that Eden is necessary for every human and that each of us deserves love, acceptance, and even privacy, then Morrison's *Paradise* argues for the opposite because, according to Morrison, the problem of evil is not found in the lack of Paradise; for most of us, it is instead in the very concept. Paradise, or Eden, for Morrison, is the ground of hatred and exclusion. Whether a secluded section of the temple or an ancient utopian ideal, it causes us to hurt each other through our various "isms" used to prohibit strangers from entering. Reflecting on this all too human habit, Morrison writes: "The matrix out of which powerful decisions are born is sometimes called racism, sometimes classicism, sometimes sexism. Each is an accurate term surely, but each is also misleading. The source is a deplorable inability to project, *to become the 'other,'* to imagine her or him. It is an intellectual flaw, a shortening of the imagination, and reveals an ignorance of Gothic proportions as well as a truly laughable lack of curiosity" (emphasis mine).[3]

For Morrison, the "deplorable inability" to imagine oneself as one with the "other," as indistinguishable from the stranger, is an abhorrent consequence of our public and private Edens. In contrast to both Saint Paul (discussed in chapter 1) and Saint Augustine (who argues that sin materialized in time and space through the pride and disobedience of Adam and Eve), Morrison implies that sin developed not only with the dominion given to Adam for naming and the scapegoating of Eve, but also in the creation of the Garden of Eden itself. The inception of Original Sin is the simultaneous creation of Paradise.

The great Fall of humanity, for Morrison, is interchangeable with *the Garden of Eden's creation*. Its seclusion is its sin. The notion of exclusion is the inauguration of its corrosion. And on that basis, I contend that Original Sin, for Morrison specifically, is a "master narrative."[4] A master narrative is a perennial idea from the dominant society that molds history and influences the practices of everyone. Thus, the notion of Original Sin is not solely a theodicy that explains the presence of both good and evil in a free and dynamic world, as demonstrated by Saint Augustine; it is also the foundation of what poisons community, the fertile soil of an exclusive utopia meant to keep Adam and Eve trapped inside.

Furthermore, the ultimate scapegoat of the Original Sin narrative, according to Morrison's novel, is Eve, the biblical figure who functions implicitly as—returning to Baldwin again—the symbol of the flesh. Eve in Christian heritage is the mascot of defilement, so much so that Christianity across the East and West categorizes the "other" as descendants of Eve.[5] These descendants often anticipate Saidiya Hartman's theory of *waywardness*, which is brought to the fore through women who threaten, in this instance, Ruby, Morrison's City of God in *Paradise*.[6] To counter this theology, to challenge the afterlife of

Saint Augustine's Original Sin, Morrison turns to religions of the black Atlantic.[7] Both African American Hoodoo and an unnamed black Atlantic religion from South America are invoked to argue an alternative idea of salvation that includes, like Baldwin, *embracing the flesh*, refusing the separation between "bone and spirit," and circumventing the concept of waywardness as a diabolical sin.

I read Toni Morrison's *Paradise*—the final installment in her classic trilogy on love—as an eco-theological counter to the dogmatic implications of the Fall.[8] By ultimately embracing a religion of the black Atlantic that causes the wayward women to reimagine the consequences of *living into the flesh* and decolonizing the religious residue of European imperialism and colonialism, Morrison provides a complicated love story mixed with a circle of conversions that reveals the healing powers of black Atlantic religions that exist and thrive in black and brown communities despite their marginalization. Nadra Nittle writes that magical realism as religion in Morrison's fiction "reflects a pan-African perspective in which the lines between the natural and supernatural worlds converge. The dead coexist with the living, signs foretell the future, and healing does not occur in a doctor's office. In short, Morrison did not feature magical realism in her literature as much as she did the reality of an indigenous African way of being."[9]

For Morrison, conversion to an unnamed black Atlantic religion serves as a decolonial transformation that causes personal and communal healing and mutual identification, and does away with the dichotomies that serve as the theological logic for seeing people as impure, outsiders, what Charles H. Long called "empirical others," or wayward descendants of Eve.[10]

In this haunting, complex, and theological novel, multiple strands intertwine to create a complex quilt of human suffering and triumph. The narrative and geographical center is an abandoned convent meant to convert indigenous girls to Catholicism, nestled within the heart of Ruby, an all-black town, which becomes the location and catalyst for the conversion of various women, each grappling with their own demons and traumas. Unexpectedly, the Convent begins to serve as a haven for a group of women who for various reasons are united by their grief. Marginalized by the norms of what's respectable, these women come and go, seeking refuge, solace, safety, and acceptance. As the stories and experiences between the women and the town unfold, the local men drive themselves to hysteria and decide to break into the Convent to kill the women who have defiled their "sacred" town. The men break in and shoot, "killing the white girl first." Yet in her usual fashion, Morrison leaves us unsure of what happened at the end of the story, considering that the women's bodies were never found.

Another story woven through the primary story is the founding of Ruby. Again, I call this town—after Saint Augustine—the text's City of God. Ruby was founded in response to the colorist exclusion that nine families traveling to the West were experiencing.[11] In this layered and haunting tale, Toni Morrison takes us back to the heart of Paradise to ask one simple question that no theologian has asked before regarding the desired utopias and heavens we are taught will be our rewards: Is this worth it? Morrison returns to the Edenic moment and instead of watching Adam and Eve move out of Paradise, she follows them outside. She takes their side after the expulsion, turns around, and asks the deity—through an engagement with Saint Augustine—was this whole Paradise thing even a good idea to begin with?

Before turning to a reading of Morrison's novel, I return to my truncated genealogy of Original Sin, beginning with the development of the thought that emerges after Saint Paul and continues to Saint Augustine. I will not be able to offer a thorough historical analysis, but provide some necessary details that will illuminate my reading of *Paradise* and of Morrison.

    I want to reiterate at the outset of my analysis of Saint Augustine's intervention that I do not wish to prop his ideas up merely to position Toni Morrison as the thinker who takes them down. Saint Augustine's ideas, I believe, are necessary to understand in his context. And as a Protestant theologian influenced by the Christian realism of Reinhold Niebuhr, I view Original Sin as a useful metaphorical framework for analyzing humanity and considering all the damage we cause.

EARLY CHRISTIAN THEOLOGIANS AND THE FALL

There are six primary reasons the history of Saint Augustine's interpretation of Original Sin is important for this chapter on Toni Morrison.

1. First, though Saint Augustine is not the sole creator of the theory, he was the theologian who created an entire philosophy of history based on its construction.
2. Saint Augustine perceived a danger and warned about the corruption of our will, along with an incomprehensible grotesque nature that requires God's grace to heal.
3. Understanding Saint Augustine's theology of Original Sin will aid us in understanding Toni Morrison's adamant refusal of its implications.
4. Saint Augustine, like Saint Paul, sees the Fall as a consequence of listening to the flesh.

5. The men of Ruby saw their community as a City of God that needed deadly protection from prideful youth and wayward women who reflected their views of the dichotomy between Eve and Mary.
6. For these reasons, Morrison turns to the insights of the black Atlantic for her characters' salvation.

As stated already, there are two common mistakes regarding the doctrine of Original Sin. The first is the assumption that the theory is a biblical claim. Like the concept of the Holy Trinity, Original Sin emerged in church history.[12] The second mistake exists at the other end of the spectrum of common assumptions. We often assume that Saint Augustine invented the theory of Original Sin, alone and independent from the insights of his contemporaries and predecessors. Despite the popularity of that notion, it is inaccurate. Saint Augustine's fully fleshed theology of Original Sin is a result of synthesizing the fragments of an idea that both the Latin and Greek early Christian theologians took for granted.[13]

In the first four centuries of the diverse Christian faith, the Edenic myth was mentioned sporadically underneath broader claims and other ideas and debates that the early Christians were developing. Yet it was Saint Augustine of Hippo who, like Saint Irenaeus, *saw an entire philosophy of history*, perceived a warning in the myth about our corrupt will and grotesque nature. Understanding Saint Augustine's theology of Original Sin will aid us in understanding Toni Morrison's refusal of its implications in *Paradise*.

Furthermore, Morrison refuses not only the dichotomy between Eve and Mary but also the dichotomy between "bone and spirit" that grounds it. She also refuses the function of the garden that makes the disobedience of Adam and Eve possible. I will begin by outlining a short history of the diversity of Christian thought on the Fall post-Paul to explain Saint Augustine's unique, and now orthodox, intervention.

HISTORICAL REVIEW

Most scholars note the glaring absence of theological attention to the Garden of Eden in the first half of the second century.[14] Neither the Didache, an instruction manual for gentile converts to Christianity, nor any of the material from Clement of Rome, the first of the Apostolic Fathers, onward makes references to Adam and Eve or the Fall; however, the myth, along with Saint Paul's attentiveness to it, gained traction in what Rondet considers the "pre-Irenaean tradition that grows in the second half of the second century."[15] Theologians like Justin Martyr, Clement of Alexandria, Tatian, and Theophilus all mention Adam and Eve in a way that links the myth to their growing ideas of salvation. The increasing attention also drew greater attention to an ancient theological bifurcation of which Morrison seeks to rid us: the division between Eve and Mary.

Interpretations of Genesis's third chapter varied widely in the first four centuries; however, there were a few common ideas taken directly from Saint Paul. One is seeing Adam's fall as corrected by Jesus's redemptive sacrifice. As stated in the previous chapter, Jesus became the "second Adam" who corrected the disobedience of the first Adam. Christian intellectuals were trying to make sense of thoughts and philosophies that question the existence of evil, the problem of flesh, notions of infant baptism, and ideas that maybe there are more gods and deities influencing our world than monotheists declare, having gleaned their insight from Judaism.¹⁶ These theologians, bishops, and apologists saw it as their duty to defend the faith from "pagan" philosophies and theologies that countered what they asserted was proper doctrine and salvific thinking. This led to employing the Adamic logic to understand the women in the gospels and Genesis. Like Jesus corrects Adam, Mary becomes the corrective to Eve. The Virgin Mother erases the failure of the first wife.

For Justin Martyr, humans are reproached by the Holy Spirit because they were made like God, meaning their creation did not necessitate pain, suffering, or death. They were created to become divine, but sin made the transformation unlikely. Thus, Christ heals humans and reconciles them with God. Justin Martyr is also significant for being one of the first Christian intellectuals to make a connection between Eve and Mary.¹⁷ "He became man by the Virgin, in order that the disobedience which proceeded from the serpent might receive its destruction in the same way it derived its origin. For Eve, who was a virgin and undefiled, having conceived the word of the serpent, brought forth disobedience and death."¹⁸ As the story of Adam and Eve grew, so did an interest in the place of Mary.¹⁹

Theophilus of Antioch was focused on ensuring that early Christian readers would understand the creation story monotheistically. He believed that the serpent was conniving enough to also trick readers into thinking that other gods exist in the cosmos. This cunning serpent, a "wicked demon," tricked Eve and continues to deceive humans to this day. For Theophilus, the fall of humanity is not a story about Original Sin as much as an example of how Satan tricks human beings into disobeying God.²⁰ The myth is a story of history, in which Adam and Eve are like children, not solely of an event that explains our current conditions.

As noted by N. P. Williams, the early theologians' reflections on the Garden of Eden reflect the debates of their time. This is especially true of Saint Irenaeus, who argued against the Gnostics' prevailing idea that the entire material universe was evil. Saint Irenaeus offers a type of systematic theology that provides a coherent narrative framework for how to think of God and God's plan for human creatures in time and space. Adam, though still considered a child unable to defend himself against the deceptive serpent, becomes the significant prototype of humanity. And through his example he becomes the center of divine providence and orchestration. In other words, he becomes a part of God's "plan." Not only is humanity redeemed through Christ, the second Adam, but also Eve's failure—following the insight of Justin Martyr—is rectified by the Virgin Mary.

These disparate ideas lead to the domineering theology of Saint Augustine, in whose shadow the ancient theologians live. The creation of the world and the overall Fall of humanity are central to his corpus. They practically consumed him, considering the frequency with which he turned his attention to the pages of Genesis. From the moment he converted to Christianity, he was working through the implications of ideas that would become orthodox in the West.

Yet before delving into Saint Augustine's groundbreaking construction of the "Original Sin," it is necessary to first outline some of the significant differences between him and Saint Paul. Following Elaine Pagels, the differences reveal some of the sources of their distinct readings of the Genesis account. First, Saint Paul was an itinerant Jewish missionary evangelist, shaped by his time as a Pharisee, his messianic and apocalyptic Judaism, and his involvement in local debates that all centered around asking him a simple question: What does it mean to become a follower of Jesus the Christ? Saint Augustine was a Roman,

North African bishop, shaped by his time as a Manichean, influenced by the popular Neoplatonism of his day, and one who carried an understanding of his faith that Paul was too early to have, though he helped cultivate it: Christianity was something interrelated with yet distinct from Judaism. Saint Paul lived and died under Roman imperial rule and believed to the point of desperation that Jesus was returning to get him, to rescue him, at some immediate time during his tenure as an evangelist, along with the followers who believed that Jesus was the anointed.

Saint Augustine, however, was born forty-one years after the Edict of Milan, which permanently established religious toleration for Christianity within the Roman Empire, and therefore lived in a vastly different world and cultural context from Saint Paul and the first-century disciples. In Saint Augustine's world, the Christians were not only a safe and legitimate class but also dominant and privileged, spending their time and intellectual labor trying to rid Christendom of gnostic ideas they considered too unorthodox. In fact, Saint Augustine was central to deciding what was "orthodox" and what was not from the fifth century on. These differences are instrumental for distinguishing the sources of their different readings of the Garden of Eden's events. One theologian focused on how Adam's sin invited death to enter time and space, a consequence of human error that Jesus's death and resurrection ultimately corrected. It is good news. The other, much later, focused on how Adam's sin marred human will to the point that it is now cursed, and that curse is transmitted to every human through sexual activity. One theologian saw the consequences of Adam's disobedience metaphysically, through "powers and principalities," while the other included and prioritized the material consequences, and the curse that no human can escape on their own.

Saint Augustine's influence is so tremendous and so expansive—and not just across Latin Christianity but across all of Christendom—that his interpretations of Saint Paul's letters have become the most authoritative Pauline analysis in history. Augustine not only overshadows the rich diversity of Pauline perspectives in early Christianity but even obscures the fact that there are substantial differences between his interpretation of Saint Paul and what Saint Paul wrote himself. This is why Augustine's concept of Original Sin, the Fall in Genesis 2, and Romans 5:12–14 are all unfortunately conflated in popular discourse; they are all—despite their diversity—considered by many to be making a univocal claim. I outline Saint Augustine's specific construction of "Original Sin" with the differences between his analysis and Saint Paul's writings in mind.

AUGUSTINE ON CREATION AND THE FALL

Because Augustine wrote a plethora of material on Genesis, which he often altered and changed, it is difficult to argue with accuracy about his positions on each component of the Edenic account.[21] What can be stated with confidence is that Saint Augustine is consistent about Adam and Eve's pride. For Saint Augustine, it is proof of an *evil will* that existed within them prior to their disobedience. Pride corrupted their will, in other words, damaged their will, and compelled them to disobey, which allowed sin to happen through each human through sexual concupiscence.

Saint Augustine both sharpens and convolutes his theory in two separate debates: first with his former teachers, the Manicheans, and second with his contemporary and rival Pelagius.

The Manicheans' literal (and perhaps reductive) reading of Genesis finds the Hebraic narrative ludicrous. In response to their dismissiveness, Saint Augustine proposes an allegorical reading in *On Genesis Against the Manichaeans* (389 CE), his first "ecclesiastical pamphlet."[22] In this text, he systematically addresses every single reductive or dismissive point that the Manicheans have asserted. For them, the Priestly (P) creation account is illogical. One can sense condescension between their words. So point by point, Saint Augustine reads their remarks, tries to bypass their disdain, and offers an allegorical response to sustain the integrity of the narrative. However, he grows dissatisfied because his theodicy is better served if the account, in particular the Yahwist (J) creation account, is read literally.

Therefore, not too long after he completed his retort, he tried to offer what he considered a literal reading in *On the Literal Interpretation of Genesis: Unfinished Book* (393 CE). He was unable to complete the project, because he found it too difficult, too heavy of a load, theologically. Saint Augustine then spent more than fifteen years writing what would become *The Literal Meaning of Genesis*. Besides in commentaries, he references creation, Adam, Eve, and sin throughout all his letters and homilies. He returns to the creation narrative in the final three chapters of *Confessions* and offers a reading of Original Sin in his classic tome, *The City of God*.

According to Augustine's theory of the creation of human beings, Adam was created by God. Adam's flesh, the physical matter that Adam occupied, was produced. But Adam became alive, animated, when God breathed divine breath into him, bequeathing Adam with a soul. This reading from Augustine counters the nondualist perspective of the body and soul in the Hebraic tradition. Influenced by Neoplatonic thought, Augustine believed that the soul of Adam, of the human being, is different from the essence and spirit of God, its source. They are connected, interrelated, as the soul is dependent upon God's essence, but they are far from identical. Therefore, it would lead to heresy to conflate them. That point is important because there Augustine develops his own spin on the immortality of the soul: the soul dies when the will decides to turn away from God. As interpreted by Bruno Niederbacher, S.J.:

> According to Augustine, the death of a human being is the separation of the soul from the body (civ. Dei 13.6). While the body perishes and dissolves into the elements, the soul is immortal. Augustine tries to establish the immortality of the soul. One argument proceeds from the fact that the soul is able to grasp the truth. Since truth is in the soul as its subject, that is, since truth is soul-dependent, and truth remains forever, the soul must remain forever as well.[23]

Hence, when the soul dies or experiences death, it is *damned*. The soul becomes *condemned to death* without being abolished to oblivion because it has, as Saint Paul stated, separated itself from God, the source of its life.

According to Augustine's earlier allegorical reading, this paradise was also a way of conveying the status of Adam's psyche. It was paradise as joy, contentment, which tied into his authority. Adam's dominion over the animals also meant that he held dominion over the animal within himself. To Augustine, Adam, i.e., human beings, are part beast. Moreover, Augustine reads Eve as created specifically to fulfill a role in the creation of Adam. Augustine does not conceive of the humanity of women as less than men; however, men are humans created in the image of God, and women are humans created in the image of men. "[Eve] was made as man's helper so that by spiritual union, she might bring forth spiritual offerings, that is, the good works of divine praise while Adam rules and she obeys."[24] To Augustine, Adam and Eve lived peacefully and could have produced children without sin. In his *City of God* reflections, he writes,

> In Eden, it would have been possible to beget offspring without foul lust. The sexual organs would have been stimulated into necessary activity by will-power alone, just as the will controls other organs. Then, without being goaded on by the allurement of passion, the husband could have relaxed upon his wife's breasts with complete peace of mind and bodily tranquility, that part of his body not activated by tumultuous passion, but brought into service by the deliberate use of power when the need arose, the seed dispatched into the womb with no loss of his wife's virginity. So, the two sexes could have come together for impregnation and conception by an act of will, rather than by lustful cravings.[25]

Augustine believed that if Adam had not eaten of the fruit and had not sinned, he would have "changed into a spiritual body, and would have passed into the incorruptible state, which is promised to the faithful and the saints without the peril of death."[26] He would not have been divested of his body but instead clothed with immortality and incorruption. And again Augustine argues that Adam and Eve were persuaded to sin because of their "pride." William E. Mann says that "Pride is also the initial evil impulse behind the Fall of Adam and Eve."[27] Mann continues with even a slight reference to Enoch:

> The devil's tempting of Adam and Eve did not coerce their Fall, for if the temptation had been coercive, then their punishment would be unjust. Adam and Eve voluntarily succumbed to the temptation because of their prideful fascination with the thought

that they would become like God. Augustine takes this similarity between the two cases to warrant the claim that sin entered the created world through pride. At the same time he is careful to insist that pride is not a component in all sins; as he points out, some sins are committed in ignorance or desperation.[28]

Adam and Eve's sin, according to Augustine, re-created all of creation, especially humanity. Through their pride and disobedience, they altered the world human beings inhabit, thus forcing an ontological guilt onto our births, attaching a condemnation that was not initially a part of God's will. This sin further altered human free will. Human beings do not have the internal tools or capacity to follow God's will on their own. We are too wretched, depraved, prideful, and selfish to accomplish consistent unending good on our own without the unmerited grace of God. This is all considered Saint Augustine's *massa damnata* theory.

Pelagius encountered Saint Augustine's teachings and concluded that he was perhaps overzealous in his focus on the depth of human sinfulness. Saint Augustine's theory of sin was not necessarily the problem; it is sin's overwhelming force that mitigates human responsibility and in a way recognizes human possibility. Eugene Teselle says that when Pelagius heard an unnamed bishop quote Saint Augustine's prayer, "Give what you command, then command what you will," his anger concerning Saint Augustine's theological anthropology compelled him to write his book *On Nature*. Then a decade later—still annoyed by Augustine's influence—he wrote a book entitled *On Free Choice*.

For Pelagius, humans are not destined to moral failure because of some curse we now know as "Original Sin"; they could—with as much moral strength as they could muster—improve, focus, augment their spiritual behavior, and ultimately perfect themselves into being what God desired from them. Pelagius, Lenka Karfíková writes, "introduced the ideal of Christian ascetism as an effort to achieve perfection in the Stoic vein, based on good nature and the free choice of the will strengthened by the gift of the law and the teaching of the Gospel."[29] Saint Augustine offered a theory that prevented the Herculean attempt to improve and then excused the disastrous failures. In fact, for Pelagius, the amount of grace about which Saint Augustine wrote was proof of accommodation of a weakness for which he refused to take responsibility. Adam sinned by eating the fruit from the Tree of the Knowledge of Good and Evil. That does not guarantee that every single human in his predicament would have made the identical decision; nor does it imply that all humans are guilty of the crimes Adam committed with his own personal free will.

Therefore, Adam's fault and guilt are his and his alone. And God offers us chances to refuse fruit that is forbidden, every day. The more we decline the temptation to disobey, the stronger our focus becomes. God's creation, to Pelagius, was good, and it is still good. It merely needs encouragement. It needs opportunities, practice, and spiritual support to continue cultivating that inherent goodness. The problem with Augustine and his reading of Saint Paul is ultimately that he refused to see his position as a clergyman as theologically endorsing human possibility, motivating and inspiring instead of discouraging with his misguidedly low theological anthropology.

For Pelagius, Saint Augustine not only misread Saint Paul but also projected his view of the human onto him and created an entire philosophy of history based on limited understanding of the holiness humans could achieve. Pelagius read the fifth chapter and twelfth verse of Paul's letter to the Romans: "Therefore, just as through one person sin came into the world, and through sin death." And Pelagius states in his commentary that Saint Paul is saying that sin came into the world "By example or by pattern."[30] This is his counter to the burgeoning widespread belief across North Africa—from Cyprian to Saint Augustine—that sin was a mysterious substance we inherited from Adam and not a disposition that we imitated because we are simply following his awful example.[31]

Though Saint Augustine respected Pelagius and thought he was a serious intellectual with invaluable insight, he was passionately against the core of Pelagius's theology. Human beings having the ability to attain perfection or come into proximity to anything resembling holiness on their own merit, by their own effort, and through their own will not only was preposterous to Saint Augustine but also failed to truly account for the sheer gravity of sin. Sinfulness is not reducible to behavior. It cannot be compared to character or activity. Sin is a complete corruption of human nature, akin to a toxin that decays the body until it dies. Saint Augustine wrote: "In the beginning man's nature was created without any fault and without any sin; however, this human nature in which we are all born from Adam now requires a physician, because it is not healthy."[32]

Pelagius and Saint Augustine's disagreement centered around this understanding of human nature. The inherent goodness and possibilities for uprightness that Pelagius wrote about had nothing to do with humans, according to Saint Augustine, who said in his response: "Indeed, all the good qualities which it has in its organization, life, senses, and understanding, it *possesses from the most high God*, its creator and shaper. On the other hand, the defect which darkens and weakens all those natural goods, so that there is a need for illumination and healing, is not derived from its blameless maker but from that *original sin that was committed through free will*" (emphasis mine). The possibility, the hopefulness, the holiness, all that is good that Pelagius saw in human nature was, to Saint Augustine, God.

However, sin, for Augustine, was neither a mythological aspect of the Genesis story nor something that Adam possessed alone after his disobedience, but was instead a permanent affliction that nothing less than the grace of God was needed to survive. Sin is so pervasive and threatening that it affects every aspect of every single human being created; even babies new to the world need God's grace and salvific work. Anyone who thinks they can achieve perfection or holiness by simply doing good has misread Saint Paul and does not comprehend the stakes at hand. Saint Augustine turns to Romans 5:12 and writes to those who agree with Pelagius:

> What other meaning is indeed conveyed than in the verse in which he says to the Romans, "By one man sin entered into the world, and death by sin"? . . . that this actual sin has not been transmitted from the first man to other persons by natural descent, but by imitation. Hence, likewise, they refuse to believe that in infants original sin is remitted through baptism, for they contend that no such original sin exists at all in people by their birth. But if the apostle had wished to assert that sin entered into the world, not by natural descent, but by imitation, he would have mentioned as the first offender, not Adam indeed, but the devil, of whom it is written, 1 John 3:8 that "he sins from the beginning."[33]

Sinfulness was such a wretched state that newborns needed baptism too, to rid their souls of the stain of having been born. Infant salvation was as necessary as salvation for an adult, because there was no difference between them as it related to their natures. And what's more, the author of salvation, Jesus the Christ, bypassed Original Sin through the immaculate conception, by being born of a woman and not a human man who carried the injury. This brings us to another important facet of Saint Augustine's theology related to Morrison's novel.

MARY AND EVE

Saint Augustine did not necessarily possess a high Mariology; he died before the Council of Ephesus in 431, where Theodosius II oversaw the doctrinal disputes between Nestorius and Saint Cyril, the Patriarch of Alexandria, over the nature of Christ.[34] Saint Cyril and the Alexandrians used the title *theotokos* to describe Mary, meaning the "God bearer" or Mother of God.[35] Since Jesus was considered the Christ, the second of the Trinity, and Mary was his mother, she too carries theological significance for her role in delivering salvation to the world. In other words, *Mary birthed God into time and space.*

Nestorius, Patriarch of Constantinople, not only was against an overly close association between the two natures of Christ, human and divine, but as a result taught that it was more precise to refer to Mary as Christotokos, "Christ bearer," not "God bearer." Such a distinction prevented confusion. It allowed people to understand that Mary birthed Jesus's human side and had nothing to do with his divinity. Saint Cyril of Alexandria disagreed vehemently and thought it heretically separated Christ's two natures. Through hypostatic union, Jesus was born with two united natures, human and divine, and it was through Mary that he—with both natures—entered the world to give salvation to the created.

The title given her officially in 431 was mostly popular for Egyptian Christians in the fourth century until the Council of Ephesus legitimized it and made it orthodox, taking Saint Cyril's side and making Nestorius's position heresy. Both the Greek and Latin churches from then on considered Mary "mother of God."[36] Again, Saint Augustine himself may not have had a strong doctrine concerning this discourse, but his homilies (along with Saint Irenaeus's and Tertullian's before him) helped elevate Mary's theological position in the church and subsequently provided fuel for the growing discourse that honors Mary in order to correct Eve.[37] Frances Young highlights that for the Alexandrians, especially Saint Cyril, elevating and honoring Mary was a direct result of the way they read the Fall. Young states:

> Mary is essentially "the temple" which allows the presence of God the Word to dwell within creation, the essential medium of the Word's kenosis. Rarely does Cyril explicitly draw out the Eve-Mary typology, but undergirding his whole understanding is the reversal of the Fall. Where Eve facilitated the entry of sin into the world, Mary allowed herself to be the "container of the Uncontained" and so the one "through whom the only-begotten Son of God gave light to those in darkness and the shadow of death."[38]

Again, Mary, the holy virgin mother, is eventually considered to have corrected the ultimate wayward mother, Eve. If Christ is the second Adam, the salvific corrective for Adam, then so is Mary for Eve. The consequence of this dichotomy existed prior to the council but proves how significant the distinction between the two mothers was to the early churches. Eve from the second century on grew into the archetype of the wayward woman.

THE CITY OF GOD

The last aspect of Saint Augustine's theology necessary for our reading of Toni Morrison's *Paradise* is his metaphysical theology of the *City of God*. Against claims that Christianity ruined the Roman Empire and brought its destruction from within, Saint Augustine puts forward one of the most fascinating and exhaustive arguments in Western history. Christianity did not ruin Rome; it was the source of its divine favor if the people would follow God's word and conduct themselves as God required. Within a metaphysical grand scheme, where a battle is taking place between the forces of good and evil, there are two cities: an earthly city where Original Sin has functioned like a disease, pushing people to give in to their pride, their desire, their lusts, and their own wills, and the City of God, the Heavenly City, occupied by Christians who have humbly followed Christ to salvation (known as the faithful), which remains standing in eternal happiness after the earthly city is damned to destruction. The Romans claimed that if the Christians had not destroyed their gods and deities, they would have advanced over goths who pursued their ruin. For Saint Augustine, Rome fell, and the entire world will eventually fall, because of the spiritual and moral decay that is internally corrupting and subsequently destroying the earth. This notion of moral decay recurs in how the men of Ruby in *Paradise* perceive the presence of wayward women in the community.

Though this rendering of Original Sin's development, along with a condensed outlining of Mariology and the City of God, may seem unrelated, my claim is that every aspect of these theological debates and arguments is displayed or at least undergirds the plot and passages of Morrison's novel. Perspectives on sin, paradise, Mary, Eve, human possibility, and/or God's grace are all significant elements of Morrison's narrative. And due to the complexity of the novel and all the different elements and theories it covers, I divide it into important sections and then explain how the theology is intrinsic to understanding my Edenic interpretation.

HAVEN AND RUBY

Our story begins in the afterlife of slavery on the two continents that compose the New World. As Lindy M. Christopher states, "[Morrison] draws not one but several narrative maps to account for the different geographies of this space."[39] I will begin by outlining the background of the North American part of the story before turning to the South American component. Through an Augustinian reading of the novel, I assert that Haven is the paradise that resembles the mythical Garden of Eden, while Ruby functions as the City of God, the heavenly city that is a paradisiacal retrieval of what was lost in Haven (Eden).

Marni Gauthier notes, "Morrison inscribes African Americans in the US mythic history of westward migration."[40] In North America, her story shows the influence of Nell Irvin Painter's *Exodusters: Black Migration to Kansas After Reconstruction* (1992).[41] During the black westward expansion, African Americans embark upon a massive exodus toward Kansas and Oklahoma, among the other states in that region. Leaving the deep South and heading west, black families of diverse complexions, accents, mythologies, and customs encounter fellow black communities that are reinscribing white supremacist hierarchies by prohibiting darker-skinned people from joining them. Colorism here functions as not only an offshoot of white supremacy but also a sin that is—as we see through the insight of Pelagius—*learned and mimicked*.

Ruby's exclusivity is explained with two historical reasons. The first reason is the townspeople's ancestors' exodus was colored by a communally traumatic experience of colorism. The second reason is the death of Ruby, the child, and the desire to insulate themselves from white supremacy and the danger of the outside world.

What the freed people who eventually became the founders of Ruby did not expect in their journey was the humiliating shunning by other black communities—other ex-slave developing territories—they chanced upon: "On the journey from Mississippi and two Louisiana parishes to Oklahoma, the one hundred and fifty-eight freedmen were unwelcome on each grain of soil from Yazoo to Fort Smith. Turned away by rich Choctaw and poor whites, chased by yard dogs, jeered at by camp prostitutes and their children, they were nevertheless unprepared for the aggressive discouragement they received from Negro Towns already being built."[42]

The other black communities' aggressive colorist discouragement causes palpable shame. This moment in their lives will become a part of their mythology, a moment adopted into the great "Disallowing" when they learned they were considered different and unwanted.

The communal pain and embarrassment has a profound effect on the freed people searching for a home. Morrison writes, "Denied and guarded against, they altered their route and made their way west of the unassigned lands, south of Logan County, across the Canadian River into Arapaho territory." In Arapaho territory—and like the Hebrews in the Pentateuch—they wander in the wilderness without proper direction. Colorism, or skin tone stratification, is a product of racism but still distinct from it. Trina Jones writes: "Though race and color are indeed related concepts, they are not synonymous. While racism may affect an individual regardless of the person's color, two individuals belonging to the same ethnoracial category may face differential treatment due to their varying skin tones."[43] The lighter-skinned person or group often receives better treatment in society due to their flesh's proximity to whiteness. One way of sustaining that preferential treatment, that proximity, is by also maintaining distance from darker-skinned people of the same ethnoracial class. The forefathers and mothers of the Edenic town appeared too dark in complexion to the strangers they met and thought they could build a life with. The strangers who shunned them saw their presence as threatening because they believed that the darker-skinned people were lesser humans or that they themselves would become indistinguishable from the darker-skinned people to white people.

Distance from white people does not always equal safety from white supremacy. On the journey, Zechariah's granddaughter, Ruby Morgan, needs medical attention. And since black children are not allowed in white hospitals, the little girl dies.[44] To honor her memory and to never forget what happens in the world out there, the community renames their new Haven "Ruby." Hence, the town is founded on the memory of exclusion, pain, loss, and migration. In Ruby, the new black settlement, residents feel the need to protect themselves, or outsiders who either disallow them or harm them will ruin their way of life.

In so many words, Ruby is not only a form of paradise but also—to the men especially—*De civitate Dei*. The founding of Haven began during the third night of wandering. Zechariah Morgan (later known as Big Papa) awakened his son Rector (who would become known as Big Daddy) and summoned him to prayer. While prostrate, and amid the sound of thunder and rain, Zechariah and Rector saw a mysterious small man walking with a satchel. Zechariah saw this as a sign from God and commanded Rector to gather the people because the mysterious walking man would show them the way. However, only they and a child were able to perceive this mysterious person's figure. So, for twenty-nine days the community followed, until Rector saw the mysterious walking man stop and open his satchel. They sped up but were not able to catch him, but Zechariah did not need to. He received the man's pause as a sign from God. The spot in the grass where the man had laid his items was the community's ultimate destination. They were where they needed to be to begin anew. "This is our place," Zechariah said, and Haven was founded.

I argue that Haven functioned in the minds of the freed people and their descendants as a paradise, a utopian land free from enslavement, a place where they could dictate their destinies, care for their young, and provide for their families. Haven was their own personal all-black town, away from the dangers of white sovereignty and vengeance on the people who rejected them. And since it was theirs and theirs alone, they took great pride in it, reveled in it, claimed it as their glory. For Morrison, the westward expansion was already poisoned by the notion of borders, of outsiders. Yet in celebration of their founding and in the spirit of their journey and life together, Zechariah Morgan commissions the building of a communal oven. This oven (which will eventually become The Oven), like rivers and special trees, operates as the cornerstone of the community.[45]

Community members talked, negotiated, argued, and enjoyed themselves near the oven. The people recounted stories at night near the oven as they cooked, they remembered humorous stories about their past, and they gathered there for no other reason than to be together, when work was no longer possible because the sun had set. They narrated the stories of their journey to find and build Haven. They recited "the signs God gave to guide them—to watering places, to Creek with whom they could barter their labor for wagons, horses and pasture; away from prairie-dog towns fifty miles wide and Satanism malefactions: abandoned women with no belongings, rumors of river bad cold."[46] Morrison writes that the citizens were so close that "[after having] been refused by the world in 1890 on their journey to Oklahoma, Haven residents refused each other nothing, were vigilant to any need or shortage."[47]

Unfortunately, Haven did not last. When the grandsons of Zechariah, Deek, and Steward returned from the war they saw a paradise lost. Yet what they had seen in the larger world during the war and outside of Haven had a larger impact on their psyches and religious consciousness. Outside Haven, "Out There," they encountered a world they wanted nothing to do with. Consequently, in 1950, fifteen families from Haven decided to repeat what their fathers and grandfathers had done and locate another settlement, which became Ruby, rather than be released into the sinful world. For these families in the Haven settlement, "Out There" meant all manner of violence, corruption, racism, and unruliness. In the outside world children did not obey parents, wives talked back to their husbands, and white people controlled the socioeconomic conditions of everyone. At least in their settlements, where they ruled, they could be "men," people invulnerable to the caprice of white domination or violence. The world "Out There" gestures toward what Saint Augustine considers the "earthly city." The people saw what life was like outside of God's paradise and preferred the insular protection and doctrines that made them distinct and safe.

These sets of conditions exist with a certain understanding of purity. The citizens of Ruby, in many ways, became *black puritans*. For the townspeople, darker skin is pure blood and lighter skin is tampered, polluted. Marrying outside of that pure paradigm has drastic societal consequences: Roger Best, the town's undertaker whose van operates as both hearse and ambulance, is ostracized because he marries a lighter-skinned African American woman from Tennessee.

Despite Roger Best's unfortunate decision, most of Ruby's residents followed their internal directives, never stepping outside of the town's protocols. In this narrative Morrison develops a story where the townspeople try to maintain the purity of their citizenship; they simply refuse to be polluted by the toxins of the outside world. Out there is much trouble and chaos, and although they lost, the initial town, a type of Eden, they built themselves a new Paradise, imagined through the typology of Saint Augustine's City of God.

THE CONVENT

Across the continent, on the other side of the New World in South America, nuns scavenge the land, looking for flesh to proselytize. Sister Ivone Gebara writes, "The Bible entered Latin America through religious instruction. As an accessory to the colonialist project of the sixteenth century, it has made its oppressive or liberating way in our history."[48] For Gebara, colonialism as a Catholic endeavor explains the presence of American and Portuguese nuns in South America. With the Holy Bible in their hands and ideas of sin and heathens in their hearts, nuns saw it as their spiritual calling to offer religious instruction and guidance to the infidels they encountered in the wild. The history of the Bible in Latin America, as outlined by Sister Gebara, is also the background of Morrison's story.

On a missionary trip in South America, Sister Mary Magna, before she became Mother Magna, comes across three children sitting in a garbage bin somewhere in an unnamed city. One of the children, Consolata, pulls at Mary Magna's heart, and she decides to take her back with her to the States.[49] Nine-year-old Connie, a delicate child only knowing the touch of abuse, is grateful for not only the rescue, but the ostensible love and concern exuded through Sister Mary Magna's countenance. At a young age, Connie paid close attention to how love was expressed through flesh. She loves Mary's "lake blue eyes," which exhibit an unfamiliar worry and concern for her well-being. Connie loves how Sister Magna's "framed face would reach over and touch [her] forehead with the backs of her knuckles or smooth her wet, tangled hair."[50] She loves Sister Mary's "hands: the flat fingernails" and "the smooth tough skin of the palm. And she loved the unsmiling mouth."[51] Sister Mary Magna introduces Connie to a world of love and protection, intimacy, and concern that was completely unknown to her.

Sister Mary takes Connie home to Ruby, Oklahoma. While Ruby was becoming an all-black settlement in 1954, seventeen miles away stood a mansion, transformed into a convent, that functions as a boarding school. It is where Sister Mary resides. The Convent was originally built by an embezzler who was arrested by a Northern lawman who attended one of his "voluptuous parties."[52] The property was taken over by nuns who built Christ the King School for Native Girls, run by Sister Mary Magna, as a colonializing project meant to rid indigenous girls of their language and culture.

Inside the Convent, Sister Mary introduces Connie to a new world with luxuries she can only deem "magic" because she has never encountered such materials before. Milk in clean glasses. Ecclesial Latin sung through hymns and prayers. Such sounds she describes as a "gorgeous language made especially for talking to heaven." This brand new "magic" combined with a foreign love overwhelms Connie. As a result, she responded to Sister Mary's generosity by dedicating her life to Christ, to living as a Christian, like a nun, transforming herself into a woman she believes is worthy of God's magic and Sister Mary Magna's rescue.

Morrison reveals in the history of Connie's kidnapping how the imagining of God's graciousness appears through, or in between, the history and project of colonialism and imperialism. Through Morrison's pen, within the dynamics of a complicated colonial history, Connie—as a survivor of colonialism's plunder—experiences some measure of benevolence to perhaps assuage the guilt of the colonizers who engineer such evil through missionary work.

In a moment of foreshadowing, Morrison writes that when Connie arrives at the Convent, her first duty is to prove her new allegiance. Connie's job is to "smash offending marble figures and tend bonfires of books, crossing herself when naked lovers blew out of the fire and had to be chased back to the flame."[53] After destroying offensive phallic figures and burning books considered sinful, she discovers the "wild bush heavy with stinging-hot peppers" and decides to cultivate them. The other nun, Sister Roberta, teaches Connie rudimentary cooking and gardening skills. These lessons help her "take over the kitchen *as well as the garden*"[54] (emphasis mine). For sure, Connie's work in the garden is a gesture toward the third chapter of Genesis where Adam and Eve labor in the Garden of Eden, toiling away before their eventual Fall. But as David Carr teaches, "Gardens and vineyards often symbolize women and female sexuality."[55]

Ultimately, Sister Mary trains Connie in a Pauline-Augustinian theology that helps her temporarily disassociate her body from her spirit. This disassociation, through traditional Catholic theological anthropology, allows Connie to separate her spirit from her flesh and disassociate from the larger world that has made her feel homeless. Pauline theology states that this world is strange to Christians. It is alien to believers and followers of Christ. Therefore, *her feeling of homelessness is given coherence* through her embracing Catholicism. For Sister Mary Magna, the body is the problem. It needs discipline. It needs bending and training to transform into an obedient instrument for the spirit.

For thirty years, Morrison writes, Connie "offered her body and her soul to God's Son and His Mother as completely as if she had taken the veil herself."[56] She proves her devotion to Jesus, Mother Mary, and the ethics required of her. Connie is faithful, dependent—perhaps even worthy of her rescue in the eyes of the nuns—until she meets Deek, the Adamic character of the story, who is the grandson of Zechariah (Big Papa). Then that faithfulness "cracked like a pullet's egg."[57]

ADAM, EVE, AND THE FIG TREES

This cracking is the introduction to the Adam and Eve aspect of our story. However, Connie transforms Deek into the embodiment of the Eucharist. She tries to consume him like the sacrament, and this causes Deek to view her, according to my reading, as a sort of witch. Moreover, the nature that surrounds them seemingly does not approve of their secret union. The heartbreak of their affair ending causes Connie to return to Catholicism with guilt, but also a brokenhearted compassion that allows her to open her doors to women in need of space and time.

Before Connie and Deek found each other in a passionate embrace, Connie's fleshly awakening was instigated by witnessing the movement and hearing the sound of black sociality. While on an errand with Mother Magna, Connie watches from afar black people "galloping" and "screaming with laughter." She watches little black children with flowers in their hair and hears their joy. She watches the younger kids enjoying horse races. She witnesses men and boys swinging their hats and moving with a black confidence and joy unimaginable in her Convent. Thus she experiences the theatrical black sociality that Zora Neale Hurston described. Morrison writes, "As Consolata watched that reckless joy, she heard a faint but insistent Sha sha sha. Sha sha sha. Then a memory of just such skin and just such men, dancing with women in the streets to music beating like an infuriated heart, torsos still, hips making small circles above legs moving so rapidly it was fruitless to decipher how such ease was possible."[58]

Connie sees people in their flesh, living, moving, and laughing—a community of people partaking, physically, in jubilance. These people are not necessarily using their flesh as much as participating in it for their shared enjoyment and communal pleasure. Yet what Connie witnesses also brings back memories of a life and time before her kidnapping and conversion. Perhaps Morrison is gesturing toward a black Atlantic environment as Connie recognizes something that feels like home, like a reminder, something lost in her new life.

For thirty years, Connie's flesh was used, utilized, prostrated, even employed as a tool to show holy obedience and deference. For thirty years, Connie was mortified by her flesh and used it as a vehicle for worship. She recognized her body as possessing the capacity to kneel in obeisance and labor in the garden. She was unaccustomed to experiencing her flesh as a partner for joy, as opposed to an obstacle to holiness. Black social life in Ruby reawakens Connie to something she remembers in her home in South America.

Morrison writes that somehow, "Consolata knew she knew them."[59] Maha Marouan writes: "By reclaiming Candomblé in her exploration of African American cultural and historical identity, Morrison is drawing the link between Afro-Brazilian and African American diasporic experiences. The novel expresses this through Consolata's meeting with the people of Ruby and with Deacon."[60] When Connie sees the physically attractive man named Deek, "the wing of a feathered thing, undead, fluttered in her stomach."[61] Whatever is inside Connie, suppressed for years in devotion to Christ and Mother, is reawakened and alive.

This experience of seeing black life and meeting Deek in passing causes Connie to conceal herself, once again, underneath her labor in the garden. She fears her sexuality. She is afraid and unfamiliar with her flesh and the sensations it is open to. She distrusts whatever is fluttering inside of her, announcing its presence. Connie refuses it. Repels it. She finds solace in her retreat until Deek arrives in the garden to buy peppers from the Convent. Deek observes her. *Sees her.* Compliments her eyes. She wonders if "she really [dropped] to her knees and encircle[d] his leg, or was that merely what she was wanting to do?"[62] For Connie, both human passion and devotion are expressed through obeisance. Love—or anything within its orbit—is understood in Connie's theology as something for which one labors, earns, sacrifices, and bows. In other words, Connie's passionate attraction to Deek—also a reemergence of her flesh's impulse—causes her to desire to prostrate before him in a holy and sexual surrender. David Carr understands her situation "on that premise—that sexuality and spirituality are intricately interwoven, that when one is impoverished, the other is warped, and that there is some kind of crucially important connection between the journey toward God and the journey toward coming to terms with our own sexual embodiment. Both sexuality and spirituality require space in one's life to grow."[63]

What occurs in their initial encounter, and continues throughout their tryst, is an unspoken, yet understood, relationship between the liturgical rituals for worshiping our gods and the physical routines we practice in expressing the love we experience. Said differently, for Morrison, theology cannot be separated from its theater.

M. Shawn Copeland attests that "The body provokes theology."[64] Consolata, unaware of that truth, finds herself embracing and creating a theology that starts with her hands. They agree to meet later that evening and, while driving together in erotic silence, Connie "let the feathers unfold and come unstuck from the walls of a stone-cold womb."[65] The mysterious force inside her fully reawakens during their excursion. Morrison employs Adam and Eve imagery again, describing "Out here where wind was not a help or threat to sunflowers, nor the moon a language of time, of weather, of sowing or harvesting, but a *feature of the original world* designed for the two of them" (229; emphasis mine). Deek and Connie's affair "out here" momentarily, and ultimately, re-creates the world with its original raison d'être. For Morrison, Deek and Connie's passionate affair restores their space to a secret paradise where the natural elements of the world are not utilized as machinery meant to measure human labor or productivity. In the context of reinterpreting the third chapter of Genesis, Deek and Connie's fall, together, reverses Adam's punishment of toiling. And for just a stolen moment, those two create their own Eden together, enjoy their own nakedness, all the while leaving the fig trees to themselves.

Their affair leaves them both speechless. "What had been uttered during their lovemaking leaned toward language, gestured its affiliation, but in fact was un-memorable, -controllable or -translatable," Morrison writes. Yet, as in the Garden of Eden, punishment soon follows. "Before dawn they pulled away from each other as though, having been arrested, they were each facing prison sentences without parole."

They agree to continue meeting every Friday at noon thereafter. Deek drives her to a burned-down farmhouse and together they "fight shrub and bramble until they reach a shallow gully."[66] They cannot speak. But Deek gestures toward "two fig trees growing into each other."[67] In the Garden of Eden, Adam and Eve realized their own nakedness and utilized the leaves from a fig tree.[68] Here, with nature as their shield and witness again, behind this burned house, the fig trees have their own relationship, their own romance and intimacy. In this Eden they are not tools for human beings but a community unto themselves. In this tale the fig trees are witnesses to love, passion, and sex. They insist on life. And when the two make love in the gully, "they competed with the fig trees for holding on to one another."[69] However, the fig trees do not support their union and do not bear fruit while they meet there. Jan Furman states that Consolata and Deek's sexual relationship "was never a convincing partnering as indicated by barren fig trees and a burned-out meeting place."[70]

Feeling the sensations of her own flesh causes Connie to simultaneously experience the longing for "home." To be home in her flesh is to be home in the world. And since Deek is the conduit through which she feels herself, through which she feels home, their union in the burned-down house becomes a new "home" in her mind and heart.

In other words, for Morrison, again, theology cannot be separated from its theater. The liturgy of Catholicism says that the love of the Lord requires consumption of Jesus's body through the Eucharist.[71] Consuming the Lord is an act of love, of honor. Morrison writes that for Connie, their "Romance stretched to the breaking point, exposing a simple mindless transfer. From Christ, to whom one gave total surrender and then swallowed the idea of His flesh, to a living man."[72] In other words, her theology causes her to *transform Deek into a sacrament*, a living and breathing Eucharist that satiates her desire for an internal reconciliation with God and home. Therefore, Connie's "gobble-gobble love" is an attempt to consume him, biting his lip and partaking of his blood.

The bite negatively affects Deek, but she is unaware of how much it impacts him in the moment. He does not tell her, but subsequently is inconsistent in meeting with her. Nature eventually intervenes and obstructs their secret place. The burnt-ash man points outside the home, beckoning them to leave. The weather worsens. The two lovers discuss the potential of a new location for their affair. Connie's desire to continue her tryst with Deek compels her to transform her cellar into a sort of altar: "The cellar room sparkled in the light of an eight-holder candelabra from Holland and reeked of ancient herbs. Seckel pears crowded a white bowl." But Deek does not appear. He stops meeting her completely, almost vanishing into thin air. Weeks later, Deek's wife, Soanne, arrives unexpectedly at the Convent, feigning a desire to abort her unborn child. Connie refuses, then demands that Soanne leave. Soanne does, but has a miscarriage while walking home. Those in the town who know what transpired collectively blame Connie.

Connie, heartbroken and shattered, cries aloud in the chapel: "Dear Lord, I didn't want to eat him. I just wanted to go home."[73] Then she unexpectedly finds her compassionate guardian, Mother Magna, kneeling next to her. Mother Magna embraces her in a loving moment of understanding. She encourages Connie, "Never speak of him again." After she partially confesses on her way out of the chapel, "a sunshot seared her right eye, announcing the beginning of her bat vision, and she began to see best in the dark. Consolata had been spoken to."[74]

With the guidance of Mary Magna, Connie regains control of her life. She has learned the value of "patience": "After arranging for her confirmation, she had taken the young Consolata aside and together they would watch coffee brew or sit in silence at the edge of the garden. God's generosity, she said, is nowhere better seen than in the gift of patience. The lesson held Consolata in good stead, and she hardly noticed the things she was losing."[75]

Connie did not realize that she has been losing "the rudiments of her first language," Portuguese or perhaps an indigenous South American language. After letting go of her embarrassment, the next thing she loses is her "ability to bear light." Initially, the sunshot that sears her right eye makes her vision in daylight, or light in general, poor. This seems to function as the beginning of a process through which Connie eventually becomes incapable of seeing light at all.

THE WOMEN OF THE CONVENT

Ruby encounters problems due to a young minister the townspeople have allowed in their midst, Reverend Richard Misner, and four women who enter by way of visiting Connie and the

Convent. Reverend Misner brings to the community a nascent liberation theology that encourages the youth to take things into their own hands. The women, however, are wayward and delinquent; therefore, they are unwelcome.

To keep Ruby isolated from the changing times outside, the men of the town blame the women for the trouble in the community. When a passerby dies in a snowstorm, the men come together and contrive a plan to scare them off. They end up breaking into the Convent and shooting every single woman in sight. The Mary and Eve dichotomy—along with the assumption that African Atlantic material culture is satanic—serves as the rationale for the violence. It is the dichotomy that makes the violence possible and the African materials that make the violence, to them, necessary.

The women of the Convent, Mavis, Gigi (aka Grace), Seneca, and Pallas, bring a host of their own issues, and Connie's home and graciousness provide each of them with something they need. Mavis's name means song thrush, a small bird or thrush that breeds across the Palearctic realm. Its Latin name, *Turdus philomelos*, connects with the name Philomela from Greek mythology, toward which Morrison gestures to contextualize Mavis's unfortunate life with her husband. Mavis accidentally killed her newborn twins (like Philomela killed her son) by leaving them to suffocate inside a hot Cadillac while she was grocery shopping. Frightened that her other children would enact vengeance against her on behalf of their siblings, she fled in the middle of the night, eventually finding herself in Oklahoma. On a narrow road she stumbled across the Convent.

Gigi (Grace Gibson) enters descending from a bus that has arrived in town. The concept of grace is reflected in Connie's reaction to hearing her name: "Grace. What could be better?" and the narrator adds, "If ever there came a morning of when mercy and simple good fortune took their heels and fled, grace alone might have to do. But from where would it come and how fast? In that holy Hollow between sighting and following through, could grace slip through it all?"[76]

Before her arrival in Ruby, Mikey, Gigi's lover, told her about a rock formation in Wish, Arizona, that resembles a black couple making love. "At sunrise, [Mikey] said, they turned copper and you knew they'd been at it all night. At noon they were silvery grey. Then afternoon blue, then evening black. Moving, moving, all the time moving."[77] Gigi needs to see this but is unable to. The people in Arizona are not aware of a rock couple making love in their midst. She decides to leave, and on the train a fellow passenger tells her about a lake in the middle of a wheat field. Nearby, "Two trees grew in each other's arms. And if you squeezed in between them in just the right way, well, you would feel an ecstasy no human could invent or duplicate."[78] Gigi asks for the location and he reveals that it is in Ruby, Oklahoma, where they also have the best rhubarb pie. Gigi boards the bus and when she arrives, notices K.D., Deek's nephew (who will eventually become a kind of lover), and other people but soon realizes there is no hotel.

Roger Best eventually gives Gigi a ride to the Convent, and through her eyes we get a full picture of what is inside. Gigi meets Connie but realizes something is different about her eyes. There is something beautiful but also something missing. Behind Connie's eyes is "a swept world. Unjudgmental. Tidy. Ample. Forever."[79] Gigi also notices that there is only a faint outline where the edge of the iris used to be.[80] Like Mavis, Gigi stays and makes the Convent a sort of home. And when Mavis arrives after some time has passed, she runs into Gigi sitting completely nude outside.

The third woman who eventually makes the Convent her home is Seneca. Her name invokes two ideas. First, and most obvious, is Seneca the Younger, the Roman philosopher and dramatist. I see little connection in terms of Seneca's tragedies; however, there is a sense in which his suicide resonates with Seneca's suffering in Morrison's novel. The other idea is stated by Sweetie who, upon hearing the name Seneca, thinks, "Sin . . . I am walking next to sin and wrapped in its cloak."[81] Abandoned by her mother who she had thought was her sister, abused in foster homes, and in love with a man she barely knows (Eddie) who is incarcerated, Seneca finds herself lost and despondent. She works for a mysterious woman named Mrs. Fox, then is dropped off at the bus station. While sneaking rides in the backs of trucks going in unknown directions, she jumps out and follows Sweetie, who is walking to the Convent.

Pallas appears in the quiet, sitting in silence in a vehicle after the women are asked to leave a party in town because of their wayward behavior. Pallas is introduced as the newest tenant in the world of the Convent. Her name invokes Athena, the Greek goddess of wisdom and warfare, who was also known as Polias. Athena's origin story usually includes an absent mother. Morrison's Pallas is a grieving child hurt by the betrayal of her mother, whom she found having an affair with her boyfriend, Carlos, an adult man several years Pallas's senior who was the janitor at her high school. Despite the inappropriateness of their relationship, Pallas is crushed and runs away. Boys assault her near a lake. While she is recuperating from the attack in the hospital where Billie Delia works, Billie Delia decides to take her to the Convent, telling Pallas, "You can collect yourself there, think things through, with nothing or nobody bothering you all the time. They'll take care of you or leave you alone whichever way you want it."[82] These four, along with Connie, are the wayward women of the town who do not belong in the paradise of Ruby. And the men make sure of that by plotting to do away with them.

LONE AND NEGRO HOODOO

One of the main characters who emerges toward the end of the novel is Lone DuPres, a midwife who conjures, whose spiritual insight allows her to see or sense the *orixas*, Yoruban spiritual entities, and powers in Connie. Lone is also the "ancestor" of the story. According to Morrison, there is always an ancestor who provides spiritual wisdom to the characters.[83] In describing African American religious imagination, Morrison states, "We are very practical people, very down-to-earth, even shrewd people. But within that practicality we also accepted what I suppose could be called superstition and magic, which is another way of knowing things."[84] This other way of knowing things is revealed in Connie's transformation, and hints of it are also sprinkled through the book. It is evident in how the women in town have a different relationship with nature than outsiders and also through Lone, whose character functions along the periphery, but not totally outside of, the community.

Morrison, with a subtle, slightly ecowomanist tone, says that "black women have held, have been given, you know, the cross. They don't walk near it. They're often on it."[85] And the women who live in Ruby are no different. For Morrison, Ruby as a paradise is a man's construct, while the women must *cultivate* their place in it. At the same time, the women in Paradise relate to nature in a way the men do not: Soane whispers to the quail to look out;[86] Anna feeds the mother cat who demands she turn away so as to feed her young;[87] Billie Delia pushes out her lips at everything occurring in Ruby but the gardening;[88] Soane, reflecting that it was a mistake to invite the wayward women to the wedding reception she was hosting, is asked by both of her dead sons: "What's in the sink?" She looks down and sees mysterious feathers. She takes the feathers and the buzzards as a sign that she should not have invited the women.[89] Furthermore, one night Dovey Morgan, Steward's wife, is inside the foreclosed home on St. Matthew Street and notices a "mighty hand" digging deeply into a giant sack and throwing a fistful of what seems to be petals into the air. Or maybe they aren't petals, but butterflies. "A trembling highway of persimmon-colored wings cut across the green treetops forever—then vanished."[90] These mystical moments illustrate that something more occurs and exists in the world of the female characters.

Yet, more explicitly, Lone DuPress *practices*. Lone is the local midwife in Ruby who was discovered, as a baby, alone in a home with her deceased mother by the original group who founded Ruby. She was subsequently adopted by the DuPres family. At the outset there seems to be a connection between Connie's and Lone's past. Like Connie, Lone was taken in by guardians who rescued her. However, she is considered "one of the stolen babies" because Fairy DuPres found her "sitting quiet as a rock outside the door of a sod house." Morrison writes, "The sight of the silent child in a filthy shift could have remained just one more lonely picture they came across, except that the desolation about the place was unforgiving. Fairy was fifteen then and bullheaded. She and Missy Rivers went to investigate. Inside was the dead mother and not a piece of bread in sight."[91]

Fairy DuPres named the infant Lone "because that's how they found her."[92] Fairy DuPres rears Lone and teaches her everything she knows about midwifery. After Fairy dies on a trip back to Haven, Lone becomes the community's sole midwife until the women in town decide to deliver their children in hospitals near Demby. Not only do the women prefer the care, rest, and technology afforded them in the hospitals, they also blame Lone for the disabilities that Sweetie and Jeff Fleetwood's children were born with.

The town believes Lone "could read minds, a gift from something that, whatever it was, was not God."[93] Not only can she read minds and sense things, but she also gathers medicinal herbs. Before the violent climax of the novel, Morrison writes that Lone was handling mandrake,[94] a plant historically connected with both European and African conjuring traditions.

According to my reading, Lone practices Hoodoo, often considered Conjuring, which, according to Raboteau, "was a system of magic, divination, and herbalism."[95] Raboteau states that hoodoo, or rootwork, is one of the "vestiges of African beliefs" that have been removed from their fully intelligible theological and ritual context.[96] According to Yvonnne Chireau, Conjuring was an "all-purpose utility,"[97] and its "practitioners experienced the invisible world as a reality rather than as a theological abstraction."[98] Lone believes that God orchestrated her presence in the garden where she overheard the men plotting their assault on the wayward Convent women. For Lone, there are no coincidences and little happenstance. Everything is in relationship through God's orchestration. God speaks through nature, through signs, through events and moments. God's word and message are thus conveyed through time and space and are direct and explicit. Lone does not, however, consider this insight unique to her, seeing it as a normal and easily accessible aspect of the world. The problem is that most human beings are "steeped in vanity's sour juice," too self-absorbed to pay adequate attention to God's natural communications.

Lone senses that Connie too has supernatural conjuring capabilities. Perhaps the African Atlantic dimensions of Lone's conjuring connect with the African Atlantic aspects of whatever is inside Connie. Perhaps there is a connection in the Old World between them, a gesture toward a similar home on West Africa's soil that understands something that Western thought categorizes as "religion" through orishas, vodun, or spirits. Nadra Nittle writes, "Through the novel's pair of healers, Consolata Sosa and Lone DuPres, the reader learns that a different type of belief system—one that considers an individual's spiritual wisdom rather than religious orthodoxy alone—is necessary for communal transformation, healing, and fulfillment."[99]

Lone meets Connie by helping her after she faints one day. After she awakens, Lone provides her with a "hot drink that tasted of pure salt." When Lone tells Mother Magna the ingredients of her herbal drink, Mother Magna admits to thinking, "baloney." Her incredulity seems, at first, to stem from disregarding the possibility of the plants possessing healing powers; however, her incredulity and dismissiveness come from something much more. Mother Magna whispers to Connie to be very careful because she believes Lone "practices" alternative religious traditions caricatured as "Black magic," a pejorative, categorical term used for religious practices derived from African traditional religions. And perhaps Mother Magna's response is what Derrida means when he says that "To think 'religion' is to think 'Roman.'"[100]

Mother Magna's response highlights how Catholicism, as a "world religion," dismisses practices and wisdom from anything outside its own paradigm.[101] Lone admits to her religious alterity and provides Connie with information that makes her "uneasy." Connie's devotion to orthodox Roman Catholicism, taught to her by Mother Magna, prohibits any other understanding of magic despite the church's connection to it through scriptures.[102] Connie says she refuses magic because "*everything holy* forbade its claims to knowingness and its practice" (emphasis mine). To which Lone responds, "Sometimes folks need more."[103]

When Connie disagrees, saying her faith is all that is necessary, Lone replies with wisdom that stems from an understanding that hoodoo is not incongruent with Christianity or other mainstream religious frameworks: "You need what we all need: earth, air, water. Don't separate God from His elements. He created it all. You stuck on dividing Him from His works. Don't unbalance His world."[104] For Lone, there is no division between spirit and nature. Spirit is what connects nature. Nature is *what reveals spirit.* Spirit moves through and within nature. Nature not only is the medium through which spirit is felt but also contains spirit, power, intelligence. Nature has feelings. Nature is the simple understanding of interconnected living. Everything alive contains an interrelated spirit that provides sustenance for and receives life from everything else.

Connie comes to this realization at the same time she discovers her own powers that emerge after a drunk driving accident in which Soanne and Deek's son, Scout Morgan, dies after their car falls off the road. Lone encourages Connie to "step inside of him" to resurrect him. She does, and everyone, including Connie, responds with shock and panic. For a while, Connie is frightened by her own powers, but time reveals that her true struggle is with how she uses them. Connie uses her powers to keep the dying Mother Mary Magna alive, although in her heart of hearts, she knows Mother Magna would not approve of this if she knew what was transpiring.

THE CONVERSION TO AFRO-BRAZILIAN RELIGION

In depression and grief over her broken heart and the anxiety she experiences from letting God down, and feeling condemned by Mother, Connie becomes ill with alcoholism. While surveying the destitution in the garden and everything that is wrong with it, filled with shame and regret, she wonders if she has lost her salvation and all its immaterial rewards. She asks Mother Magna, "Where is the rest of days, the aisle of thyme, the scent of veronica you promised? The cream and honey you said I had earned? The happiness that comes of well-done chores, the serenity duty grants us, the blessings of good works? *Was what I did for love of you so terrible?*" (251 [emphasis mine]).

While she is questioning her Christian God, sulking in the guilt of her sins, she looks and wonders at the gold and blue-green plumage in the sky, "*strutting* like requited love on the horizon" (emphasis mine).[105] This represents the peacock, which is sacred to the Yoruban *orixa* Oxum. In Candomblé—as well as other Yoruban religious traditions—Oxum is the goddess of love, divinity, and beauty. This reveals that Connie feels Oxum *inside of her*, beckoning her to return from her depression so that she can experience pleasure and freedom through her flesh.

While she is sitting outside, an *orixa* in the form of a mysterious man in a hat arrives and declares that Connie knows him. As he is speaking flirtatiously, trying to convince her, Connie slides "towards his language like honey oozing from a comb." Suddenly, she begins losing her standard American English: "You have your glasses much more me." Morrison writes, "He took off his glasses then and winked, a slow seductive movement of a lid. His eyes, she saw, were as round and green as new apples."[106] This encounter changes Connie, and she organizes a communal initiation with the women in the Convent. She reintroduces herself as Consolata and, like a new "reverend mother" or *mai-de-santo* of Candomblé, transforms the Convent from a former Catholic mansion intended to rid children of their indigeneity into a *terreiro*, a place of community worship, meant to heal women and return them to themselves, wholly/holy and cleansed.

Toni Morrison stated that part of the inspiration for this novel was a false story that a man walked into a *terreiro* and killed all the women practicing. Sheila S. Walker writes that "Candomblé is an Afro-Brazilian creation, a system for worshiping the Orishas, the Yoruba spiritual entities responsible for the elements and dynamics of natural and human reality, on soil distant from the African homeland, and developed within the oppressive social and cultural context of slavery."[107] I am focusing on Afro-Brazilian religions within black Atlantic religions, although Morrison never explicitly says that Consolata was taken from Brazil or returns to practices of Candomblé or Umbanda, another Afro-Brazilian religion that is at times blended with Catholicism and indigenous beliefs.

Therefore, though I make use of what Rachel E. Harding describes as the "significant commonalities" of Afro-Brazilian religions and various insights from black Atlantic religious scholarship, I concentrate on Candomblé. This is not to suggest that there are no differences among Afro-Brazilian religions or among the Candomblé nations. In fact, there are many distinctions across cities and regions in Brazil. For the sake of simplicity, I will utilize the scholarship on the Nago nation.

I claim that Consolata converts into a *mai-de-santo*, a priestess in Afro-Brazilian religions such as Candomblé, Umbanda, Quimbanda, and Macumba, among others.[108] Translated, it means "mother of the saints" or "mother of the holy." The *mai-de-santo* is the priestess responsible for the *terreiro*, the sacred space for the adherents of Afro-Brazilian religions.[109] There the altars of the *orixas* (*orishas* in Portuguese and Yoruba), Yoruban spiritual entities, are housed.[110] Every *terreiro* is different in South America, but these are the overlapping aspects. This reveals that Connie's conversion to Consolata also resulted in the spatial conversion of the Convent itself.

When she reintroduces herself to the women of the Convent, she asserts, "I call myself Consolata Sosa. If you want to be here you do what I say. Eat how I say. Sleep when I say. And I will teach you what you are hungry for."[111] The women are hesitant at first. They do not quite understand why Connie, now Consolata, is so different. Her facial structure has changed. Her demeanor has altered. She is speaking with an unfamiliar accent to which they are unaccustomed. The women seem to only partially recognize her. However, out of love and trust for a woman who has only ever cared for them, they decide to stay.

Melville J. Herskovits says that the *mai-de-santo*—or *iyalorixa*, the traditional Nago title—"exacts, and receives, the respect and obedience of all functioning members of the group on the basis of authority derived from the control of supernatural power and demonstrated competence in administering its affairs and counseling its personnel."[112] Despite the Convent women's ignorance of Consolata's powers, her prior love and graciousness toward them allows her to function with authority—not necessarily because of deference to her abilities, but because of trust. The women trust her because of what Morrison scholars consider an "excessive goodness" in her actions.[113] Not long after their decision to remain in what I am classifying as the new *terriero*, and to follow the priestess's rules, they realize that deciding to stay meant an initiation for them as well into the unnamed African Atlantic ritual that Consolata organized. An event in the story mirrors an initiation:

> Then they ringed the place with candles. Consolata told each to undress and lie down. In flattering light under Consolata's soft vision they did as they were told. How should we lie? However you feel. They tried arms at the sides, outstretched above the head, crossed over breasts or stomach. Seneca lay on her stomach

at first, then changed to her back, hands clasping her shoulders. Pallas lay on her side, knees drawn up. Gigi flung her legs and arms apart, while Mavis struck a floater's pose, arms angled, knees pointing in. When each found the position she could tolerate on the cold, uncompromising floor, Consolata walked around her and painted the body's silhouette. Once the outlines were complete, each was instructed to remain there. Unspeaking. Naked in candlelight.[114]

According to Maha Marouan, "The Convent women, under the leadership of Consolata, undergo rituals reminiscent of Candomblé . . . Although the rituals of Candomblé can be both male and female directed, Candomblé remains a female-centered religion. Women were the first establishers of Candomblé temples in Brazil in the early nineteenth century, and the majority of temples are still run by women."[115]

While conducting the ritual, Consolata explains her religious odyssey. She reveals to the women that her hurt child body leaped into the arms of the the nun, who taught her the dualism that states—once again through Pauline and Augustinian theology—that her "body is nothing . . . spirit everything."[116] She listened, and followed the teaching. She focused on her spirit until her body collapsed into everything she wanted to avoid. She tells them that she followed this theology until she "met another" who taught her differently. Taught her otherwise. And whatever lessons she learned from this "another," the *orixa* that visited—maybe returned—to her changed her perspective on herself and what she thought she had lost. Her faith now also includes her flesh. It does not reject it. This bears out what Karmen Mackendrick says: "The world does not name God by either logical argument or empirical inference, but in a delight that calls out first to the senses."[117]

This *orixa* altered the assumptions of her Catholic theology. She learned that the body, the flesh, is not only "something" as opposed to nothing, it is also a part of creation. It is good, important, invaluable. There is no difference in significance between flesh and bone. There is no separation between the sacred spirit and sinful skin. And as Lone stated when they met, for Consolata now, bones are as important as the spirit. Consolata says that her body was so hungry for itself, a self she shunned in the name of Christ, that it tried to eat the man we know as Deek.

In Morrison's novel *Beloved* (1987), Baby Suggs fervently preaches a homily to the formerly enslaved folk in the Clearing about loving and accepting their flesh despite the outside world's hatred and desire to wound it. Morrison's *Paradise* replicates this moment, depicting an elderly mother in the community who delivers a radically liberating message to the women about refusing the dualism that has wreaked havoc on people considered unworthy in the eyes of the (supposedly) sinless. This passage is not only meant to console the women in the Convent, but it is also *Paradise*'s rebuttal to Saint Paul's pseudepigraphical pastoral letters and Saint Augustine, and a theological challenge to the impetus behind and grounds for the argument between Nestorius and Saint Cyril.

Against Saint Paul, Saint Augustine, and the Council of Ephesus in 431, Consolata asks, Where is the division between spirit and bones? She warns the women against this theology: "Hear me, listen never break them in two. Never put one over the other." And after she teaches this lesson, she makes one of the most important claims for this chapter that addresses the history of original sin and mariology. Consolate says, "Eve is Mary's mother. Mary is the daughter of Eve."[118] Mary is not the Virgin Mother who rectifies the disobedient Eve, she is not the woman of purity who remedies Eve's waywardness; she is Eve's daughter, a fellow mother who experienced loss, who endured tragedy, who loved a life. Consolata, the new holy *mai-de-santo*, does not reject the women in the Convent after her conversions. She does not refuse the women who seem to represent the various derogatory descriptions of Eve; her priestess theology and worldview include them, and she worships with them, sees them, and refuses separation from them. Nadra Nittle says, "As she does in *Sula*, Morrison complicates the virgin-whore dichotomy, arguing that the archetypes are inextricable from one another."[119]

Following the Yoruban protocol, I argue that this initiation transforms the women into *filhas de santo* or "daughters of the holy," "daughters of the saints." These initiates become the life of the *terriero* because they serve, through their flesh, as ritual embodiments for the *orixas*.[120] *Their flesh becomes the source of divinity*. Rachel E. Harding explains that "initiates are prepared to embody the presence of their dominant *orixa* and are taught the specific means by which the ritual relation is to be continually cultivated."[121]

The women share in one single dream of release. Together as one they process the pain that has pursued them until their unity helps cultivate the love and liberation that has perhaps always evaded them. One remarkable facet of their conversion is found in the moment of their cooking and eating, no small gesture, considering Morrison writes that they eat "food without blood." This embodies what Elizabeth Perez calls "kitchen work," which is integral to the overall transformation of the women in the Convent. Much attention, according to Perez, is given to the ways the study of black Atlantic religions includes rituals of sacrifice and spirit possession, practices that are perhaps the easiest to correlate with "world religions," an invented classification Tomoko Masuzawa asserts is a reshuffled category from the

European episteme.[122] But Morrison opens space for Perez's theory of "kitchen work," a seeming micropractice at first glance, but truly functional as a robust and significant part of the changes and bonding that the women in the Convent experience.[123]

One of the final moments of their initiation—which lasts for a few months—is a key aspect of Afro-Brazilian ceremonies: dancing. In the rain, together, they move. Candomblé etymologically means "dancing in honor of the gods." In Umbanda, according to Reginald Prandi, "The spirits of Cablocas (Indians) and Pretos Velhos (Old Slaves) manifest themselves through the bodies of initiated when they are in a ritual trance in order to dance, give some advice and cure those who look for any religious or magical help."[124]

On one of these nights of dance, the men of Ruby decide to strike. They have assumed the role of both the deity and the cherubs in the second creation story. They have decided among themselves that the women in Paradise must be not only expelled but also executed to ensure they never return to continue the town's unraveling. Lone DuPres arrives too late to warn the new initiates. The men have successfully shot and killed all the women inside the Convent, although they claim otherwise until Deek admits that they committed the crime. Nadra Nittle explains, "With no knowledge of African spirituality, the posse of men can't deduce that these objects have ties to Yoruba spirituality. Instead, they view the altars as 'satanic' and further justification to annihilate the Convent's defenseless residents."[125] To the community's surprise, however, there are no dead bodies. The soil holds no record of them. They have completely disappeared, and readers only encounter them again in spiritual appearances in the final chapter. Consolatais peacefully resting her head on the lap of Piedade, a black woman who sings to her in paradise. This moment in the novel is the culmination of Consolata's entire religious journey, and perhaps an alternative eschaton that comprises an atonement based on reconciliation, a salvation of love and reclamation. After her conversion, her transformation, she rests with Piedade. She is embraced. Loved. *Consoled*. Piedade, a Portuguese name, "displays Jesus in Mary's arms after his crucifixion. In Morrison's rendition, the mother and son image is replaced by a mother and daughter—Consolata in Piedade's arms. The association with the ocean, the ships and the shores, suggests Piedade's connection with the Candomblé Goddess, Yemanja, the patron of the sea and the protector of ships and fishermen, and with the Virgin Mary, another manifestation of Yemanja in Candomblé."[126]

Maha Marouan continues, "Piedade, whom Morrison also describes as 'black as fire-wood' (318), alludes to the Egyptian goddess Isis. This vision where Yemanja, the Virgin Mary, and Isis are blurred suggests another level of syncretism across religious traditions with a focus on the feminine as a common bond. Morrison said that she intended the final word of the novel to be 'paradise with a lowercase 'p' and asked the publisher to make the correction for later editions."

I agree, and also add that this invokes all of the more than four hundred images of the Black Madonna across the globe—images of black mothers holding their child that represent sacredness, power, and worship.[127] All these aspects are now present in and for Consolata.

For Morrison, it is the men in Ruby who must live with the consequences of their Paradise. What they did to maintain it is a burden reminiscent of the mark of Cain. Trying to remove what they registered as sinfulness in wayward women's bodies compelled them to murder, to a frenzy, to a thirst for the women's demise that they never registered as wrong or awful or terrible. Their interpretation of sin stopped with what they determined as the Original Sin, or the fall of humanity—for Morrison, a theological master narrative. This narrative declares "what is ugliness, what is worthlessness, what is contempt."[128] It is the value system of Christendom imposed on the subjects and survivors of Christian colonialism. The ugliness that characters across her oeuvre experience, the pain they feel at the hands of the white hegemonic imagination's proclamations, is a result of a theology that states humans are discardable upon arrival, unless redeemed by the colonial Christ.[129]

Morrison asks, "How do individuals resist or become complicit in the process of alienating others' demonization—a process that can infect the foreigner's geographical sanctuary with the country's xenophobia? By welcoming immigrants or importing slaves into their midst for economic reasons and relegating their children to a modern version of the 'undead.'"[130] As Lindy M. Christopher explains:

> [Morrison] traces the single road that leads north from Ruby, the all-black town, to the Convent where desperate women struggle with their ghosts, and beyond that into wild grasslands and forests. And while creating these multi-layered geographies, she also provides several versions of the garden: an Edenic paradise where men hold dominion over all; a safe haven for women recovering from damaging relationships; bountiful, bounded gardens that provide food and aesthetic value to their growers; and a wild, flat landscape full of beauty. Immediately we recognize there are multiple cartographies, multiple maps, and many ideas of paradise.[131]

For Morrison, the idea of the Garden of Eden is dangerous. Its danger, for the most part, is not about human frailty or disobedience, not so much about forbidden fruits or trees of knowledge. The Garden of Eden's danger centers around the barriers erected that block off the rest of the landscape. The Garden of Eden is about the forces outside that prevent entrance to whoever is not allowed. The Garden of Eden is not meant to be shared, which Morrison declares is dangerous, because "the destiny of the twenty-first century will be shaped by the possibility or the collapse of a shareable world."[132] Such a shareable world is diametrically opposed to the Garden of Eden's portrayal as a divinely constructed paradise. This means the notion of human or divine utopias will operate as the source of the collapse.

Nadra Nittle writes, "While Paradise doesn't condemn Christianity, it argues that for it to be a tool of liberation, it can't be a reproduction of white religion. It must recognize the cosmologies of people of color and the social conditions that fuel oppression; moreover, it must include the divine feminine."[133] Paradise, according to Morrison, is made appealing through exclusion. Its allure is found in its inability to be shared, in its ability to signal massive discrimination. And the idea of paradise, of the utopian, that is lodged in our religious and political consciousnesses through the timeless Garden many a time justifies the violence we wield to establish and sustain it. In other words, the Garden of Eden that existed outside of time has influenced the miniature Garden of Edens in our midst to require not only walls and barriers but dogmatic bloodshed. "It may be that the most defining characteristic of our time is that, again, walls and weapons feature as prominently now as they once did in medieval times. Porous borders are understood in some quarters to be areas of threat and certain chaos, and whether real or imagined, and enforced separation is posited as a solution. Walls, ammunition—they do work. For awhile."[134]

3

ADAM AS THE OUTSIDER

Is this not the illusion of freedom: that one can determine tomorrow?
—Richard Wright

No, in possibility all things are equally possible and anyone truly brought up by possibility has grasped the terrifying just as well as the smiling.
—Søren Kierkegaard, *The Concept of Anxiety: A Simple Psychologically Orienting Deliberation on the Dogmatic Issue of Hereditary Sin*

James Baldwin, through a direct encounter with Saint Paul and his aversion to the flesh, reframes Adam and Eve's punishment and subsequent expulsion from the Garden, suggesting that all of us deserve a private and ever-expanding Paradise of our own, through self-acceptance and allowing ourselves to feel and to love. In contrast, Toni Morrison, through an engagement with Saint Augustine, perceives the very idea of Paradise as the singular problem. Another writer, Richard Wright, is not so much invested in thinking of Eden spatially or as a site of human and animal activity but rather is compelled by

Eden's characters. In other words, moving away from the location of the Garden of Eden and what it provides or prevents, we now look more closely at how Wright thinks through and with the Genesis characters Adam and Eve, especially Adam.

My central argument in this chapter is that Richard Wright uses the Adamic archetype in his second novel, *The Outsider* (1952), in two specific ways. First, through Kierkegaardian analysis, Wright uses Adam to interrogate the concept and consequence of "freedom." Second, Wright uses the answers from his interrogation to offer a warning about the dangers of the capitalist world, an entire world seized and ravished by god-men, a planet brutally governed by human deities who use the concept of freedom to carry out their own will to power.[1] Wright's main character stumbles upon "freedom" but finds it challenged and strained as he meets other men whose freedom is contingent upon the domination and deceit of others.

It may seem odd at first to turn to Richard Wright, whom some regard as explicitly secular, for a theological text that explores biblical depictions, but Tara T. Green is correct in her claim that "Although Wright rejects organized religions, whether Christian, tribal, or communism, he, ironically, uses the figurative language similar to that of sermons, including biblical stories and symbols, to appeal to his readers and to develop his themes."[2] Wright's classic books, *Native Son* (1940) and *Black Boy* (1945), include much on the problem of religion, and he stated in his own terms that *Man Who Lived Underground* (1944) was his way of exploring the religious consciousness of his grandmother. But I turn to his undertheorized novel, *The Outsider*, to investigate how Wright not only engages in systematic theology with great care but also engages with the Garden of Eden.

Furthermore, unlike Baldwin and Morrison, Wright does not exclusively turn to canonized theologians or early Christian writers considered theological architects of Christianity. Instead, like most of his contemporaries, Wright relies on the popular continental philosophers of his day and the nineteenth-century intellectuals who inspired them. Along with figures like Saint Paul and Saint Augustine, Wright turns to Martin Heidegger, Jean-Paul Sartre, Albert Camus, Simone de Beauvoir, Friedrich Nietzsche, and, most importantly for our study, Søren Kierkegaard, the Danish philosopher whose popularity exploded in the twentieth century.

There is no shortage of materials that detail Wright's early and emphatic disregard for religion. His earlier and more popular works, *Uncle Tom's Children* (1938), *Native Son* (1940), and *Black Boy* (1945), often criticized unlettered or apolitical black preachers and superstitious black women. Wright argued that Afro-Protestant doctrine held a mental grip on black people's religious consciousness. In *Black Boy* (1945) and *Native Son* (1940) especially, black religion, to Wright, is a relic of slavery that keeps black Americans subjected to white political sovereignty. Wright's second novel, *The Outsider* (1952), however, no longer limits that criticism of religion to black people pathologically but expands it to suggest that theology, the very notion of the sacred and salvific, leaves humans vulnerable to mass manipulation. An imagination that includes the capacity for thinking theologically is what allows "the sacred" to be twisted and placed into various ideologies that promise secular versions of not only salvation but also Eden. In an unpublished draft essay Wright considers this move a "shrinking," in which people have "surrendered their human sovereignty in exchange for 'security.'"[3]

I will begin with Wright's connection to Kierkegaard, then delve into a reading of Kierkegaard's *The Concept of Anxiety: A Simple Deliberation on the Dogmatic Issue of Hereditary Sin* (1844).

These explanations will illuminate how Kierkegaard's existential reading of Eden serves as the primary source of Wright's second novel, how Wright uses Adam, and his presentation of Eve. I will also show how Wright connects Cross Damon to Nietzsche's *Übermensch*, or Overman, a hypothetical figure who transcends typical morality and values for existential self-actualization. Wright follows Nietzsche but ultimately shows the consequences for an individual in a society filled with men who create according to their own whims and thirsts. So, where and when did this connection begin?

WRIGHT AND KIERKEGAARD

Even though Wright was not a fan of religion, he studied theologians across various time periods. Søren Kierkegaard seems to have spoken to something deep within Wright, in ways that other theologians did not. Perhaps this was because Kierkegaard reads the Garden of Eden sequence differently from both Saint Paul and Saint Augustine. There was something in his unique account that Wright found not only useful but also insightful for thinking through his work in progress at the time, as well as his earlier material.

Kierkegaard's work resonated with Wright so much that he told C. L. R. James, "Everything that [Kierkegaard] writes in those books, I knew before I had them."[4] Furthermore, Wright did not come across Kierkegaard's work by mere happenstance. Both Wright and Ralph Ellison were attentive to the popular continental philosophy sweeping the cafés and classrooms of post–World War II Europe. Both, but especially Wright, were involved in the development of existentialism in the United States.[5] Wright was involved in a cosmopolitan intellectual culture that interrogated and addressed the human condition by returning to figures like Kierkegaard and Nietzsche.

Wright was so influenced by Kierkegaard's philosophy that he contacted his friend Dorothy Norman to help him locate European intellectuals in New York City with whom he could discuss both Kierkegaard and Heidegger. Norman, excited about this moment of intellectual collaboration, orchestrated a meeting with Paul Tillich, a systematic theologian and professor at Union Theological Seminary, and Hannah Arendt, a political philosopher and director of the Commission on European Jewish Cultural Reconstruction, at a café in Brooklyn.[6] There is no documentation concerning this meeting in Wright's diary or anything written about it from either Norman, Tillich, or Arendt. This event does reveal that though many consider Wright an emphatically areligious writer, he studied and pursued rich engagement with theologians and philosophers who were interested in rereading classical doctrine.

Before delving deeply into a textual analysis of *The Outsider*, I will analyze the way Kierkegaard reads the "Fall of Humanity" in the third chapter of Genesis to create a foundation for my reading. Examining key sections of Wright's novel, I make a few theological claims about the text to show how Wright offers a humano-centric theology. *The Outsider* reworks the Adam and Eve story by using Kierkegaard's interpretation of it, along with elements of Nietzsche's protagonist Zarathustra and Albert Camus's Arthur Meursault, to argue that the very structure of modernity—of the Western world particularly—is devoid of genuine morals, laws, ideologies (or perhaps even theologies) that guarantee human connection and intimacy.[7] Every ideology, no matter how romantic, well-intentioned, humanistic, Marxist, left, right, or religious, not only is subject to corruption and distortion but also inevitably leads directly to it through humanity's insistent will to power. Without human connection and intimacy, life becomes a constant process of alienation. Wright suggests that becoming a "bridge for man," a phrase he borrows from Nietzsche, is the key to creating a better world.[8]

SØREN KIERKEGAARD ON ANXIETY

Kierkegaard wrote *The Concept of Anxiety* in 1844, under his pseudonym, Vigilius Haufniensis, the "Watchman of Copenhagen."[9] It is undoubtedly one of his most difficult works. However, at its core, the book closely interrogates the nature and complexity of human anxiety, which, for Kierkegaard, is a result of human freedom.

To be human, for Kierkegaard, is to have anxiety—to possess angst—to be ever aware of the responsibility and burden of one's freedom. It is to understand the possibility of a dizzying affect. And this anxiety, angst, or dread was introduced to Adam through the prohibitions from the deity in the Garden. This reading both examines and contrasts the orthodox conclusions of Original Sin. Haufniensis interprets the Original Sin myth as a "fanciful dialectic" illogically promulgated by the Catholics and a historical fantasy erroneously explained by the Lutherans. For Erik M. Hanson, Kierkegaard evaluated both traditions—Catholic and Lutheran—when outlining his position because while "[the] medieval and Scholastic theologians followed Augustine in holding that original sin entailed a loss of only original righteousness, the Protestant Reformers returned to a more rigorous view of Original Sin: The fall led to not only the loss of original righteousness, *but the absolute corruption of the human rational and volitional capacities*" (emphasis mine).[10]

For Haufniensis, a robust sense of freedom for humanity was not possible through Saint Augustine's concupiscence, or at least his Edenic timeline of its corruption. The Lutherans went as far as to say that Original Sin demolished the possibility for humans to think or behave righteously. Hanson clarifies the exact tension that Kierkegaard was trying to address:

> Kierkegaard's ultimate commitment to human freedom and a broader Augustinian understanding of faith required that he balance two contrasting views that shared the rejection of the Augustinian account of hereditary sin. On the one hand was the perspective of ethical rigorism, a perspective which he held with Immanuel Kant that rejected inherited culpability. Yet defending human moral freedom also required that he avoid intimations of Pelagianism—that the individual alone was capable of overcoming evil and attaining righteousness without divine assistance.[11]

It was important for Kierkegaard not to overly assert the human ability to grasp our own salvation and to avoid using Original Sin as a justification for human fault. In other words, if the flesh with which we are born is the ultimate cause of all our failings, then our failings cannot possibly or logically be our fault.

Describing the traditional idea of the relationship and overall conditions for living between human and deity before the Fall, Niels Jorgen Cappelorn writes, "The idea is that before the fall of Adam, God established a *covenant of nature with Adam* in his role as a plenipotentiary of the whole race. After the fall, humankind diverged from this covenant and is consequently damned as a penalty for breaking the covenant of nature."[12] For Saint Paul and Saint Augustine, Adam's consumption of the forbidden fruit from the Tree of Knowledge engineered the entire destruction of God's originally created order. From their vantage point, Adam's disobedience shattered a prior congruency among creator, creature, and all of creation. In most orthodox interpretations, it was Adam's radical defiance, his clandestine desire for possible equality with God, that destroyed the divine bond between God and person. In other words, sinfulness and its serpent-like shrewdness seduced the untainted nature of Adam. Thus, sinfulness was conjured by disobedience. To place Saint Augustine's equation in existentialist terms (to the chagrin of Kierkegaard): sinfulness—in its essence—preceded sin.

Kierkegaard, however, interprets the Edenic myth a bit differently. He sits with the psychological ongoings of what he calls the "qualitative leap" and the theological consistency necessary for seeing the expulsion from Paradise as an explanation for our human condition.[13] A clarification is in order, according to Kierkegaard, to sustain the myth's integrity. For him, Saint Augustine's dogmatic theory of Original Sin was not necessarily incorrect in trying to maintain a sense of human guilt and culpability. There is some truth in its intentions, but it does not address properly Adam's freedom and the anxiety/angst it conjures. Sitting with Adam's psychological state would render a more complete explanation of sin than the orthodox dialectic that makes its case too strongly. Gregory R. Beabout states, "By psychology, Kierkegaard does not mean empirical psychology in the contemporary sense. Rather, he uses the term 'psychology' in the classical sense to mean the study, description, and explanation of the human soul, or of the human being and that which is essential to being human."[14] Kierkegaard writes: "Through Adam's first sin, sin came accordingly into the world. This statement, the common one, contains however an altogether external reflection that has without doubt contributed greatly to misty misunderstandings. That sin came into the world is quite true, but this is no concern of Adam's. To put it quite pointedly and accurately one must say: through the first sin, *sinfulness entered Adam*" (emphasis mine).[15]

For Kierkegaard, the language confuses more than it clarifies. The concept of Original Sin rightfully presupposes "sin" but inadequately explains it. He continues, "Hereditary sin is . . . not to be explained by dogmatics; the explanation is that it is something presupposed, like that vortex that the Greek speculation about nature talked so much about, a moving something which no science can get a hold of."[16] Although Augustine's dogma fleshes out a fully formed theology of Original Sin through his historical arguments with Pelagius, Kierkegaard believes dogmatics is the improper "science" to address some of the central questions that surround presuppositions about sin. The "what" is rightly and dogmatically assumed. Kierkegaard believes that his readers know that sin entered the world. He is less convinced that they know how. Therefore, he wants to explore not only what happened on that fateful mythological day for Adam but also what happens on all our fateful days. There must be some consistent explanation that does not place Adam outside of history, outside of the human race. Plus, Kierkegaard reads the Fall like the Hegelians in his day and other intellectuals who favor a more allegorical interpretation. Therefore, Adam must remain connected to humanity for humanity to remain meaningfully a part of the story. Otherwise, the entire schema of Original Sin falls to the wayside. What is said about Adam must also hold the possibility of being said about us for the myth to ultimately matter.

Therefore, Kierkegaard wants to interrogate the consequences that Adam faced, to analyze the consequences that *we* face: to ask what salvation is and how it helps us deal with the ramifications of sin. He pursues these questions because he wants to ensure that we reconnect with God and overcome despair/sin. For Kierkegaard, it is not about disobedience in the same way as for Saint Paul, Saint Augustine, and the theologians before them. It is about anxiety through the awareness of possibility. And this possibility forces one to face the responsibility of freedom. Kierkegaard is focused on an understudied component of the Genesis legend that requires more thought than the pious declaration of Original Sin, which is explicit about its irrationality:

> The present work has taken as its theme the psychological treatment of "anxiety," in such a way that it constantly keeps *in mente* [in mind] and before its eye the dogma of hereditary sin. It has therefore to take account, although tacitly, of the concept of sin. Sin, however, is not a theme for psychological interest, and it would only be to abandon oneself to the service of a misunderstood cleverness if one were to treat it thus. Sin has its definite place, or rather it has no place, and that is what characterizes it.[17]

With this stated, I will examine the primary idea in the *Concept of Anxiety* to illustrate Kierkegaard's concept of Original Sin or, more appropriately, his theory of anxiety, which undergirds the Edenic myth. This will show how Wright used Kierkegaard to explain the choices and condition of Cross Damon—Wright's Adam/monster—in *The Outsider*.

THE FALL AS THE LEAP INTO SIN

According to Haufniensis, anxiety (introduced psychologically) must keep sin in mind as a concept because *anxiety precedes sin*. And we learn from Kierkegaard, or Anti-Climacus in *Sickness Unto Death*, that *sin is despair*. And despair—an undeniable aspect of life—is what every human confronts and must encounter to embrace the self. Said differently, anxiety precedes sin, which is despair. Haufniensis's overall argument is that if we think critically about the theology of Original Sin, especially as it relates to the myth used to explain it, then we will be able to see that anxiety preceded the Fall, or the "qualitative leap," of Adam. However, the illogical explanation of Original Sin through this narrative has been an "ethical and illogical heresy" because we place Adam outside the history of humanity while also making him responsible for humans.[18]

So, how does Kierkegaard explain the consequences and lessons of the Edenic myth? For the Watchman, according to Kierkegaard, and against Saint Augustine, "the human being" or, in this case, the example of Adam pre-Fall, "is not characterized as spirit but is psychically characterized in immediate unity with its natural condition. Spirit is dreaming in the human being." He means that spirit is not yet posited in the formulation of the human being's concept of the self. A self is not quite present yet. It is abstract. This is the foundation for conceptualizing Adam's innocence. It is a spiritless ignorance, like a plant or an animal (in Kierkegaard's framing). Adam, however, is not reduced to an animal because spirit exists in him as immediate or dreaming. We must take Adam's blissful ignorance about freedom, good, and evil as primary. Also, we must maintain a grip on the concept of anxiety as being a part of the dreaming spirit that exists as *potentiality* for Adam.

God prohibits Adam from partaking of the fruit of the Tree of Knowledge of Good and Evil. This does not teach Adam about freedom, necessarily, but "The prohibition makes him anxious, because it awakens in him freedom's possibility. What innocence let slip as the nothing of anxiety now enters him, and here again it is a nothing—the anxious possibility of *being able*."[19]

George Pattison writes, "It is in this possibility that anxiety is found, insinuating itself between the prohibition and the desire. If desire is conceived of primarily in terms of its object, then anxiety is primarily to do with the subject's sense of self and its own intrinsic possibilities."[20] Moreover, Kierkegaard says, "The infinite possibility of 'being able,' which the prohibition awakened, now draws nearer through this possibility as its accompaniment."[21]

Saint Augustine argues that sin enters the world through Adam's disobedience. For Kierkegaard, anxiety was induced by God's prohibition, which preceded the ultimate "disobedience" and introduced "possibility" into Adam's universe. The very notion of possibility, the very actualizing and dizziness of his "freedom," creates the condition of possibility for sin to enter the world through Adam. *For God to declare what Adam should not do introduced Adam to the possibility of what he could do; and possibility always comes with a burdensomeness, an anxiety attached because it is a new opening.* This burdensomeness, this dread, this opening, is also the guilt that rids the human of their innocence. To be aware, to be fully awake to the possibilities of good and bad, morality and sin, and the subsequent ramifications of our choices that could determine so much, is to be free. Yet this freedom is what engenders the possibility of guilt. Pattison says: "It is not a matter of a simple, centred subject desiring some external object, but rather of an internally differentiated subject discovering the diverse possibilities of relating to its world made available by this internal differentiation."[22] This is why, through Kierkegaard and Heidegger, Jean-Paul Sartre states that "Man is condemned to be free; because once thrown into the world, he is responsible for everything he does."[23] Kierkegaard describes anxiety as "a sympathetic antipathy and an antipathetic sympathy." Humans are both attracted to and disgusted by this freedom.

We are drawn to it. We are happy for it. We want it. We hate it. We don't want it. Give it here. Give it back. And this is one of the main reasons it is distinct from fear. To fear something is to be afraid of a something, to have an object of the fear. Anxiety is the fundamental human condition, a feature of existence. It is close to experiencing fear without being directed toward anything. Furthermore, we are also somewhat attracted or drawn to the possibilities of our freedom. Most scholars use looking over the abyss and not wanting to fall but also wanting to jump as an example. This is what I mean by the disgust and the attraction.

Kierkegaard's positioning of Adam in history is imperative for his conception of Adam's choice to eat the fruit with Eve. The decision is the leap. Adam participates in his freedom, and most would categorize this as the Fall, but Kierkegaard (Haufniensis) considers it the "qualitative leap" into sin. The decision altered Adam's existence. He went from innocent in an ignorant, dreaming way to guilty in a free, burdensome way. This point is critical for Wright. Cross Damon views his life—prior to engaging existentialism—as a sort of ignorant sequence of dreams.

Concerning whether hereditary sin, Adam's first sin, and Saint Augustine's "Fall" are identical, Kierkegaard states that because of the difficulties of explanations and proposals, a fantastic presupposition is introduced: Saint Augustine has a sexual way of explaining Original Sin. But it is through this fantastic presupposition that questions are raised about Adam's connection with the rest of the human race. This connection is important for understanding every human being's participation in sin. The way sin entered the world through Adam is the same way sin enters the world through us as individuals who are a part of the "nexus of history." Therefore, we all—every single one of us—make a qualitative leap into sin.

Kierkegaard understands that anxiety is a necessary, although painful, passageway to faith. Going through anxiety is an unavoidable aspect of life if one is to have spirit, to be human with psychic and physical components. And unfortunately, the only place of rest is faith. Kierkegaard believes that one must learn to be anxious, to cope with the anxiety and not succumb to it. He believes anxiety is informing: it consumes, embraces, reveals, and destroys anything that is insignificant and finite. One must be fully aware of the weight of possibility to understand the complexities and experiences of it. Kierkegaard acknowledges that to be educated by possibility, to cope with anxiety, is a dangerous feat. Those who experience anxiety sometimes succumb to it and unfortunately fall into despair. On the other hand, others in fear of anxiety often avoid it and thus circumvent living an authentic interior life. Kierkegaard calls this a life of spiritlessness. Thus, he believes only faith, a faith that traverses through anxiety and does not give in to despair, is significant for the life of the human who is both infinite and finite.

THE OUTSIDER: THE CRUSHING GOD, THE WRECKAGE, AND THE QUALITATIVE LEAP

Richard Wright's novel illustrates how he used these ideas to offer his own political theology. Following the insights and structure from Albert Camus's *The Stranger* (1942), *The Outsider* tells a story about a man named Cross Damon. Cross is an intellectual who suffers from alcoholism.[24] He works at the post office. He pores over existentialist literature. His first name, according to his mother, is derived from the "Cross of Jesus."[25] His last name, according to Margaret Walker, stems from "daemon."[26]

Lewis Gordon too claims—again through Nietzsche—that "Damon represents what it means *really to go outside*, to go beyond values."[27]

Most critics suggest that Cross Damon reflects Richard Wright more than *Native Son*'s Bigger Thomas. Like Wright, he is on a constant quest for meaning and finds himself diving through the corpus of European continental philosophers and theologians. Unlike Wright, Cross was admitted to the University of Chicago but stopped attending when he started having children. Like Wright, he worked for the U.S. post office and had a religious mother who wanted him to accept Jesus Christ and join a church.[28] Unlike Wright, Cross Damon accidentally stumbles upon the freedom for which he yearns and later regrets the decisions and choices he makes with it.

Like Bigger, Cross has friends who are black and jovial. They laugh and make jokes. They play the Dozens. The novel begins with Cross and these four friends walking through the snow. This friend group offers him reprieve. They pay attention to his health. They notice his change in attitude since his deep dive into existentialism and offer him guidance. There is an intimacy between male friends across Wright's oeuvre that has gone overlooked and taken for granted. Cross has been drinking heavily, and his friends try to intervene. He jokingly throws his weight on them and asks if they can carry him. Jokingly they respond, but each takes notice of how cold his flesh has become, remarking that he is "Mr. Death." After they tell him that he needs to quit drinking, Cross says he needs the alcohol because it helps him "feel less." Humorously, the conversation turns into a sort of memorial, a collection of memories of what the "old Cross" was like. He was playful. Alive. Vivacious. In fun he would prank groups of people. His friends said his jokes were so good it was like he was God standing outside of time. This opening scene with Cross Damon's friends offers a glimpse into who he was before existential reading revealed that the meaninglessness of life was not just possible but certain.

Using Wright's nonfiction essays to interpret his Adamic protagonist, I believe that the depression Cross feels but does not necessarily describe is an example of what Wright believes is a consequence of white political sovereignty. The consequence is thus an indoctrination into a sort of "spiritual void." Like countless black and brown people across the West, Cross fails to find meaning and purpose to counter this void and sinks into a depression, a profound grief that forces him to drink to numb whatever pain or thoughts bombard him about his place in life.

The beginning of the story also shows the social and familial conditions that metaphorically strangle him. Cross is legally married to a woman he no longer loves, Gladys, and is trying to convince the younger woman he does love, Dot, to have an abortion. He realizes that he never desired either of them, he just desired *desire*. And "desire" manifested itself in the form of the women around him.

Cross Damon's mother—like Bigger's mother and Wright's grandmother—symbolizes not only Afro-Christianity broadly construed but also a version of what I consider to be Wright's depiction of the "Black Madonna," which is in stark contrast with Toni Morrison's artistic image of the Black Madonna discussed in the previous chapter. *Paradise* concludes with an image of the Black Madonna that offered mercy and peace to Consolata. Wright sees this differently: black mothers and the imagery of the Black Madonna are not identical. And one consistent idea across his work is that black mothers are in fact the human conduits through which white supremacist Christian practices and theological doctrines are imposed on the consciousness of black children.[29] The older black mothers with broken hearts and stifled sexualities carry the message of Jesus, along with what Wright considers to be the senseless doctrines of their religious institutions.

These doctrines and religious perspectives—existential absurdities—are not only taught but also indoctrinated through manipulation, chastising, physical abuse, and constant rebuking. In other words, everything there is to know about God's condemnations, prohibitions, and expectations is voiced through black mothers' ceaseless scolding. Everything there is to know about God's absence, broken promises, and lack of meaningful interventions is reflected in their embarrassing pleading. Wright states, "This frigid world was suggestively like the one, which his mother, without her having known it, had created for him to live in when he had been a child. Though she loved him, she had tainted his budding feelings with fierce devotion born of her fear of a life that had baffled and wounded her."[30] For Wright, black children in particular are hammered by their mother's religious consciousness before they are given a choice to develop their own beliefs: "[Cross's] first coherent memories had condensed themselves into an image of a young woman whose hysterically loving presence had made his imagination conscious of an invisible God—whose secret grace granted him life—hovering oppressively in space above him. His adolescent fantasies had symbolically telescoped this God into an awful face shaped in the form of a huge and crushing NO."[31]

Wright's portrayal of the black mother furthers my claim that Cross Damon is an archetypal Adam, through the Kierkegaardian framework. He was created from his mother's flesh like Adam was created from God's breath. The connection between Cross and his mother started to break down because of her divine prohibitions in the same way, as Kierkegaard outlines, God's prohibitions awoke in Adam the mere possibility of severance.

Cross Damon's mother and her "crushing GOD" awakened in him sexual and sensual desires that were "paradoxically given him."[32] In order to reject this deity, to break free and do something despite the restrictions imposed on him, Cross had "slain the sense of [his mother] in his heart and at the same time had clung frantically to his memory of that sense."[33] This psychological murder of his mother is—in so many words—Cross simultaneously murdering God.

Cross never expected to feel love from God, nor did he expect *to desire* to feel love from God. For Cross, this was a God "whose love seemed somehow like hate."[34] Here Cross Damon's philosophy of religion in many ways mirrors that of black philosopher William R. Jones. Through his pioneering text, *Is God a White Racist? A Preamble to Black Theology* (1973), Jones criticizes the traditional depictions of God as loving, compassionate, involved, and moral. For Jones, African American faith has been slow to question the morality of the deity because of its commitment to orthodox ideas. There is a lack of statistical or experiential evidence that God is omnipowerful, omnibenevolent, or omniscient, especially considering that most black people live in poverty, are incarcerated at higher rates than white people, and struggle with all manner of other societal injustices. For Cross Damon, his mother's God might actually prefer the current condition of the world and might be—perhaps most likely is—the primary engineer of the order of things.

Like Bigger's mother, Mrs. Damon functions as the voice of God, the one who asserts a theodicy, the defender of God's righteousness, and the one who foreshadows Cross's eventual demise: " 'You can laugh!' she stormed at him. 'But God'll punish you! He *will*! You'll see before you die! You'll weep! God is a just God! And He's a hard and jealous God! If you mock Him, He'll show you His Power!' "[35] After scolding him, she concludes,

"To think I named you Cross after the Cross of Jesus."[36] But his mother's oppressive religious tenets are only the first cause awakening Cross's freedom.

Everything comes crashing down on Cross once he discovers that his girlfriend, Dot, will not proceed with an abortion. His situation worsens once Dot confesses that she is not the age she initially claimed when they met. She is only a teenager. Aware of the illegality of their romance, she threatens to contact the police if he does not marry her and commit to their family. Cross, however, cannot legally marry Dot because he is already married to Gladys, who has refused to grant him a divorce. Once Gladys is made aware of Dot's plan to have him arrested, she contrives a scheme to extort money from him before his inevitable incarceration. Cross's arms are tied. His life is closing in on him. He sees no escape. While heading home from work at the post office, holding the money he received as an advance from his job, he abruptly finds himself upside down, hurt, and barely conscious after a deadly Chicago subway wreck.

The train wreck in the novel is another prime example of black writers using biblical imagery to make theological points. Wright uses the wreck to reimagine the famous Johannine conversation about soteriology between Jesus and the curious pharisee Nicodemus. In the Johannine story, Nicodemus emerges from the "darkness" and meets with Jesus "in the light" to inquire about the process of salvation and redemption that he heard Jesus explaining to his followers. Nicodemus is genuinely confused about the physiological details of Jesus's metaphorical demand that one "must be born again."[37] He rightly understands that humans cannot "reenter their mother's womb." Wright invokes the imagery from this pericope in the train wreck passages to reflect a rebirthing process. Cross is trapped around flesh and blood and pushes himself through a small window to crawl onto the ground, which will ultimately result in him becoming a born-again, new person.

The old him is publicly pronounced dead, and everyone who knew him prior to the collision considers him dead too.[38] Jennifer Elisa Veninga makes an interesting point in saying that this subway wreck, where Cross Damon, the man, dies—from a Kierkegaardian perspective—"frees Cross from the guilt of sinfulness that Adam brought into the human race."[39] In these moments, Cross exists outside of the human. I agree and categorize the phenomenon in these terms: Cross Damon is freed from the guilt of sinfulness that he brought into the world and ultimately, even if for just a moment, finds salvation in pure possibility.

As Cross slowly makes his way to a bar where the news is covering the accident, he realizes he is missing his wallet. Unbeknownst to Cross, his wallet, containing all his identification papers, fell on a corpse in the wreckage. Therefore, when the hospital and police announce the deceased victims, his name is mentioned. Cross takes this as an opportunity to re-create himself and his life. He sneaks around the city like a ghost, watching his funeral, spying on his family, slowly shredding whatever connections he has to his former life.

Cross pays to sleep in a brothel, where he tells people he is from Memphis and just arrived in Chicago, but he runs into Joe Thomas, one of his friends from the beginning of the novel. Joe says, "What the hell is this? . . . I've got to touch you to believe it." Lewis Lawson comments on this part of the story: "To Joe, a miracle has occurred; he sees a man who has risen from the dead; thus a scene from the Gospel is reenacted, with Joe as Doubting Thomas and Cross as the risen Christ [or what I would call the second Adam]. Joe says, 'I've got to touch you to believe it.' Right here in the novel we see another enemy of Wright that isn't talked about much."[40]

Lawson further writes that "Joe is the very picture of the traditional Negro: jolly, optimistic, content in his belief in a personal Christian God. He cannot conceive that he is really looking at a new man, one who must kill him to retain the freedom that he has chosen. Cross crushes Joe's skull, then topples him out of the window so that it will appear as if Joe might have leapt to his death."[41] I argue that Cross's murder of Joe and staging of it as suicide is Wright toying with Kierkegaard's language. This is specifically Cross Damon's quantitative leap. Before a full day has passed, he has bitten the forbidden fruit and allowed sin to enter into him, effectively changing him, transforming him into a person who kills, who takes power into his own hands and does what is necessary to maintain it.

Cross thus severs his connection to his friends and support system. Afterward, he gets on the train headed to New York City. Tommie Shelby writes that once Cross finds his freedom, "He lives as a thoroughgoing *nihilist*—an atheist who is fundamentally amoral and who, through his choices, self-consciously imposes order and normative significance on an inherently meaningless life in the world."[42] Eberhard Alsen states, "Cross Damon not only accepts Nietzsche's contention that God is dead, but he also considers himself one of Nietzsche's 'last men' who place themselves beyond good and evil in their pursuit of power."[43]

CROSS DAMON ON THEOLOGY AFTER THE FALL

We first encounter Cross's view of religion as the narrator reflects on the Afro-Protestantism of his mother. However, Wright does not limit his critique of religion to black culture; he also extends it to Christianity and religion writ large. While Cross is traveling on the train, he finds himself sitting near a Catholic priest. For Cross, religious adherents—especially religious leaders—are trapped in a premodern world that ties the political order of things to a divinely appointed calculus, of which their interpretations justify their behavior and sovereignty. Wright writes, "Cross's anxieties now condensed themselves into an attitude of sullenness toward the priest. He disliked most strongly all men of religion because he felt that they could take for granted an interpretation of the world that his sense of life made impossible."[44] His sense of life cannot be reflected in a Christian world where a salvific story offers a particular coherence and ultimate meaning. Furthermore, Christianity, and religion more broadly, only make logical sense to the white people who colonized the world in the name of God. Wright states:

> The priest was secure and walked the earth with a divine mandate, while Cross' mere breathing was an act of audacity, a confounding wonder at the daily mystery of himself. He felt that the attitude of the priest was predicated upon a scheme of good and evil ordained by a God whom he was constrained out of love and fear to obey; and Cross therefore regarded him as a kind of dressed-up savage intimidated by totems and taboos that differed in kind but not in degree from those of the most primitive of peoples.[45]

For Wright, religious leaders' thoughts and understandings of politics, science, and history are controlled by unreal forces that they mistakenly believe make them conceive of themselves as moral people. Wright believes that religious people avoid dread by living in a permanent state of what Sartre called *mauvaise foi*.[46] They ultimately take no responsibility for finding or cultivating meaning in their lives. They take no responsibility for their actions. Yet "Cross had to discover what was good or evil through his own actions which were more exacting than the edicts of any God because it was God alone who had to bear the brunt of their consequences with a sense of absoluteness made intolerable by knowing that this life of his was all he had and would ever have. For him there was no grace or mercy if he failed."[47]

However, this assumed morality is disrupted when the passengers are confronted with the evils of their day. This priest rises to the aid of a white woman who attacks a black worker, Bob Hunter, on the train while shouting that he's a "nigger" because he almost, unintentionally, spilled coffee on her.[48] For Wright, regardless of or with the encouragement of religion, the Catholic priest reveals his firm commitment to the white supremacist order of things. Wright also rightfully understands that Christianity was the primary thought used to justify Western colonialism. He begins his classic essay in *White Man, Listen!* by stating:

> Buttressed by their belief that their God had entrusted the earth into their keeping, drunk with power and possibility, waxing rich through trade and commodities, human and nonhuman, with awesome naval and merchant marines at their disposal, there are countries filled with human debris anxious for any adventures, psychologically armed with new facts. White Western Christian civilization during the fourteenth, fifteenth, sixteenth, and seventeenth centuries, with a long, slow, and bloody explosion, hurled itself upon the sprawling masses of colored humanity in Asia and Africa.[49]

This history causes Cross Damon to see the Catholic priest as a "savage," a word that Catholics and Protestants historically used to demean and describe the Africans and Asians they pillaged.[50] After they both return to their seats, a friend of the priest, a New York City district attorney with a hunched back named Ely Houston, joins Cross to philosophize about the "outsider" status of black people. Ely, whose name also represents, according to my reading, the Hebraic God and the moment of Jesus announcing his being forsaken, has a hunchback, representing the nature of both the divine and earthly law. As Sandra Adell writes, "The one person who understands Cross and to whom he is most attracted, is, ironically, the hunchback district attorney, Ely Houston. Houston shares Lionel's status as an outsider (Lionel is the name Cross gave him so I will henceforth refer to him as Lionel); but he is also a man who possesses a keen insight, not only into the psychology of Black Americans, but into that of modern western man."[51] Ely Houston says to Lionel (Cross),

> Negroes, as they enter our culture, are going to inherit the problems we have, but with a difference. They are outsiders and they are going to know that they have these problems. There are going to be self-conscious; they are going to be gifted with a double vision, for, being Negroes, they are going to be both inside and outside of our culture at the same time. Every emotional and cultural convulsion that ever shook the heart and soul of Western man will shake them. Negroes will develop unique and specially defined psychological types. They will not only be American or Negroes; they will be centers of knowing, so to speak.[52]

Cross finds himself enamored with the conversation but also realizes that he must keep his distance because he is, in fact, a criminal on the run.

Cross arrives in Harlem. He stays with Bob Hunter and his wife, Sarah, and discovers that Bob is a black communist. Bob invites leaders from the Communist Party, Gil and Eva Blount, over to meet him. Gil is a leader in the party and wants Cross to move in with them to annoy their fascist landlord, Herndon. Yet what is most important is that in Harlem, Cross meets Eva, for whom Eve is the archetype in this tale.

EVA AS EVE

Eva is a member of the Communist Party not by choice but through marriage. Her marriage to Gil, unbeknownst to her, was planned by the party to claim prestige because she is a successful artist. She does not discover this until a gossiping Trotskyite, not knowing who she is, inadvertently reveals her standing in the party. This information disheartens and changes her. It also, according to my reading, reinforces my theory that if Cross Damon follows the Adamic archetype, then Eva Blount follows the archetype of Eve.[53] Eva is presented as innocent and childlike and winds up being deceived. Cross sees this naivety and innocence in Eva and becomes intensely attracted to her because of his own guilty conscience.

Orthodox Christian interpretations of Genesis suggest that Eve was deceived by the serpent. Her naivety and gullibility, combined with Adam's pride and desire, are understood as the "cause" of the Fall of humankind. In parallel, in the novel Eva is deceived by the treacherous Communist Party, and Cross's love and desire for her lead to his end.

At some point on the night Cross and the Blounts meet, while Gil is downstairs discussing party business, Eva reveals to Cross that she is a painter. His interest is piqued. He tells her he would love to see her artwork. She shows him. He sees that she paints nonobjective paintings. These reveal an innocent woman who is not corrupted by the modern world or its politics, like everyone else.

Moreover, Eva's artwork reveals to Cross their mutual condition of alienation. They are both outsiders. The difference between them is that Cross has given in to his desires, which have caused him to lie, kill, and deceive. Eva, however, is completely innocent, not giving in to her desires, and copes with the life that she lives. Therefore, through some personal and psychological and theological equation, Cross sees the possibility for his redemption in her.

Cross tells Eva that her paintings express "the dominant consciousness of man," which is godlessness.[54] He means that the cosmos is utterly empty of a divine or supreme creator. All that exists in this world are humans, who are essentially alone. And since we are alone, we project "our moods, our consciousness, onto nature and our outer worlds."[55] Following Freud, Cross asks, "Now, my notion is that since this is true, that the world we see is the world we make by our manual or emotional projection, why not let us be honest and paint our own projections, our fantasies, our own moods, our own conceptions of what things are. Let's paint our feelings directly. Why let objects master us?"[56] After Eva leaves him with her art, "[Lionel] had the illusion, while studying them, of standing somehow at the center of Eva's ego and being captured by the private, subjective world that was hers, a world that was frightening in the stark quality of its aloneness; and he knew that it was out of sense of aloneness that these bold, brutal images, nameless and timeless, had come with force of compulsions."[57]

Cross feels that he has discovered an artistic entry point into Eva's ego, but he does not stop there. When visiting the Blounts' apartment, he steals her diary from her room and reads her personal confessions. These, along with her art and overall innocent comportment, compel him to fall madly in love. As Jane Davis notes, "One major factor in his attraction to her is that unlike the other women in his life, she has no power over him and is non-threatening."[58]

Out of nowhere a fight erupts between Herndon, the fascist owner of the building in which the Blounts live, and Gil. Cross runs downstairs and pretends to protect Gil. While Herndon is threatening Gil with a poker in his face, Cross grabs a heavy oaken leg from the table and smashes it on Herndon's head, crushing his skull. Afterward, while Gil is completely unaware, Cross smashes the oak "on the left side of Gil's head." In a moment of passion, disgust, detachment, and anger about the ideologies and godlike manner the two fighting men claim, he kills them both. "[Cross] killed two little gods . . . There was in him no regret for what he had done; no, none at all. But how could he have done it? He too had acted like a little god. He had stood amid those red and flickering shadows, tense and consumed with cold rage, and had judged them and had found them guilty of insulting his sense of life and had carried out a sentence of death upon them."[59]

Cross realizes that he has made the same mistake he charged them with. "But if he resented their being little gods, how could he do the same? His self-assurance ebbed, his pride waned under the impact of his own reflections. Oh, Christ, their disease had reached out and claimed him too. He had been subverted by the contagion of the lawless; he had been defeated by that which he had sought to destroy."[60]

Cross knows that he took things too far. Wright begins book 4, "Despair," with this beautiful passage:

> The seductions of vanity have lured countless men to destinies that have confounded them, left them straightened and undone. After an arduous journey of experience it is not good to stare in dismay at a world that one was creating without being aware of it, and there is no chastening of the spirit so severely sobering as that rankling sense of guilt that springs from a knowledge of having been snared into the mire of disillusionment when one thought that one was soaring on wings of intellectual pride to a freedom remote from the errors and frailties of the gullible. At times there come into the lives of men realizations so paralyzing that, for the first time, their hands reach out fumblingly for the touch of another human being.[61]

Wright's use of "vanity" and "pride" invokes the Augustinian conception of Original Sin to home in on how Cross's pride caused his actions—his prideful murders. Wright further suggests that the double homicide also compels Cross to rethink the concept of community, or at least to desire the touch and help of another person. Eva, who was already the focus of his affection, becomes the human touch, the understanding and, I would even venture to say, the salvation for which Cross yearns to heal his "wounded pride."

Ely Houston discovers who "Lionel" really is and assumes that he is the one who committed the double homicide. Houston convinces Cross's family to come to New York City to identify him, since they think he is dead. Cross pretends not to notice them and refuses to respond to their cries. Houston invokes Camus's *The Stranger* (1942) and says that Cross is a man who has transcended morality. After Cross returns from Houston's office, having seen his family and heard the news of his mother's death, he rushes to Sarah Hunter's home to locate Eva. He realizes that the party has told Eva about his background. She confronts him, and he does not deny any of the details and tries to communicate the reason, or the lack of reason, for murdering Herndon and Gil. Cross pleads for Eva to forgive him, to embrace him, to redeem him. She not only refuses to provide the salvation he pleads for but also rushes out of the window and commits suicide, signaling that she felt completely alone and trapped in a world of never-ending deceit.

Cross is once again alone. Ely Houston tells him that Eva's diaries, taken after her death, reveal the truth about who and what Cross Damon is. When Houston reads her mistaken interpretations of Cross's innocence, he realizes what Sarah Hunter already discovered earlier: that Cross is a "genuine atheist."

> A genuine atheist is a real Christian turned upside down; God descends from the sky and takes up abode, so to speak, behind fleshy bars of his heart! Men argue about their not believing in God and the mere act of doing so makes them believers. It is only when they do not feel the need to deny Him that they really do not believe in Him . . . You went all the way! You have drawn all the conclusions and deductions that could be drawn from the atheistic position and you have inherited the feelings that only real atheists can have. At first I didn't believe it, but when you stared so unfailingly at your sons, when you laughed when your poor wife could summon enough strength to identify you, I knew that you were beyond the pale of all the *little* feelings, the *humble* feelings, the *human* feelings. I knew that you could do anything![62]

Houston surmises that Cross Damon is an inhuman human being, not because he is an atheist in the normative sense but because he does not believe in any transcendent or universal laws at all. Tommie Shelby states: "What makes Cross special—that is, atypical . . . [is that] He confronts the human predicament with eyes open, without the consolations of religion or political ideology."[63] Cross does not believe in any values, ideas, ethics, or mores that require cooperation among all human beings. That is why in reflection, he thinks that "He had broken all of his promises to the world and the people in it."[64]

What Houston reveals to Cross, however, is the ultimate argument of *The Outsider*: "But Damon, you made one fatal mistake. You saw through all ideologies, pretenses, frauds, but you did not see through *yourself*." Wright, through Houston, thus invokes Saint Augustine. Houston continues, "How magnificently you tossed away this God who plagues and helps man so much! But you did not and could not toss out of your heart that part of you from which the God notion had come. And what part of man is that? It is desire."[65] Shelby comments:

> Cross lies, betrays, steals, invades others' privacy, commits adultery, covets another's wife, and refuses to honor his mother. Mostly, he kills or indirectly causes others to die. As murder is considered the greatest wrong one can do to another human being (showing disrespect to God might be worse), an existentialist meditation on killing gives Wright a perfect opportunity to think about the rational basis for a purely secular ethics. Cross desires to act on an unrestrained libido and to be free from the surveillance and punishment of his superego. Though he does not believe in God, he chooses to become a "little god" himself, deciding by a pure act of will what is right and wrong; judging others and dispensing punishment; and treating others either as obstacles to the achievement of his aims or objects to be used to satisfy his cravings.[66]

Cross has stripped all illusions about the world from his mind and transformed himself into sheer naked desire. This, however, is what caused his terror. Houston asks: "Is desire not a kind of warning in man to let him know that he is limited? Is desire in man not a kind of danger signal of man to himself?" He answers himself by declaring, "Desire is the mad thing, the irrational thing . . . Man's decree is ultimately to be a god . . . Man desires *everything.*"[67]

It seems that Original Sin as a concept is a problem for twentieth-century black writers (and for twentieth-century liberal theologians). Most progressive intellectuals stay clear of the idea, considering all its implications. Baldwin's and Morrison's novels take different stances and offer alternative readings of the entire Eden narrative. Yet might the doctrine of Original Sin itself—made official during the Council of Carthage in 418— have something helpful, positive, or redemptive about it? For Saint Paul, Saint Augustine, and Søren Kierkegaard, the notion of sin causes a robust self-examination that does not conclude favorably. Saint Paul dramatizes his inability to do right, Saint Augustine's confessions are drenched in guilt and gratitude, and Kierkegaard's work, especially *Sickness Unto Death* (1849), also sees the terrible, the awful, the corruption that sits in the corner of all of our hearts. Reinhold Niebuhr's Christian Realism, indebted to Saint Augustine, is helpful here. For Niebuhr, everyone assumes the worst in their neighbor and the best in themselves, without considering that all of us participate in some form of injustice every day of our lives. Cross Damon is able to experience freedom but can identify the will to power and desire for sovereignty in everyone but himself. The New York district attorney's question begs the question, how well are we seeing ourselves if the worst and the awful are always externalized? Reinhold Niebuhr says:

Neither the devil nor man is merely betrayed by his greatness to forget his weakness, or by his great knowledge to forget his ignorance. The fact is that man is never unconscious of his weakness, of the limited and dependent character of his existence and knowledge. The occasion for his temptation lies in the two facts, his greatness and his weakness, his unlimited and his limited knowledge, taken together. Man is both strong and weak, both free and bound, both [sightless] and far-seeing. He stands at the juncture of nature and spirit; and is involved in both freedom and necessity. His sin is never the mere ignorance of his ignorance. It is always partly an effort to obscure his [imperception] by overestimating the degree of his sight and to obscure his insecurity by stretching his power beyond his limits.[68]

Houston refuses to arrest Cross because he knows he does not have sufficient evidence to convict him. Furthermore, Houston says he would not incarcerate him because that would help him. He wants Cross to suffer. He wants Cross to experience what it is like living outside the boundaries of the community, to *feel his freedom*—a punishment that mirrors the punishment of Cain in Genesis chapter 4. Cross's punishment is to suffer alone. Houston asks, "Didn't you know that gods were lonely?"[69]

Cross finds himself roaming the streets, disconnected from all human life, until he feels a bullet rip through his chest as he is running toward a taxicab. Nearing death, he awakens in a hospital bed with Ely Houston standing over him like a judge. Before Cross dies, he says that he always thought he was innocent and wishes that he—invoking Zarathustra—could have been a bridge for humankind.

For sure, Nietzsche's will to power existentialism is all over the text by way of Cross Damon's constant reimagining of himself, his persistent transformations and reinventions that coincide with adapting new values and insights. The bridge reference is an explicit nod to Zarathustra's teachings, but from a different angle, intentionally more political than Nietzsche intended. In other words, I read Wright's *The Outsider* and Cross Damon's final words as occupying an opposite stance to Nietzsche's position. For Zarathustra, the bridge would have led humans to evolve away from faux religious and political morals, freed them from a cultivated subjugation, and made them transcendent, powerful, forceful, like an *Übermensch* who knows another register of freedom and experiences a more vital existence. Wright sees where Nietzsche wants to go and believes that Camus's Meursault is perhaps a contemporary version of the *Übermensch*, but one whose life is determined by his disassociation. Meursault, the emotionless protagonist from Albert Camus' *The Stranger* (1942), feels nothing. He does not yearn for anything. He has embraced that he lives in a meaningless universe without any metaphysical demands, requirements, narratives, or promises. He is therefore indifferent to the values, ethics, and expectations placed on him. He does not weep at his mother's death and he kills without rationale. Therefore, Wright writes Cross Damon as a clarion call, almost a warning not to become a human without connection, community, and reason, not to disassociate from the positive side of humanity and shared life. I read Cross Damon as attempting to be a bridge "for man" like Zarathustra, but leading in the opposite direction.

According to Cedric Robinson, "The novel is a parable. It is a moral, philosophic, and political exercise. Like the myth in phatic groups, the purpose is to demonstrate the terrible consequence to the human spirit as well as to the social organization of a total exorcizing of social ideology."[70] Wright attempts to warn humanity, through theological anthropology and continental philosophy, about the invisible danger of our created society.

His thesis, overlooked by many critics, is that the modern industrial world is run by faux god-men—little demigods—who sacrifice fundamental aspects of being human to sustain the dehumanizing oppressive structure of the modern capitalist world. Cross Damon is a product of that system; he is not a hero. He is Wright's philosophically Marxist plea. Wright's novel argues, in many ways, that the very structure of modernity—of the Western world particularly—is devoid of genuine morals, laws, ideologies, and perhaps even theologies that guarantee human connection and intimacy. Every ideology, no matter how romantic, well-intentioned, humanistic, communist, left, right, or religious, not only is subject to corruption and distortion but inevitably leads to it through humanity's insistent will to power.

Cross Damon, a black American who considers his race the least important component of his identity, has a marginalized perspective that allows him to see the intricacies and mechanics of this structure. Instead of building community, delving into the social relations of the world, and using his experiences to build bridges to other human beings, he cultivates the part of him that furthers the consequences of modern industrialism.[71] Cross Damon is outside the experience of freedom his country declares. He is even outside the black cultural practices that are used to help him live in what Sartre calls "Bad Faith" and what Heidegger calls "inauthenticity."

Moreover, theologically, Cross is outside the very intention of his name but inside the paradoxical ways his name can be understood. His mother says, "And to think, I named you Cross after the cross of Calvary." The beauty of the cross to Christians is accepted and valorized if it is theologically tethered to some form of redemption; otherwise it is just another form of meaningless lynching.[72] This "cross" was his mother's gift to him, a theology that did not "deny him life" per se—following James

Baldwin's quip—but showed him the burden of existing in a meaningless world where black people await another oncoming world where they will be able to experience safety and joy.[73] I argue that the cross in his name is not solely an allusion to the death of Jesus of Nazareth but also a symbol that points beyond itself, to a Cross representing not just Adam but also the risen Christ, "the Second Adam." For Wright, *this is the return of Christ after the Fall*. In other words, Cross Damon—the crucified demon—returns from the dead while fully aware of the world that caused his murder.

Cross Damon follows an "Adamic archetype" and realizes his dizzying freedom through the prohibitions of his mother. He then becomes what Saint Paul calls the "Second Adam," "born again" after surviving the train crash. This second Adam (aka Lionel Lane), aware of the absence of the Absolute and any genuine morals and ethics, lives in this spiritual void and reacts according to his brute, naked desires—until Ely Houston, the detective in Harlem, discovers his identity before Cross is killed by the communists he shunned.

For Wright, the communal connection between human beings, which is slowly being destroyed by industrial capitalism, is what maintains a sense of morality and cultivates intimate community and social relations. Cross Damon's murders and his own death are warnings. If humanity does not wake up from its capitalist and imperialist slumber, then countless Cross Damons who feel no allegiance to community or society will continue to be created.

To Wright, this "death of god" evolution is more than dangerous. Ideologies that promise salvation not only deify the white intellectuals promulgating them but even demand obedience and conviction from the black and brown people who are merely using them to alleviate their subjugation. This means that in the modern world, God—as a theological idea—is not necessarily dead (per Nietzsche) as much as superseded. And the spirit that emerges after God's demise is assumed by political ideologies that claim they can take better care of the world than its previous (over)Lord. This is not a defense of religion or theology for Wright but an argument that the "death of God" has created a smoke screen or veil for God's replacements to function like demigods who control the world through their selfishness, desires, and what Nietzsche outlined as their will to power.

These demigods, to Wright, are responsible for the history of wars and strife. They are responsible for all manner of terror. They are fascists emerging with growing numbers of followers who believe in human domination; Stalinists who spy and purge their own adherents if they are deemed untrustworthy. They are Christians of various races and ethnicities who see the concept of God through a whiteness that demeans blackness to constitute its holiness. They are brute capitalists, subscribing to the doctrine of the day that transforms every organism into a machine or tool for the ruling class. Wright turns to Kierkegaard (along with Simone de Beauvoir, Heidegger, Sartre, and Nietzsche) and the Garden of Eden, to the concepts of creation, sin, and human free will, to offer what William R. Jones calls a "humano-centric liberation theology" through the form of the novel. Tommie Shelby writes that "*The Outsider* is not agitprop or a defense of any political ideology. It is about the individual quest for meaning and freedom in a world without a god to love and guide us."[74] He is correct in that the novel is not a defense, but I argue *The Outsider* is also a humano-centric theological critique of the twentieth century's invention of the "individual."

The novel is a counter theology to the death-of-god drama orchestrated by modern demigods governing the world. More specifically, this humanist theology can most clearly be seen in Wright's use of Kierkegaard's analysis of Adam, the metaphorical first human being, to construct his own existential creation story and warning.

I argue that *The Outsider* is Wright's artistic way of reinterpreting the Fall of Man in Genesis and of offering a philosophical example of William R. Jones's humanocentric theology to counter modernity's will-to-power ethos. *The Outsider* is a theological corrective for future generations, who he believes are in danger of becoming like his protagonist, disconnected from all human relationships and all universal concepts of ethics. This Adam, known as Cross Damon, makes compulsive decisions based on prideful naked desire. And like *Native Son*'s Bigger Thomas and following Lewis Gordon's insights, this Cross Damon, according to my reading, is Wright's monster—his Frankenstein—created to caution humankind against the effects of modern civilization's order of things. Gordon writes that Cross Damon is "a double critique. The first is the presentation of these 'monsters' as a call for America to fix itself. (Recall the historical critique of the Soviet Union of its becoming the monster it was fighting.) If America ignores these warnings, the second message is evident: advancing itself as a daimon, it becomes them and takes its place as a monster, as a warning, to the rest of humanity."[75]

Cross Damon, Wright's antihero and symbolic literary warning, like the Yahwist strand's Adam, becomes aware of this pervasive conundrum of ideological domination through his "guilty reading." Nietzsche, Heidegger, and other continental philosophers reveal a world where humans have killed deities and erected statues of themselves and the depth of the human soul is twisted and distorted by the capitalist industrial society that nurtures it. Through his existential literature, Cross Damon is made aware of a "spiritual void" that is a particular consequence of the white supremacist world he inhabits. Yet instead of using his knowledge, his guilty thoughts, to build communities, coalitions, and connections, he too embraces his desire and will to power and becomes a demigod, a "crucified demon" who transcends the absolute and acts on his own spontaneous motives and naked desire.

Many critics of *The Outsider* considered the novel overwhelmingly smothered in continental philosophy, thus marking a period when Wright "lost touch" with African American culture and consequently published material below his usual standard and talent. According to Hazel Rowley's biography, James Baldwin wrote to James Campbell that "Wright did not know whether his hero was right or wrong," and "Personally, I did not find Cross Damon remotely real. Wright clearly intended it to be read as a novel of ideas, but the ideas had nothing to do with the action."[76] Furthermore, in the same letter, Baldwin suggests that Campbell read Wright's book and offers his final remark: "His boys are always trying to redeem the world with one murder."[77]

Margaret Walker, who had assisted Wright in the early stages of writing *Native Son* (1940), expressed displeasure with the author's constant negative depictions of African American women. Ralph Ellison stated that existentialism caused some bad tendencies in Wright's writing (despite being one of the first people to suggest that he read about the philosophical movement), even though there are noticeable commonalities between *The Outsider* and *Invisible Man* (1952), which Wright recorded in his personal journal, detailing his admiration for Ellison's work. And finally, Ellen Wright, his wife, reportedly said *The Outsider* was "overly intellectual and not a good story."[78]

Shelby, on the other hand, once again understands the questions with which Wright is wrestling:

> If there are no sacred commandments promulgated by a deity, then human beings have to figure out on their own how to treat one another and how to live. To be driven by mere libidinal desire or caprice is to live like an animal, which is an undignified way for a free being to move about the world. Our capacity to deliberate and choose, like our mortality, is inescapable, and so we are responsible for our actions and are appropriately judged for how we use our freedom. But on the basis of what principles can we decide how to live, and what gives these principles their authority? The character of Cross Damon is the vehicle through which Wright explores these questions.[79]

Wright was a polarizing figure who achieved a level of success without black literary predecessors. But even that success, while highlighting his literary genius, also highlights the racism of the industry. For most reviewers, Wright's perspective on the bleakness of black life was overbearing and downright untruthful. At the same time, most who examine his entire oeuvre would assert that his works written between 1938 and 1945, prior to his move to Paris in 1946, are his best. I disagree.

In 1946, Wright and his family migrated to Paris, France to fully escape the tension and burden of white supremacy. They returned shortly but couldn't cope with American racism and left again permanently in 1947. From then until his death in 1960, he was what I call "the latter Richard Wright." This move marked a change in his intellectual curiosities and an overall expansion of his perception of the world and the injustices that mark it. The latter Richard Wright became enamored with existentialism. He moved away from a primarily American political analysis to one that included the "darker subjects of the world." And therefore, my overall argument is that the latter Richard Wright, the Wright of Paris, the homeless cosmopolitan, the Wright whose reputation was ruined by aligning himself too closely with Simone de Beauvoir, Jean-Paul Sartre, Albert Camus, and the works of Martin Heidegger, Karl Jaspers, Friedrich Nietzsche, Edmund Husserl, and Søren Kierkegaard, sought to answer the initial striking and popular criticisms of James Baldwin, Margaret Walker, Ralph Ellison, and others. To do so, he returned to theology, the biblical figures Adam and Eve, and the mythological location of the Garden of Eden.

Wright's earlier but more popular works are thought to suffer from a burdened racial consciousness that is unable to see black life outside of the pervasiveness of white supremacy, struggles with seeing the value of black cultural resources, and ultimately "accepts a theology that denies him life," as Baldwin declared. The latter—albeit less popular—Richard Wright is a black existentialist travel writer in search of resources that can be employed and embraced, even through what he calls negative loyalty, to initiate international human freedom, particularly for black and brown peoples, even if those resources fail in the long haul and need to be constantly reimagined and revaluated.[80]

In other words, Wright's 1953 novel, *The Outsider*, is a corrective to and departure from—although not complete refutation of—his earlier material. It is a corrective because despite his consistent bleak perspective of blackness, Wright starts to see that this is a product of modernity, a violence enacted on peoples across the global south, an inherent part of the structure of the world against the operation of demigods who are opposed to freedom, human dignity, and the individual. This causes him to explore the concept of free will and evil much more theologically.

In a 1953 interview before *The Outsider* was published, he was interviewed by a French newspaper that asked him about the theme of his new novel. Wright answers: "Man without a home, without rest, without peace, in an industrial culture. The main character is a Negro, but he, in contrast to Bigger Thomas in *Native Son*, does not react as a colored person in a dominating white world, but as a human victim of social circumstances. The background is Chicago and New York."[81]

This quote may seem to suggest that Wright was trying to reduce the significance of race for Cross Damon. However, he is saying that the industrial culture, which is one of human domination, does something to humans across the board. The theological structure of the industrial world engineers manipulation and subjugation.

Jane Anna Gordon says that "Wright brought an unflinching racial realism and brilliance to his unremitting exploration of freedom."[82] And because of that, Wright reads the book of Genesis's second creation story and the creation of Adam and Eve as a tragedy. A tragedy where freedom—wherever it originated—allowed for a regret-filled descent and could have been avoided, had God's prohibitions not caused the possibility of severance. In this overlooked and unpopular novel, Wright returns to figures in the Garden of Eden and—through Kierkegaard—explores sin and free will. Wright believes, according to my reading, that human connection and intimacy prevents people acting solely from their selfish desires and impulses. He returns to the figure of Adam to suggest that the Fall of Man is not just a mythological theology in Abrahamic faiths but a consistent event in all our lives. And the modern, technocratic, industrial world is engineering it, causing it. By becoming aware of this and paying attention to the direction we are headed as a society, we can still turn the ship around, if only we use Cross Damon as a warning—a warning we perhaps should have noticed long ago through Adam.

4

THE SERPENT/LILITH'S LIBERATION THEOLOGY

Now the serpent was more crafty than any other wild animal that the Lord God had made. He said to the woman, "Did God say, 'You shall not eat from any tree in the garden?'"
—Genesis 3:1 (NRSV)

One of the most famous and compelling examples of a black theological novel that vigorously sifts through the debris left in Eden's wake is Alice Walker's incomparable *The Color Purple* (1982). Walker's novel, at its core, is an intimate engagement with Eden that returns to the carnage, sees the fog in the atmosphere produced by Adam and Eve's tears, and reimagines orthodox theology and doctrines to prevent what happened from ever occurring again.[1] Following the lives of two young black sisters who grow up and grow old in a complicated world, Celie and Nettie, the narrative unfolds through Celie's letters to God—letters inspired by the prayers of Sojourner Truth—and Nettie's long-lost letters to her. In this story of traveling and lost papers we learn about how their lives developed after Nettie fled from torment at the cruel hands of Alphonso (Pa) during their mother's illness.[2]

Celie, the protagonist in Walker's tale, is by all accounts sold into marriage to a man initially known as Mr. ____, but later the name Albert echoes across the pages. Albert is a sharecropper from rural Georgia whose wife was brutally murdered by her secret lover.[3] Sick and ruined in his own ways, he violently pursues Nettie, who refuses, runs away, and hears him scream that she will never see her sister again. Nettie ends up on the doorstep of a missionary family while Celie remains stuck, captured by Albert, who ensures that the two remain apart. The cruel and enforced separation, along with the sisterly yearning to reunite, is the heart of the story and drives both women's behavior in their individual lives. The separation is the grief of the novel. The world that caused it is the problem of evil both characters must navigate as they craft a kind of life without each other.

In Celie's life with Albert, she works tirelessly to please him and his children but only experiences their cruelty in return. She experiences no love, no intimacy, and no care. Her life is unfortunately and overwhelmingly lamentable until she forms a bond with Sofia, her stepson Harpo's wife, who not only represents strength and fortitude but also provides an example of unflinching dignity. Harpo and Sofia's marriage offers a glimpse of what's possible when two parties decide their own roles and their own duties in their own relationship, regardless of gendered expectations. But that example, though prominent and informative, does not last. Harpo tarnishes their unique relationship and attempts to emulate the power and authority of his father and grandfather. Harpo tries to dominate, to rule over Sofia, but she fights back. Finally, one day, Sofia takes their children and leaves, leaving Celie once again alone in the world, grieving another separation from a sister she loved and by whom she was encouraged.

Celie eventually meets Albert's lover, Shug Avery, a blues singer who is unwell and needs care. Celie nurses Shug back to health, and they too develop a bond, even a sisterhood, but one that includes a transformative erotic experience. Shug Avery is Celie's first lover, her first paramour. She is Celie's partner, helping her navigate her own sexuality and also reconceptualize everything she thought she knew about her flesh, her place in the world, and the larger natural world around her. What occurs between Celie and Shug is the opposite of what transpires between David and Giovanni in James Baldwin's *Giovanni's Room* (1956). While David refuses the queer futurity Giovanni is inviting him into, Celie wholeheartedly jumps in and embraces another life, another way of being alive. To follow the existentialist thread established by Richard Wright, Shug Avery loves Celie into Celie's own self-realization.

After Shug discovers international mail from Nettie to Celie, she helps Celie locate the hidden box that holds every one of Nettie's letters that Albert took throughout the years. Celie takes them and reads all of them. The letters affect her beyond measure. She becomes spiritually reconnected with her long-lost sister and writes back. The process of writing itself also contributes to a growth in consciousness. In rage and disappointment, Celie eventually curses Albert for all the terror he caused. She moves out and into the home her parents left her. She starts a business sewing trousers, all the while thinking she has lost her sister for good. But one day, thanks to Albert and the conversion he makes after Celie's curse, and their new friendship, she meets Nettie and her children, Olivia, Adam, and his wife, Tashi.[4]

Nettie's story—which is an integral part of the overall narrative—is about her complicated escape to a kind religious family who embraces her as one of their own. After gaining their trust and support, she joins them as their nanny on a Christian missionary trip to West Africa. There they work with the Olinka people, an African linguistic community invented by Walker herself. Little does Nettie know that the children the couple have adopted are the children of her sister, Celie, including a son named Adam, whom Celie thought Pa had murdered in the forest.[5]

Nettie encounters the various issues and impact of European colonialism. Struggling with "traditional" norms and gender roles in the Olinka community, she also comes to see them as equally complicated as Western traditions. On the continent (Africa), she grows. She loves. And despite her distance and her new life across the Atlantic, she never forgets her sister, Celie. She writes to her constantly, though the lack of any response makes her unsure if Celie is still breathing, let alone receiving her messages.

Walker created this story and these communities from a photograph of her grandmother. She wanted to re-create the lives of that black community who survived hell and tried to build a life and society together. But like Toni Morrison, she did not want to create a black Paradise devoid of human flaw and error. So she wrote unflinchingly about all the music, violence, sex, and language she imagined present in that one photograph, and in doing so initiated a literary-theological paradigm shift. This helped initiate not only womanism and its most ecological elements but also an entire reconceptualization of God and the biblical characters across Genesis.[6]

Therefore, in reading this classic text—the author of which is the first black recipient of the Pulitzer Prize in Literature—I want to offer a different view than is normally rendered. Many reviews of *The Color Purple* have focused exclusively on either its gender or its class aspect. Gloria Steinem's popular review focuses on how great the novel is because it is not only "about the poor" but also "for the poor."⁷ Trudier Harris, in contrast, sees the novel as stereotypical, unmeasured, and worshiped by white feminists in problematic ways.⁸

These readings and historical debates are significant, rich with a certain texture that beckons us to analyze what it means to read, to feel, to think; however, I limit my scope to the black and womanist theological tradition that agrees with what Delores Williams said in 1993: "Nobody had paid attention to Alice Walker's portrayal of the protagonist Celie's understanding of God's relation to her life."⁹ Such a claim might be too strong now considering the wealth of theological readings of the text, but it does bear mentioning that even Walker was confused by the absence of religious engagement. She reminds her readers in the preface that this is a work of theology.

My reading acknowledges the novel's prior interpretations but is hyperfocused on the specific Edenic elements that have gone unnoticed. Walker's novel, I contend, is like Morrison's *Paradise* (1997) in that it is a theopoetic text. It offers an intervention into systematic theology by offering an alternative theology of God. But this text is different from Morrison's in that it is not against Paradise as a concept, just the version of Paradise cultivated by the entity Mary Daly called "God the Father."¹⁰ In Walker's novel we are invited to leave the Garden of Eden, to go in search of another garden that is open to a more robust consciousness and spirit indistinguishable from the natural world—a mother's garden. And Walker crafts one where a Lilith isn't discarded in the shadows of mythological history, where the serpent is not only telling the truth but also helping us all escape from a deity who prefers our ignorance.

Through this insight, I contend that the alternative reading of Eden is centered around the person I call Walker's "Lilith-Serpent" character, Shug Avery, who mirrors the activity and character of the serpent by helping Celie question the authority of the deity she writes to. As Pamela B. June notes, "The snake appears in several of Walker's writings, and it is evident that she hopes to restore respect to the creature who has been maligned following the Genesis story."[11] Shug Avery's gentle cajoling encourages Celie to reconsider how her theology and allegiance to doctrines affect the way she navigates life. She is encouraged to see herself as one with nature, part of a larger divine family that includes everything we can sense in the garden.

Shug Avery's religious beliefs assist Celie with embracing an eco-womanism that envisions God as participating in the pleasures of life and the flesh. She helps Celie accept a theology that refuses a distinction between secular and sacred, body and spirit, or earth and heaven. As a result of Shug's words and music, Celie embraces a spirit who loves her into self-actualization. My argument is that through the theological insight of Shug Avery—read through the Latin American ecofeminism of Ivone Gebara and her contemporaries—Walker offers the world a radically beautiful theopoetics of a God who takes seriously the aesthetics of life. Shug introduces to Celie and to readers a God who loves life, loves the folk, and not only responds to messages but also sends return messages. Before delving into the novel, I turn back to the Genesis myth to draw the strongest possible connection between the Hebraic tale and Walker's novel.

THE SERPENT

The previous chapters used James Baldwin to focus on Eden as a concept, studied Richard Wright and his use of Adam as an existential archetype, and read Toni Morrison to investigate the problem of Eden and how it relies on a scapegoating of Eve. Now I turn to the other primary character in the history of the Abrahamic myth that the other writers, perhaps, left out of their novels: the animal, the serpent.

In both Jewish and Christian interpretations, the serpent, or the Naschash, has functioned as a devious character—even Satanic in some traditions—who exploited Adam and Eve's blissful naivety.[12] If Richard Wright focused primarily on Adam and the literary Adamic representation, and Toni Morrison's attention was mainly on Eve and her historical implications, then I argue that Walker kept an eye on the animal who is (perhaps unfairly) infamous in the myth. I want to return to the Genesis text to focus on the serpent and all the implications of the orthodox interpretations to show how Walker reconceptualized the creation myth to unearth a deeper truth about life and our relationship to everything around us.

The story says that in the Yahwist (J) narrative of Genesis, the serpent was craftier than any other animal that Yahweh created.[13] The craftiness seems to be associated with the serpent's ability to uniquely communicate with humans. However, there is no indication that this ability is extraordinary or uncommon in comparison to the other animals. So it is reasonable to assume that the world of the myth includes the possibility that all the animals at one time could in some way, verbally or otherwise, communicate directly with and understand humans. John F.A. Sawyer writes, "The serpent here is one of the 'beasts of the field,' a common or garden animal, like the fox and the crow, the ant and the grasshopper, the hare and the tortoise and all the other ordinary animals that appear in Aesop's fables. Such animals appear in the biblical Wisdom literature too, not in fables, but in proverbs."[14] Yet in the myth, the serpent conveys a message that Eve comprehends.

At some point in the discussion, the serpent questions Eve's confidence in God's regulations, asking, "Did God say, 'You shall not eat from any tree in the garden?'" In the J narrative, Yahweh stipulates that Adam may feed off every tree in Eden save one, the Tree of the Knowledge of Good and Evil. This decree is lodged before Yahweh creates Eve from Adam's flesh and bones. Therefore, it was more than likely Adam who disclosed to Eve the rules and customs of Eden. She responds to the serpent with her understanding: "We may eat of the fruit of the trees in the garden, but God said, 'You shall not eat of the fruit of the tree that is in the middle of the garden, nor shall you touch it, or you shall die.'" The serpent reveals to Eve that she will not die. In fact, she has been woefully deceived. The truth is, according to the serpent, Yahweh knows that once she eats the forbidden fruit she will be able to distinguish between good and evil.[15] The Genesis text states: "So when the woman saw that the tree was good for food and that it was a delight to the eyes and that the tree was to be desired to make one wise, she took of its fruit and ate, and she also gave some to her husband, who was with her, and he ate. Then the eyes of both were opened, and they knew that they were naked, and they sewed fig leaves together and made loincloths."

Adam and Eve's consciousness changes. They experience a dramatic metamorphosis, and their "eyes were opened." They are transformed into conscious beings, awakened to their own nudity. At some point they hear Yahweh surveying the Garden and hide, which reveals the intervention of new thoughts that were not possible in their prior ontologies. Yahweh calls for Adam, and his response reveals the transformation. Adam expresses feelings that should be unusual for his state of being, like fear and self-consciousness in his own nudity, and Yahweh knows that they have partaken of the forbidden fruit. Yahweh is incensed. He gave clear instructions, and they disobeyed. In response to the interrogation, Adam refuses responsibility, and his ability to do so once again reveals a new consciousness. He retorts, "The woman whom you gave to be with me, she gave me fruit from the tree, and I ate." It is not his fault. The deity is the one to blame for creating the condition of possibility for his insubordination. Furious at what he hears, but possibly granting some credence to Adam's rebuttal, Yahweh looks to Eve and asks, "What is this that you have done?" And, like Adam, Eve places the blame elsewhere. She scapegoats the serpent and protests, "The serpent tricked me, and I ate."

This response causes Yahweh to punish the serpent before punishing Adam and Eve. Yahweh looks directly at the serpent and declares:

> "Cursed are you above all livestock
> and all wild animals!
> You will crawl on your belly
> and you will eat dust
> all the days of your life.
> [15] And I will put enmity
> between you and the woman,
> and between your offspring [a] and hers;
> he will crush [b] your head, and you will strike his heel."[16]

Saint Paul sees the serpent as "cunning," skilled in the art of deception.[17] Saint Augustine too believes the serpent was deceptive, and a part of his cunning intelligence was his approaching Eve instead of Adam because he knew Eve was "less rational."[18] Though the Judeo-Christian tradition, biblical literature, and postbiblical material—especially the writer of Revelations—conflate the serpent, Satan, and the devil into one figure, Ivone Gebara and Alice Walker take a different position.[19]

Gebara argues that the serpent is not the adversary, or the deceiver as depicted in Revelations or church history, but the liberator in the story. This is not too far off base. As Sawyer writes, "In biblical literature, serpents seem to have been proverbial for their wisdom. Best known is Jesus' advice to his disciples when they were about to go out into the world: 'Be wise as serpents.'"[20]

Therefore, I am reading Walker's novel—and especially the moments between Celie and Shug Avery—through Gebara's radical and creative intervention. The first moment is a conversation in a beautiful garden of flowers. My claim is that Shug Avery is a serpent figure who also helps Celie question the theology she has learned. The second moment is closer to the end of the novel, when Celie explains to Albert the Olinka people's origin myth, which inverts and reconceptualizes not only what nakedness means but also who Adam was and what it meant for him and Eve to be created, yet fully aware of what and who they were. I will explain Gebara's reading of the Fall and the actions of the serpent to create the hermeneutical foundation for my reading of *The Color Purple*.

IVONE GEBARA ON THE SERPENT IN EDEN

In a chapter entitled "The Face of Transcendence as a Challenge to the Reading of the Bible in Latin America," Ivone Gebara reads the Edenic myth much differently than Saint Paul, Saint Augustine, and Søren Kierkegaard.[21] Gebara reads the scriptures symbolically. In *Out of the Depths: Women's Experience of Evil and Salvation* (2002), she says that she prefers to work from the perspective of theological anthropology.[22] Therefore, she reads scriptures in a way that constructs new human relations across races and genders. Gebara takes seriously not only the words of the serpent but also what the serpent may have intended by suggesting that Eve partake of the fruit. The fruit does not represent the site of disobedience. It represents deliverance. It is the symbol of liberation for a humanity held captive by an impassable deity. Therefore, countering every other theologian we have studied, Gebara believes that to construct theologies that prioritize relation and interconnection, we must "take the risk of the serpent."[23] We must go after the fruit. Search for it. Find it. Bite it passionately and relish the new consciousness it galvanizes.

As stated earlier, Gebara argues that women in Latin America have embraced the Bible and used it to envision themselves anew: to create a critical distance between seeing themselves as mere objects of the world and as human subjects with value and worth for which they should not have to argue. They have taken the Bible and Christian theology as instruments to engender that value and self-esteem. This hermeneutical technique, though understandable, is not enough for Gebara. Using the Christ figure to cultivate value means that women are only as valuable as Jesus maintains. And even that is subject to translation and interpretation, which leaves no room for interrogating the ways Jesus treated women differently in the Christian scriptures. What's more, "In various contributions based on their readings of the Bible, women have attempted to criticize the androcentric and patriarchal structures of our society, our churches, and ourselves. But even in criticizing them, these readings unconsciously retain and utilize the androcentric and patriarchal basis for their new interpretations."[24]

For Gebara, the residue of patriarchal imaginations still undergirds not only feminist interpretations of the Bible and new theologies but also the imaginings of God more broadly. One of the primary challenges in liberation theologies surpasses not only the pronouns used to address or refer to God but also—and more poignantly for her—the characteristics of God:

> This means that the vision of the cosmos, the practical "anthropovision," and the basic theology continue to be those that understand *God* as a self-contained spiritual being, limitless and independent of the "creature" but at the same time "limited" to God's own being. According to this vision the "spiritual body of God" is separate from and higher than other bodies. God has God's own purpose or plan for humanity, and ultimately the final responsibility for everything that happens is God's.[25]

The theologies, the ways people imagine God, are especially significant. Analogical language is taken as an independent reality in practice. Therefore, what one says about or how one describes God bears material consequences for adherents. Gebara notes the danger in this: "In Latin America various groups with various ideologies present 'plans of God,' schemes for salvation, and manipulate the people according to their immediate interests."[26] Focusing on the image of God and the political commitment of that image has been a primary methodology of both black and Latin American liberation theologies.[27] Yet, as Gebara notes, though the liberation theologians pride themselves on their sociopolitical commitments, they cannot be absolved of responsibility; they are still integral to the issue at hand.

> The liberator God, in spite of the attractiveness of the concept, sometimes seems as dangerous as the God of reason, who governs the world from a throne of glory. In practice this image of

God as liberator excludes women as much as does the image of God as "the Other," insofar as women continue to be the *pietas* of war games, accepting on their knees the murdered bodies of husbands, lovers, brothers, sisters, children, parents . . . who possess no decisive responses to the "masculine reason" that governs the world; who are accomplices in plans for development by weapons and profits, accomplices in the cold logic in which human tenderness and mercy seem extinguished.[28]

For Gebara, there is no freedom in black and Latin American liberation theologies if they stop at vengeance. Defending oneself against white supremacy and colonization is fundamental to reclaiming a sense of dignity, but if liberation theology is reduced to battle, to combat, to the spark of revolution, then it is not unlike the theologies it is countering, those with imperialist commitments. Gebara wants to know if there is more to liberation than the sword used to achieve it. Surely there must be an eschaton of justice that does not necessitate bloodshed to establish. Therefore, through this desire and logic, she says that she is suspicious of the mighty, omnipotent God. And she is implicitly suspicious of the "God of the Oppressed."[29] She posits that God's eternal aseity in these liberating theologies does not evoke anything other than more authority.

For Gebara, if this cosmic liberator deity is beyond the earth and the cosmos, then it is also beyond everything that needs care. And care cannot be experienced from a deity that sits on a throne and points, chastises, controls but never feels. Care can never be experienced from a god who commands but never receives, who punishes with severity and never has a gentle conversation. This god of liberation and revolutions is "very much like humans, the celestial 'double' of powerful men; whether of the right or the left."[30] Gebara declares: "The god on high, in heaven, on a throne, the father of men, the god of blind obedience, the god who punishes and saves, is no longer useful—even when he presents a liberator's face—to our world, to the humanization of the human, to women, to the future of the poor."[31] She sees no use for a deity without sensitivity, an apathetic father completely unable to feel anything toward his children: "He too is the fruit of an authoritarian religion experienced by the masses, a religion that produces sentimentalism and consolation as faith's response to the nonsense of an existence reduced to survival, the existence today of thousands of humans scrabbling for a wretched loaf to exist."[32]

For Gebara, this image and construction of God is not only prevalent in the liberation theologies but also prominent in a corruption of feminist theology. To make her case, she invokes the deuterocanonical text about Judith, who decapitates the Assyrian general, Holofernes, as an example of a hermeneutic, or at least a tradition, that celebrates violence.[33] Judith is praised and highlighted for her retribution. Gebara is interested in more: she wants a different tradition that does not bear the traces of or make room for violence. "To create another tradition in obedience to the history of today signifies the possibility of constructing egalitarian anthropological and theological foundations that respects men and women living in reciprocity and in respect for their differences."[34] In other words, Gebara demands the construction of a theology that reflects nothing less than mutuality. Mutuality between creator and created would mean that both God and humans learn about and from each other; both God and humans participate collectively in the world's unfolding. She refuses a theology that states God has a will. Any form of a teleology contributes to the unfair power dynamic at play between God and life:

> In this sense *he* does not have a will for us; *he* does not have a pre-established design or plan; *he* does not take sides; *he* is not a

self-sufficient being; *he* is not a person as we are persons. Our entire theology has imprisoned this God, *this he*, and has made of it *his* being and *his* place of existence. This prison has also been that of the Christianized Latin American masses, who now find themselves prevented from escaping it. It has almost become a part of their being; of their skin, but in spite of everything little pathways have opened up, revealing new possibilities.[35]

Therefore, Gebara invites feminist theology in Latin America to purify itself of a feminizing patriarchal theology that is feminist in its language but bears no distinctions in its character. To distance themselves from the oppressive theology that they have assumed, liberation and feminist theologies must go further.

The way to construct a new theology that is not a product of "patriarchal orthodoxy," Gebara states, is to think of transcendence outside of the standard classical metaphorical categories. The liberation and feminist theologies must "take the risk of the serpent."[36] Gebara writes, "I would like to open a dialogue with tradition, the tradition that belongs to our heritage, to see what possibilities it can welcome for new interpretations generated from the study of different human groups who invoke the Christian faith but wish to live it on the basis of other interpretive foundations."[37] She is declaring that she wants to return to the Garden. For Gebara, new interpretations of what occurred in Eden open new possibilities upon which to build new theologies and cultivate new insights.

What if the serpent, the Naschash, was not an evil character or the adversary in animal disguise? What if the animal was after freedom for all of creation?[38] For Gebara, the serpent was not satanic but a fellow creature who saw the danger in following the deity's order of things. In this schema, it warned against obeying unlimited power and suggested civil disobedience toward the Creator. Every other theologian of the Fall discussed in this book expresses fidelity to the reading of the forbidden fruit, but Gebara instead sees the fruit as representing the liberation that feminist and liberation theologians write about. It is the freedom they yearn for. She says we must not only partake of the fruit but "must even eat it with relish, passion, gluttony, and let it become our new flesh. The transformation is slow and progressive, as was the structuring of our present religious images."[39]

Where the classical theologians see a descent, Gebara sees transcendence. And this transcendence allows for a radical reinterpretation of relations. Reading the Fall differently, as an escape instead of a plunge, as fugitivity rather than delinquency, opens new horizons for the stories we tell ourselves and the stories we share. For Gebara, reading scriptures in ways that counter the tradition is contingent upon reading the Bible symbolically as a resource that goes beyond itself. The Bible does not need to be discarded because the classical interpretations counter the concerns of our day and age; it can be read in light of our desires and concerns and used in a way that brings about abundant life and better relations with the rest of creation.

Shug Avery, the blues woman and theologian of Alice Walker's *The Color Purple*, not only offers an ecotheology like Gebara's but also functions as a Lilith-Serpent character. She is perceived as a sensual villain in the community, but in the reality of the text, she delivers an eco-womanist theology that reveals the spiritual interconnection of living beings.

SHUG AVERY AS THE SERPENT

After Shug Avery discovers Nettie's letters and hands them to Celie, there is an immediate change. Celie grows frustrated. She is discontent, angry with the severe conditions of her life. All the wretched experiences she has endured finally break the faith she had in the god she imagined was reading her messages. She expresses a theodical question: How could her God allow her to not receive messages from the one person she loved the most? Celie was at first communicating with a deity who cared, who loved, one she envisioned would one day open the gates of Heaven and swoop down to wreak vengeance upon the forces that were trying to crush Miss Sofia.[40] No matter what, God loved her. God was the only personality who saw her and cared. Yet the experiences of her life became too much to bear. Her personal theodicy no longer allowed any defense that interwove God's omnibenevolence and divine might. Celie could have believed that God loved her and was powerless to change her situation. However, the problem was not God's might or power. It was not God's strength or competence. It was God's commitment. This resembled her experiences with men. Thus, she writes to Nettie: "I don't write to God no more. I write to you."[41]

Shug, however, is surprised by Celie's words and asks, "What happen to God?" Celie responds with: "Who that?" "What God do for me?" After she confides in Shug about her denouncement, Shug's reaction introduces a brand-new theology. But before Shug tells her what she thinks, she comments, "Celie! Like she shock. He gave you life, good health, and a good woman that love you to death."[42]

According to Shug—who perhaps does not take Celie's words fully into account as sensitively as she should—there is more to life than what Celie endures. Her arguments about the richness of existence might not be appreciated in that moment but set up the introduction to her eco-theology. Shug suggests that there is much in life for which to be grateful. There is life itself. There is the function of the lungs. And there is love.

Yet for Celie, this is no time to wax poetic about the things in life that should be givens. So she states every aspect of her story that prevented her from knowing the pleasures of life. She tells Shug that God gave her life, but along with it came "a lynched daddy" and a mother who fell ill, "a lowdown dog of a step pa and a sister I probably won't ever see again." In recounting all she learned about Nettie's life from her letters, plus the fact that those letters were hidden, Celie reveals what's unspoken in the novel: she has experienced profound sorrow and grief. And through her grief she tried to write to God, but that God has been absent. In her letter to Nettie, Celie reveals that she told Shug: "Anyhow, I say, the God I been praying and writing to is *a man*. And act just like all the other mens I know. Trifling, forgitful and lowdown."[43] For Celie, God is like all the men she's ever known, so hardened by their own lives that they've no soft place for the women around them, so emotionally unavailable that her pleas and cries are met with a vindictive coldness. So the "God" she met in an unwelcoming church is nothing special or different from what she has been used to all her life. The great god in the sky is not a loving deity or a compassionate creator but a literal, Aristotelian, unmoved mover with the same limitations and shortcomings of every other man. For Celie, God is just a man, a simple man in the heavens who is unmoved by pain that does not directly concern or affect him. Celie writes to Nettie about Shug's response:

> She say, Miss Celie, You better hush. God might hear you. Let 'im hear me, I say. *If he ever listened to poor colored women the world would be a different place, I can tell you* . . . All my life I never care what people thought bout nothing I did, I say. But deep in my heart I care about God. What he going to think. And come to find out, he don't think. Just sit up there glorying in being deef,

I reckon. But it ain't easy, trying to do without God. Even if you know he ain't there, trying to do without him is a strain. (emphasis mine)[44]

The first thing Shug Avery teaches Celie is what Giovanni was trying to teach David in *Giovanni's Room*, what Consolata learns from Lone DuPres in *Paradise*: her inherited theology of sin is all wrong; Saint Paul, Saint Augustine, and Søren Kierkegaard's views of sin were misguided and counter to the true experience of creation. Sin, for Shug Avery, is not about reigning in one's concupiscence. Instead, the flesh of nature reveals that *pleasure pleases God*, that God shares in the satisfaction of the natural world. For Shug, the theological concept of sin and its conflation with human gratification is a theological and historical error.

Celie had assumed that Shug's sexual life and the music genre (blues) she performed all indicated a refusal to consider God's existence.[45] Celie believed, wrongly, that Shug Avery chose a life of sensuality over and above a life tethered to an ontological conception of God's existence, or at least a moral conception of God's expectations. These assumptions bear the traces of a spirit-versus-flesh dichotomy that is reflected in the division between spirituals and the blues. Angela Davis makes this point clear when she describes how the blues became the most successful "secular" genre in the early part of the twentieth century. It eventually displaced the religious, or "sacred," music in black culture and signified a new popular consciousness. "This consciousness interpreted God as the opposite of the Devil, religion as the not-secular, and the secular as largely sexual. With the blues came the designations 'God's music' and 'the Devil's music.' The former was performed in church—although it could also accompany work'—while the latter was performed in jook joints, circuses, and traveling shows."[46] Because of

Shug's artistic passion, Celie assumed she did not think of the sacred or theological at all.

Shug disagrees: "Us worry bout God a lot."[47] She and the other people who see God and the world of nature amorously worry if God too feels the absence of or disappointment in love and life when they experience it. She continues, "But once us feel loved by God, us do the best us can to please him *with what us like*" (emphasis mine).[48] According to Shug Avery, worshiping God feels closer to an orgasm than a refusal of one. In other words, God experiences the orgasm with humans as a form of worship. Walker says in an essay, "All people deserve to worship a God who also worships them. A God that made them and likes them. That is why Nature, Mother Earth, is such a good choice."[49]

These theological ideas sound strange to Celie. They rupture her earlier thoughts. Even though the epistolary text does not offer a robust account of what she believes from any Christian teaching, it is clear that Shug's beliefs do not reflect—and are directly contrary to—anything that Celie has ever come across in her parish. She reacts first with incredulity: "You telling me God love you, and you ain't never done nothing for him? I mean, not go to church, sing in the choir, feed the preacher and all like that?"[50] Celie's retort shows the influence of Max Weber's Protestant work ethic, which follows lessons from the Epistle of James.[51] For James, if one has faith in God, then laboring motivated by their faith would ensue. James writes: "What good is it, my brothers and sisters, if someone claims to have faith but does not have works? Surely that faith cannot save, can it? If a brother or sister is naked and lacks daily food and one of you says to them, 'Go in peace; keep warm and eat your fill,' and yet you do not supply their bodily needs, what is the good of that? So faith by itself, if it has no works, is dead."[52]

Therefore, to prove one's love, devotion, and unequivocal commitment would entail a religious grind or activity. Faith needs chores. A religious allegiance without an exertion that exhibits it is unfathomable to Celie. But not to Shug:

> But if God love me, Celie, I don't have to do all that. Unless I want to. There's a lot of other things I can do that I speck God likes.
> Like what? I ast.
> Oh, she say. I can lay back and just admire stuff. Be happy. Have a good time.[53]

That God cares and wonders about human joy, human pleasure, human glee, is a paradigm-shifting thought to Celie and maybe even to Walker's readers. At this point in the conversation, Shug invites Celie to a different Eden, a different Garden, one where God is not just involved in the affairs of the human but also involved in all of life, from the plants and animals to the rocks and the ocean. Shug Avery's God is not moved by onerous human labor. It does not delight in self sacrifice. It does not thrive off pain. Shug Avery's God is not bound to the churches, mosques, temples, or synagogues but is only as present in those buildings as the people who bring it. That means God is present only in the people who share, give, and exchange God. People who love people in the name of God and people who love God in the name of other people. All these theological ideas finally compel Shug to ask directly how Celie envisions her deity—not because she does not know, but because she wants Celie to announce her beliefs aloud to herself. Celie writes:

> Then she say: Tell me what your God look like, Celie.
> Aw naw, I say. I'm too shame. Nobody ever ast me this before, so I'm sort of took by surprise. Besides, when I think about it, it

don't seem quite right. But it all I got. I decide to stick up for him, just to see what Shug say.

Okay, I say. He big and old and tall and graybearded and white. He wear white robes and go barefooted.

Blue eyes? she ast.

Sort of bluish-gray. Cool. Big though. White lashes. I say.

She laugh.[54]

After Shug laughs at Celie's description, she confesses that she too once imagined God as an old white man in a white robe. Celie asks from where their images of God stem, and Shug reveals to her what Emilie Townes calls the "White hegemonic imagination," which undergirds and determines the racial hermeneutics of their Bible.[55] But this is not her fault. Shug Avery's theology overlaps with Walker's religious views. Walker says:

> As a college student I came to reject the Christianity of my parents, and it took me years to realize that though they had been force-fed a white man's palliative, in the form of religion, they had made it into something at once simple and noble. True, even today, they can never successfully picture a God who is not white, and that is a major cruelty, but their lives testify to a greater comprehension of the teachings of Jesus than the lives of people who sincerely believe a God must have a color and that there can be such a phenomenon as a "white" church.[56]

According to Ivone Gebara, there is an implicit social hierarchy in the knowledge production of the world that is ingrained in all of us and is the foundation for us to imagine God and everything else. Accepting such knowledge means we participate in reproducing what she calls a "patriarchy heritage."[57] In other words, the ways the Bible was taught to black people across the diaspora include the characteristics, concerns, heritage, and implicit imagery of white epistemic domination.

This is a new idea for Celie. Her understanding is that God wrote the Bible himself, but through the hands of human actors. The entire biblical text is "god breathed," a direct revelation that avoids any human mistakes. Celie tells Shug that the Bible cannot be a human product. Shug responds, "How come he look just like them, then? she say. Only bigger? And a heap more hair. How come the bible just like everything else they make, all about them doing one thing and another, and all the colored folks doing is gitting cursed?"[58] For Shug, the theology that has been given to black people in the Americas reflects a metaphysical enslaver who governs the world through divine white supremacy. Yet there is a womanist hermeneutic that exists and is formed underneath this perspective, and she introduces Celie to it. "Ain't no way to read the bible and not think God white, she say . . . When I found out I thought God was white, and a man, I lost interest. You mad cause he don't seem to listen to your prayers. Humph! Do the mayor listen to anything colored say? Ask Sofia, she say."[59]

Shug addresses William R. Jones's classic hypothetical question, *Is God a White Racist?* (1973) with first a guffaw and then a resounding yes, so strong that it suggests she sees the question as foolish and the answer as painfully obvious. God is undoubtedly, and by colonial design, a racist. His whiteness and its implications are synonymous with the declaration of his holiness. He is divinely set apart from blackness. White Euro-American Christianity for Shug is the most effective colonizing weapon in their arsenal. But here she begins to explain the decolonial tenets of her eco-womanist faith.

First she removes God's colonial transcendence. "God is inside you and inside everybody else."[60] Everyone and everything that is created is interconnected with God. However, that connection must be accessed by people who search for it, cultivate it, pursue it with a profound sense of love, not obligated by doctrine or forced into obedience. For Shug Avery, being created with an attached threat of punishment is insufficient. The relationship with the divine must be sought after, and one must be open and vulnerable to its manifestation. This provokes the question, what makes or compels people to search for God? Shug says it could be anything, but most of the time it's trouble. Sometimes it's sorrow, "Feeling like shit."[61] Yet what catches Celie most off guard is that Shug refers to God as "It."

> But what do it look like? I ast.
> Don't look like nothing, she say. It ain't a picture show.
> It ain't something you can look at apart from anything else, including yourself. I believe God is everything, say Shug.
> Everything that is or ever was or ever will be. And when you can feel that, and be happy to feel that, you've found It.[62]

The dialogue between Celie and Shug exemplifies what Karmen Mackendrick identifies as an enticing form of theology.[63] Celie is not only compelled by these ideas and counter-ideas, feeling liberated slowly by the heretical aspect of her insight, but is ultimately being seduced by the truth of what Shug is saying. Shug's words are opening new avenues for Celie. Her world is becoming undone. The process of this new form of thinking is illustrated by Gebara: "Ecofeminist epistemology is not, then, a fashionable mode of thought that can be put on like a new hat; neither is it knowledge that can be acquired like a new book. It is a stance, an attitude, a search for wisdom, a conviction that unfolds in close association with the community of all living beings."[64]

Shug's second decolonial step away from classical theology is a result of how she started seeing the trees. After the trees, it was the air. After the air, it was the birds. Then after the birds, she declares, it was other people. The natural elements of the world eventually made her feel at one with nature and herself. She envisioned herself as one with creation. And not a creation that is cursed or has fallen, that is enduring a punishment or a comeuppance, but a creation that simply is. She began to erase the boundaries between her flesh and the flesh of nature. "I knew that if I cut a tree, my arm would bleed." According to Pauline ecclesiology, humans who have accepted Jesus Christ as Lord are henceforth considered the "body of Christ." As a collective, Christians are the physical presence of Christ in the material world. However, Shug removes Christianity from an exclusive divine pedestal and draws a naturalistic connection among all of nature. When she says that if she cuts a tree her arm will bleed, the inverse is also true. Cutting her arm will also affect the tree. Therefore, rather than seeing the church as the body of Christ, Shug sees the earth as the flesh of God, and God, or the spirit, as the flesh of the earth.[65]

This eco-womanism of Shug Avery is one against the Anthropocene: the era in which humans have dominated the world into an unfortunate re-creation. An abhorrent geological alteration has transpired thanks to the thirst of "man," a creature who only knows the dangerous word "mine." For Shug, the rest of creation, beginning with women and then excused and ordained by the second creation account in Genesis, has been consumed by this creature of dominance. And liberation, freedom, revolution, and all that is good and kind and connected in the world begins with the color purple, because purple reflects God's true intentions—summed up as noticing beauty, embracing interconnection, and existing gently.

After explaining the beginning of her conversion to a new conception of life, nature, and divinity, Shug rubs Celie's thighs to explain how the erotic is ever present and inherently a part of the spirit. When Celie responds, shyly, to this erotic touch, Shug says,

> Oh, she say. God love all them feelings. That's some of the best stuff God did. And when you know God loves 'em you enjoys 'em a lot more. You can just relax, go with everything that's going, and praise God by liking what you like.
>
> God don't think it dirty? I ast.
>
> Naw, she say. God made it. Listen, God love everything you love—and a mess of stuff you don't.[66]

One of the primary theological ideas that I contend Walker is trying to expunge is based on Celie's genuine question, which I believe David desperately wanted to ask Giovanni in *Giovanni's Room* but did not, because his mind was already convinced: "God don't think it dirty?"[67]

What is fascinating about *The Color Purple* and distinct from Baldwin's novel is that there is not a trace of queerphobia anywhere. No one in the community bats an eye at the love between Celie and Shug. It is not a secret. Celie freely explains to Nettie via letters her love and her experiences and the unique pleasure she is encountering. The community understands and accepts their love without reservation. All that is left for Celie to do is to, in a Baldwinian sense, accept a theology that does not deny her life or love but encourages it. God, as Shug believes, is not disgusted with Its creation; instead, It yearns for adoration. It desires reciprocity. It craves affection from creation. It wants admiration for Its art, for its little surprises, to the point that it even "pisses God off if you walk by the color purple in a field somewhere and don't notice it."[68]

Shug Avery's God is an artist. Shug Avery's God is beautiful, and invested in beauty as such. Beauty that can be embraced as a spiritual practice, inspires life, and is for everyone to behold. Shug tells her that her theology is not easy to sustain given the length of time man has centered himself in their religious imaginations, but whenever she is struggling to remember where God is and what It wants, she should "conjure up flowers, wind, water, and a big rock."[69] According to Tara Tuttle, "Shug's knowledge-giving expands Celie's spiritual consciousness and her physical possibilities. The patriarchs effectively castrated, Celie's body becomes hers for the first time."[70]

As mentioned earlier, Walker admits that *The Color Purple* for her is primarily a theological book, in which she examines "the journey from the religious back to the spiritual."[71] In the religious she finds constrictions and limitations, the residue of domination, but says, "Having recognized myself as a worshiper of Nature by the age of eleven, because my spirit resolutely wandered out the window to find trees and wind during Sunday sermons, I saw no reason why, once free, I should bother with religious matters at all."[72] For Walker, trees and wind were the sermon. Their existence and communication were a homily. The sermon from the preacher was based on a religion that subdued the earth, used it as a prop for human dominion.

The theology that directly undergirds her text was overlooked for so long and for the sake of so many other arguments, and the discourse caused by this monumental book was significant. But Walker finds this curious: "I would have thought that a book that begins 'Dear God' would immediately have been identified as a book about the desire to encounter, to hear from, the Ultimate Ancestor. Perhaps it is a sign of our times that this was infrequently the case."[73] For her, the book is ultimately about a spiritually erotic yearning, an ostensible craving for a mutually beneficial divine acknowledgment between nature and humans, to the point of being obvious. She believes the issue is not missing the theological, but rather how limited is our understanding of it. We can only see the theological through the ancient and distantly patriarchal views handed down to us. "Perhaps it is the pagan transformation of God from patriarchal male supremacist into trees, stars, wind, and everything else, that camouflaged for many readers the book's intent: to explore the difficult path of someone who starts out in life already a spiritual captive, but who, through her own courage and the help of others, breaks free into the realization that she, like Nature itself, is a radiant expression of the heretofore perceived as quite distant Divine."[74]

This novel is about Celie's salvific transformation, but that transformation is attached to a larger ecological argument: the theology and overall image of God as a distant impassible deity contributes to her conditioning. She and Nettie are surrounded by a society where humans are conditioned to mistreat Earth through an identical theological framework. Earth, to Walker, is also held captive. Earth is also damaged. And the declaration in Genesis of Earth's distinction from the heavens makes it finite and unholy and ripe for anthropocentric exploitation. Once Shug Avery, the serpent, reveals to Celie that she is her own forbidden fruit, that she is an intricate part of nature and that nature is divine in and of itself, there is a theological rupture that forces the transformation that serves as the anchoring part of the text.

METAPHYSICS

Monica Coleman's process metaphysics also provides an insightful framework that aids in comprehending not only Shug Avery, but also Lone DuPres in Toni Morrison's *Paradise* and the broader concepts of interconnectedness and relationality.

Coleman helps parse out the multiple strands of these characters' theologies—and Walker's theopoetics more broadly—that bear traces of an ecology influenced by the "invisible institution," secret religious practices of slaves in safe "hush harbors," as well as ideas from African traditional religions. In other words, Shug Avery and Lone DuPres's theology is akin to braided hair: strands of thought and meditations beautifully intermingled in a way that displays a rich diversity of insight and wisdom. Following Coleman means seeing Shug and Lone in the tradition of process theology, influenced by the mathematician and metaphysician Alfred North Whitehead. In Whitehead's philosophy, all of life and every single part of the material world are interconnected and synthesized.

For Whitehead, the planet is not a lifeless ornament bestowed for the purpose of dominance or human control, nor an object intended to serve human needs or desires. Like theologian Sallie McFague, process thought sees planet Earth as a living organism deserving of dignity, love, and good treatment.[75] And as a living organism, it is a part of the fabric of life, warranting relational care and concern. Everything that exists in the universe is alive, interconnected, and interdependent. As humans, as living beings, we are in relationship with all our surroundings; we are not closed entities maneuvering through the world but are affected by all stimuli, whether we know it or not. Understanding, accepting, and then embracing our interconnectedness is the first step to understanding Shug Avery's naturalistic theology.

When Shug says that anyone can see that God just wants to be loved, she is in accord with Coleman and Whitehead, who interpret the attention God pours into the world as God's way of beckoning us toward Its vision. For all the theologians discussed in this chapter, God is not an authoritative transcendent Father who solely desires to control humans and demands that we control and dominate nonhuman species; God is a being who lures us into harmony with goodness, beauty, and novelty. And if we can follow Lone DuPres and become listeners of God—listeners who follow our spiritual intuition—then we are tasked with thinking critically about all our decisions and responses because we are interconnected with the entire world. Coleman's process metaphysics and Shug and Lone's organic eco-womanism show that anthropocentrism, at the expense of the rest of life, is deadly.

Furthermore, since Shug does not mention a Christ or a messiah, neither Jesus nor a crucifixion functions in her religious naturalism. Process metaphysics creates theoretical and theological distance between Jesus and God to include other deities and religious insights.[76] Coleman states, "As a philosophical metaphysics, process thought offers a depiction of reality as a whole, including atoms, amoebas, dolphins, humanity and God . . . it explains the constant sense of change in the world and how we exist in the midst of stability and instability."[77] Although Whitehead does not explicitly refer to his conclusions and responses to evil within his metaphysics as *salvific*—as the place of the soteriological—Coleman nevertheless sees his intervention in this way. For Coleman, Whitehead provides a framework that opens numerous possibilities for black women's multiple and complex understandings of salvation.

SHUG AVERY AS LILITH/LILLIE

Lilith—an entity whose name is derived from a Sumerian word that loosely translates as "female demon" or "spirit of the wind"—has been haunting the world for over five millennia. This demon, through Sumerian and then Babylonian folklore, was feared not only for the possibility of her terrifying presence but also for her infamous reputation of hunting down and devouring pregnant people and children. Her first recorded appearance in literature is in an epic poem from ancient Mesopotamia that bears similarities to the Garden of Eden tale. Discovered on a tablet in Ur, this poem is an episode in the *Epic of Gilgamesh*, "Gilgamesh and the Huluppu Tree." Lilith prevents Innanu, the goddess of love and war, from using the wood of the huluppu tree to build both a holy throne and a holy bed. Samuel N. Kramer translates: "The tree grew large but she could not cut off its bark. At its base, the snake who knows no charm had set up for itself a nest, in its crown the Zu bird had placed his young, in its midst Lilith had built for herself a house."[78] Innanu's brother Utu, the god of the sun, refuses to help her. However, her other brother, the mighty Gilgamesh, courageously slays the snake (or dragon in some translations) and scares the she-demon Lilith into fleeing toward the desert.

The evil and demonic Lilith persists from Babylonian Talmudic mythology to the Dead Sea Scrolls. She appears briefly in First Isaiah as an owl, referencing the bird-like imagery that is hinted at in the translation of her name (wind spirit). In ancient Mesopotamia people believed that incantations and amulets could protect them from Lilith's carnage. However, the *Alphabet of Ben Sira* reveals another interpretation of Lilith's origin. According to this medieval Hebrew text, Lilith was not a random deity or lost demonic goddess but the woman created alongside Adam in Genesis's first creation story. This depiction eventually inspired a feminist embracing of Lilith's stance against Adam's assumed superiority. Lilith not only refuses what is presented in the story as a sexually submissive position but also rejects any assertion that she is less than Adam or was created for his domination. Lilith grows so angry with Adam's attempts to subdue her that she says God's name aloud, a forbidden act in Judaism. After committing this self-destructive sin, she flies toward the Red Sea with the wings that she is depicted as having in Sumerian mythology.[79]

A Mesopotamian terra-cotta plaque called the "Burney Relief," or "The Queen of the Night," features a woman standing on top of lions and possessing wings. Some scholars suggest that this is a Babylonian depiction of Lilith, while others argue that it is not Lilith but the goddess Ishtar. Another possible and disputed image of Lilith is found on the Sistine Chapel's ceiling. The "Temptation and Expulsion of Adam and Eve" section of Michelangelo's magisterial "Fall of Man" painting shows a serpent that is half woman at the top of its body. Whether or not Michelangelo portrayed Lilith is not as important as the fact that it is a possibility. The view of Lilith as demonic from the vantage point of God and Adam, as connected in some way to the serpent, and as unable to be dominated persists with countless variations.

Alice Walker contributes to this persistence. Shug tells Celie: "One thing my mama hated me for was how much I love to fuck, she say. She never love to do nothing had anything to do with touching nobody, she say. I try to kiss her, she turn her mouth away. Say, Cut that out Lillie, she say. *Lillie Shug's real name. She just so sweet they call her Shug*" (emphasis mine).[80]

Shug is simply short for "sugar," and her independence and overall appetite for affection are the source of her nickname and complicated relationship with her mother. I have argued that Shug Avery functions as the serpent character in the text, and the other half of my argument relates to Jewish folklore: she is a character in the Lilith heritage. For some modern feminists, Lilith represents freedom from a divinely mandated chauvinism. She represents total defiance of the God of the Garden and will blaspheme if needed to fly away. To understand how Walker invokes the Genesis myth in the latter half of the novel, we will investigate Nettie's experiences with the Olinka people. Celie tells Albert the Olinka version of the Edenic myth, which has an alternative understanding of what it means to be naked and what it means to be created with awareness.

NETTIE'S STORY

The first letter Shug Avery takes and delivers to Celie proves that Nettie's love for her sister has withstood the tests of time, silence, and distance. With every reason to give up on the possibility of communication and the chance of their reconciliation, Nettie writes to Celie every Christmas and every Easter, hoping the letters will arrive, but resigning herself to a devastatingly low probability. However, if by some slim chance this letter makes it to Celie's hands, then she wants her to know one particular thing: that she is alive. And she still, across land and water, and through every letter, aims to communicate her aliveness to her sister. Nettie writes:

> Dear Celie, I know you think I am dead. But I am not. I been writing to you too, over the years, but Albert said you'd never hear from me again and since I never heard from you all this time, I guess he was right. Now I only write at Christmas and Easter hoping my letter gets lost among the Christmas and Easter greetings, or that Albert gets the holiday spirit and have pity on us. There is so much to tell you that I don't know, hardly, where to begin—and anyway, you probably won't get this letter, either. I'm sure Albert is still the only one to take mail out of the box. But if this do get through, one thing I want you to know, I love you, and I am not dead. And Olivia

is fine and so is your son. We are all coming home before the end of another year. Your loving sister, Nettie.[81]

The first discovered letter reveals an unimaginable message. Not only is Nettie alive, not only has she been attempting to contact her, but Celie's children, whom she thought were lost, are there with her sister. What is more, they are eventually returning to the States, and there are other letters with more critical information, updates and reflections on a life Celie thought had ended. Celie and Shug find the other letters in Albert's drawer hidden in his closet. They read them one by one.

Nettie's first letter shows that as soon as she was able to flee from Albert, she wrote to Celie imploring her to get away too. Fugitivity seemed to be the only freedom for them. Albert threatened Nettie with the possibility of never hearing from Celie again. By Nettie's third letter, she realized that Albert would keep his word and stand in the way of their reconciling. While Nettie was fleeing, she was by chance pointed in the direction of a minister and his family, and as soon as she reached the home, she met a child whose eyes bore a striking resemblance to her sister.

The family, Reverend Samuel and Corrine, are kind people. They are devout black Christians who are members of a Christian evangelical group called the Missionaries, part of the American and African Missionary Society. Celie has already met Corrine, though. While walking slowly inside a local store, Celie notices a young black woman holding a little girl who draws her in and reminds her of the child she delivered into the world. Nettie confirms what Celie suspected that day: that the baby girl was not just any child but Celie's, one who Nettie helped bring into life.

Nettie writes that Reverend Samuel and Corinne have "ministered to the Indians out west and are ministering to the poor of this town. All in preparation for the work, they feel they were born for, missionary work in Africa."[82] As in Morrison's *Paradise*, the indigenous element of the novel cannot go unnoticed. While Celie labors in her church and writes letters to a silent god in hopes of being heard, Nettie joins a devout Christian family dedicated to evangelical missions and charitable pursuits. With their family, she sees what would have been possible if she had been reared in a home with love and tenderness.

One of the missionaries who is supposed to travel to Africa with Corinne and Samuel to help with the children and set up their school suddenly marries a man who refuses to accompany her there, and Corrine and Samuel invite Nettie to replace her. What begins as charity work, a favor to a woman less fortunate, turns into an invitation into not only their missionary efforts but also their lives, home, and family. This opportunity also gives Nettie the time and proper circumstances to be near her niece and nephew, a secret she keeps from everyone around her. Yet the separation from her sister weighs on her. Nettie begins one informative letter: "I wrote a letter to you almost every day on the ship coming to Africa. But by the time we docked I was so down, I tore them into little pieces and dropped them into the water. Albert is not going to let you have my letters and so what use is there in writing them. That's the way I felt when I tore them up and sent them to you on the waves. But now I feel different."[83]

The missionary work is not the first time Celie and Nettie have heard of the continent. Their teacher, Miss Beasley, whom they adored, told them explicitly that Africa was composed of savages. This idea is, to some degree, shared by Corrine and

Samuel and galvanizes their theological impetus to conduct missionary work in the region. Nettie, however, is reluctant to arrive at such a conclusion. She reads several books about Africa from Samuel and Corrine's bookshelf and is surprised by not only how expansive, diverse, and historical the continent is but also her own lack of knowledge. She writes to Celie: "Did you know there were great cities in Africa, greater than Milledgeville or even Atlanta, thousands of years ago? That the Egyptians who built the pyramids and enslaved the Israelites were colored? That Egypt is in Africa? That the Ethiopia we read about in the Bible meant all of Africa?"[84]

Her love for her newfound education becomes compromised by the time she learns about the history of the transatlantic slave trade. She writes to Celie that Africans sold other Africans because they were greedy and "loved money more than their own sisters and brothers."[85] She learns about the trading, the auction block, the enterprise of African human trafficking. Learning about Africa is a simultaneous confrontation with the worst of human history.

Nettie is not the sole beneficiary of her educational quest. It extends far beyond her own personal growth and inquiries. In passionate letter after letter, Nettie shares her insights with her sister. She also offers her own interpretations and critical analysis of her discoveries. The process of letter writing helps Nettie critically engage with both her new experiences and the books she is studying. This is a key reason Alice Walker was disappointed in the film depiction of Celie. Director Steven Spielberg reduced the significance of letter writing, which is crucial for her growth in consciousness in the novel. Celie is not only gaining an education alongside her sister across town (and eventually across the Atlantic) but also gaining insight into the larger world that Nettie discovers. The letters function as windows through which Celie can imagine and envision another life, another world, one still riddled with problems but also filled with love, family, languages, and the joy of her own children. Overall, Nettie's letters to Celie are fervent epistles of transformation. They are Nettie's New Testament to Celie. Unknown to the author, they beckon a powerful metanoia.

Nettie's traveling and books reveal to her and her sister that there is a world of possibility, of kindness, with people who are not cruel or vicious but open and encouraging of growth, adventure, and the pursuit of knowledge. In emphatic glee that leaps off the page, Nettie writes: "Oh, Celie, there are colored people in the world who want us to know! Want us to grow and see the light! They are not all mean like Pa and Albert, or beaten down like Ma was. Corrine and Samuel have a wonderful marriage. Their only sorrow in the beginning was that they could not have children. And then, they say, 'God' sent them Olivia and Adam."[86]

Nettie lets Celie know that their childhood is not indicative of what or who is in the world. There is beauty. There is tenderness. Her children are alive, unharmed, well taken care of. Nettie, a newly devout Christian, recognizes God's providence as the reason for her fortune. According to Nettie, "God" orchestrated a divine plan, and this allowed her to locate her niece and nephew, "lavish them with love," and find safety and solace for herself.[87]

I argue that their correspondence through the letters reveals how Celie's and Nettie's experiences parallel each other in a decolonial conversion: gaining new insight into and ideas about blackness, gender, and religion, through vastly different diasporic experiences. Nettie's time in West Africa changes her theology in the same way that Celie's experiences with and conversation about Shug Avery's eco-theology alters hers.

Nettie's transformation begins with Samuel and Corrine rescuing her, and it is cultivated further by an introduction to Garveyism. Their congregation actively takes part in a process that resonates with Judith Weisenfield's concept of "religio-racial self-making," a significant practice for black individuals during and after the Great Migration.[88] This movement saw the emergence of African American figures, congregations, and organizations that intricately interwove their ancestral lineages and cultural legacy into sacred landscapes across time. Though many figures were central to this movement even before the twentieth century, Marcus Garvey appeared as a formidable catalyst with singular influence on the creation of not just a black nationalist identity but a royal one, of profound history and significance. Inspired by Garvey's genius and conviction, individuals across diverse religious and nonreligious backgrounds not only embraced their heritage but also adopted a regal and dignified perspective that reframed their narrative. The influence of Garveyism is displayed in Nettie repeating the church's saying: "Ethiopia shall stretch forth her hands unto God."[89] This challenges Nettie's image of God. Like Celie, Nettie imagined God as white and gray-haired, through the visual culture of American Protestantism. She never questioned the whiteness of God or the biblical characters. Whiteness was normal in any image of holiness.

While she travels and reads, Nettie's worldview continues to expand. She walks around British museums looking at the relics of Africa's material culture. "They have thousands of vases, jars, masks, bowls, baskets, statues—and they are all so beautiful it is hard to imagine that the people who made them don't still exist. And yet the English assure us they do not."[90] She encounters the writings of J. A. Rogers, who opens her eyes to white supremacy as an ideology. She learns about the historical ideologies that contributed to destructive notions of African inferiority. She begins to connect the dots and finds herself face to face with the European responses to questions surrounding the history of modernity and the vapidness of missionary work. She senses that something is amiss but still holds on to some of the preconceived notions and ideas she was taught. Before concluding her letter, she tells Celie, "Today the people of Africa—having murdered or sold into slavery their strongest folks—are riddled by disease and sunk in spiritual and physical confusion. They believe in the devil and worship the dead. Nor can they read or write."[91] In Liberia, She discovers that the Dutch own the cocoa. She takes note of how the black president says "Natives" when referring to African-born Liberians. Something is amiss.

She travels through the jungle to get to Olinka. The Olinka people were not sure if the children belonged to Nettie or Corrine because they resembled Nettie. In one of the most significant parts of Nettie's introduction to West Africa, she learns about the importance of the Roofleaf. As the Olinka myth goes, the people believed that their location would always be fertile for them. It yielded many crops. One day, one of the Olinka people became greedy and wanted to grow more than necessary to sell to the white men. There were complaints about his intentions, but no one tried to stop him because he compensated them with the materials he was buying. Then a great storm came and destroyed all the roofs in the community, and there were no more roofleafs for repairs because of the greedy Olinka seller. Rain and wind later destroyed their homes, children were sick, and they lost countless lives. "Cold rocks, shaped like millet balls, fell from the sky, striking everyone, men and women and children alike, and [gave] them fevers."[92]

They endured their lot for six months while praying to their gods for relief. When the rain stopped, they searched for more roofleaf to protect them but were unable to grow a substantial amount until five years later. During that time the community experienced relentless calamity but were finally able to grow enough. They celebrated, remembered the error of their ways, and took it as a warning against greed and selfishness. After Nettie and the others learned the importance of the roofleaf, they were presented with their own for their home. Nettie tells Celie,

> As it approached, the people bowed down. The white missionary before you would not let us have this ceremony, said Joseph. But the Olinka like it very much. We know a roofleaf is not Jesus Christ, but in its own humble way, is it not God? So there we sat, Celie, face to face with the Olinka God. And Celie, I was so tired and sleepy and full of chicken and groundnut stew, my ears ringing with song, that all that Joseph said made perfect sense to me. I wonder what you will make of all this?[93]

Nettie sees value, or truth, in worshiping the roofleaf as God. Just like Celie forms a bond with Ms. Sofia, Nettie forms a relationship with an Olinka mother in the community, Catherine. And Olivia forms a bond with Catherine's daughter, Tashi.

Tashi and Olivia's relationship resembles the sisterhood between Nettie and Celie. Whatever Olivia learns in school, she shares with Tashi, just like Nettie does with Celie. Nettie wants to educate Tashi along with Olivia but learns that the Olinka people do not prioritize girls' education. Yet after Tashi's father dies, Catherine allows it.

Nettie also experiences European colonialism firsthand when the Olinka community learns that their region, without their knowledge or consent, has been sold to a rubber manufacturer in England who bulldozes the area, knocking down the school, the church, and numerous homes. When the chief travels to the coast to find out what is happening, he is shocked to see hundreds of other communities also cleared and destroyed by the English. Nettie writes to Celie, "The ancient, giant mahogany trees, all the trees, the game, everything of the forest was being destroyed, and the land was forced to lie flat, he said, and bare as the palm of his hand.... But the worst was yet to be told. Since the Olinka no longer own their village, they must pay rent for it, and in order to use the water, which also no longer belongs to them, they must pay a water tax."[94] When trying to prevent further destruction and desecration of their land, they find out that the British have been instructed to shoot and kill any African who tries to stop them.

Nettie writes that several Olinkans joined the *mbeles*, the fighters who resist European colonialism through combat and resistance, but nothing is powerful enough to fully prevent the exploitation of the land. Forced to pay for corrugated tin, which they now must buy for cover instead of using the roofleaf that was grown freely and chopped down due to the rubber farms—the Olinkans acknowledge defeat.[95] After their time in Africa, including confrontations with the Europeans and complications with the Olinkas, Reverend Samuel and Nettie go through a theological shift. Nettie writes to Celie, around the same time that Celie is writing to Nettie: "God is different to us now, after all these years in Africa. More spirit than ever before, and more internal. Most people think he has to look like something or someone—a roofleaf or Christ—but we don't. And not being tied to what God looks like, frees us."[96]

Nettie and Samuel want to start a new church in the United States when they reconcile with Celie. There will be no idols or images and no clergy, and everyone will be encouraged to "seek God directly."[97] Once again, Walker creates a dual decolonial conversion where the sisters, though separated, each have found an inner freedom from doctrines they inherited. Returning more explicitly to Eden, Celie and Albert discuss the Fall tradition directly and Celie teaches him not the Genesis account, but the little-known Olinkan interpretation.

One significant transformation erased from Spielberg's cinematic depiction is the complexity of Albert's change and his return to the community. Though Spielberg shows the dire consequences of Celie's curse on Albert and how he is ultimately the orchestrator of her reconciliation with Nettie and her children, Walker's novel depicts an even more intimate friendship that blossoms between the two central characters. Spielberg's gesture and concluding depictions of Albert function like a cinematic grand apology. However, the latter half of Walker's novel focuses on detailing a slow but compelling communal redemption. It is hard to imagine redemption and restoration for a man who has done harm, who has done wrong, in our day. Although many readers bemoan Walker's depiction of men in her narrative, they fail to acknowledge the beautiful grace, the complexity of forgiveness, and the sheer effort in allowing a man who was once terrible back into the fold. Though neither Walker, nor Celie, nor Nettie has to extend such grace, they recognize the monstrosity that affected him, saw and experienced the monster that he turned into, and yet still open their hands after his conversion. *The Color Purple* rightfully centers the women, but on the periphery, it also provides an example of a world where black men can live and receive something akin to another chance. Albert is not slain. The curse was not one of death. In other words, *The Color Purple* challenges what might seem like obvious moments of justice and punishment and instead looks for something restorative.

While discussing clothing and gender, and knitting together in her new home, Celie tells Albert an Olinkan origin myth that resembles the Nation of Islam's Yakub legend: Adam was not the first human being created but the first white man. Before Adam's creation, all of humanity was black. Then, unexpectedly, a mother delivered a white baby. Suddenly, everyone giving birth was delivering white children and the people did what they could, in fear, to try to kill all of them because they represented future domination of the world. Celie does not say whether the myth asserts they were successful, but she then turns to the Genesis myth and how the missionaries tried to tell the Olinkas the standard creation story: "So these Olinka people heard about Adam and Eve from the white missionaries and they heard about how the serpent tricked Eve and how God chased them out of the garden of Eden. And they was real curious to hear this, cause after they had chased the white Olinka children out of the village they hadn't hardly thought no more about it."[98] Celie and Albert misunderstand the story to mean that West Africans throw out anyone who does not look or behave like them, including African Americans.

Next, Celie explains that the Olinkas also have a different interpretation of what transpired after the serpent convinced Eve, and then Adam, to partake of the forbidden fruit. Genesis states:

> When the woman saw that the fruit of the tree was good for food and pleasing to the eye, and also desirable for gaining wisdom, she took some and ate it. She also gave some to her husband, who was with her, and he ate it. Then the eyes of both of them were opened, and they realized they were naked; so they sewed fig leaves together and made coverings for themselves. Then the man and his wife heard the sound of the Lord God as he was walking in the garden in the cool of the day, and they hid from the Lord God among the trees of the garden. But the Lord God called to the man, "Where are you?" He answered, "I heard you in the garden, and I was afraid because I was naked; so I hid." And he said,

"Who told you that you were naked? Have you eaten from the tree that I commanded you not to eat from?"[99]

Celie tells Albert that the Christian missionaries used this story to try to enforce the wearing of clothing but, to their chagrin, the Olinkas had their own interpretation: it was not the Hebraic deity who expelled Adam and Eve from the Garden, it was they who expelled Adam and Eve from their village. And they did so because nakedness meant the absence of racial color. In other words, Adam and Eve were expelled because of their whiteness. Celie explains, "They said anybody looking at a white person can tell they naked, but black people can not be naked because they can not be white."[100]

For the Olinka people, according to Celie, this expulsion created a world of rejection and violence. The Olinkas believe that the serpent in the story represents African Americans. And the desire to crush the heads of serpents is how white people in the world justify their cruelty. They are getting revenge for the expulsion. Celie tells Albert, "And something else, I say. Guess who they say the snake is? Us, no doubt, say Mr. _____. Right, I say. Whitefolks sign for they parents. They was so mad to git throwed out and told they was naked they made up they minds to crush us wherever they find us, same as they would a snake. You reckon? Mr. _____ ast."[101] Both Celie and Albert understand white supremacy and colonialism to stem from this divine desire to step on the head of the serpent.

Celie tells Albert that this will be the history of the world until humans evolve into something else, perhaps living beings with two heads instead of one. Yet even then there will be some rejection, some destruction, some violence, some reaction to humans rejecting and expelling other humans from community. However, there is a cure: "the only way to stop making somebody the serpent is for everybody to accept everybody else as a child of God, or one mother's children, no matter what they look like or how they act."[102] Finally, Celie tells Albert one more thing that is fascinating. The Olinka people—like the people across Benin who practice Vodun—worship the serpent and even believe it is possible to see the serpent as one of them. "They say who knows, maybe it is kinfolks, but for sure it's the smartest, cleanest, slickest thing they ever seen." Celie's son bears the name of this story, but more importantly, he bears the name of the refusal to be considered naked. Albert asks what they named Adam, and Celie tells him "Omatangu," "an un-naked man," which is a covered man. And there is a connection somehow between his covering and his self-awareness, his consciousness. Celie tells Albert that Omatangu was close to being one of the first humans God created, but there is a difference between him and Adam. Omatangu "knowed what he was. A whole lot of the men that come before the first man was men, but none of 'em didn't know it."

In the never-ending debates about Walker's treatment of black men in this novel, my reading is that she extends one of the most difficult theological concepts to us: grace. According to the Olinkan interpretation of the Fall, which Celie explains to Albert, a man who was cruel but changed and grew, there is a chance to be something else. And even the traditional God of the classical doctrine played a part in their dehumanization.

Walker asks, "And what kind of God would be so cruel as to curse women and men forever for eating a piece of fruit, no matter how forbidden?"[103] This is not only preposterous but severe. Perhaps she takes the myth too literally and stretches it to the point of becoming ridiculous. But for Walker, this is necessary to counter its material consequences: "It is fatal to love a God who does not love you. A God specifically created to comfort, lead, advise, strengthen, and enlarge the tribal borders of someone else. We have been beggars at the table of a religion that sanctioned our destruction."[104]

For Richard Wright, thinking theologically is intricately a source of our problems. For Walker, though, the problem is that we do not extend the sacred to nonwhite entities, be they gods or humans. Man's overrepresentation, to borrow from Sylvia Wynter, is stuck in our psyches. Therefore we must, in the words of Shug, "git man off [our] eyeball, before we can see anything at all."[105] For James Baldwin, we all deserve a private Eden of our own, but Walker believes Eden should be public and shared, participated in, cultivated. In contrast to Morrison, she does not find paradise a terrible concept. "The truth was, we already lived in paradise but were worked too hard by the land-grabbers to enjoy it."[106] The Garden belongs to us all. It is a shared space for every being to thrive and live. Each tree has the possibility to reach skyward on its own if we leave it alone and view it as one of us. And upon every branch hangs fruit, a bountiful and delicious offering accessible to every form of life seeking sustenance.

CODA

Lucille Clifton's poetry can topple an edifice. Stanzas of only a few words can make you rethink myths that have been held sacred for a considerable amount of time. With less than five words she can change your mind, reframe the way you read your most preciously held scriptures. Her voice is not one of force. Her pen is delicate. She never raises her voice on the page. What Clifton does is merely stun the reader with her unique subtlety. The poems masquerade as uncomplicated; they come across as basic, modest, and straightforward, all the while demolishing and reconstructing theological convictions you were committed to keeping without knowing it.

In fact, no other poet in the twentieth century exerted more artistic genius to convey, with an unmatched sensitivity for life, the hidden insights in between the Bible's various languages. As I conclude this project, I am in awe of a poem I never intended to include in my analysis. Even though my focus has been on the African American novel, Clifton's work bears mentioning. The poem that I have been reading repeatedly is spoken through the voice of Lucifer, who is having a heart-to-heart with God. "Brothers" reintroduces Lucifer and causes me to envision his relationship with God through another lens, which suggests that he—like every single one of us—has encountered and survived loss.¹ This perspective reminds me that they shared a relationship prior to the celestial rebellion. They were close. They were family, *brothers,* before the angelic upheaval.

In this poem, Clifton takes us back to the wreckage after the Garden, when the man and woman were exiled and nothing was left but crumbs, footprints, and the gloom of staggering disappointment. She allows us to listen to a conversation between Lucifer and God, sitting at the site of the wreckage, and beckons us to sit with what we all might have missed in our reading of stories of the Fall.

In the first stanza Lucifer invites God to "coil" with him, to be with him in "creation's bed," to be with him in the place where everything went wrong. Clifton writes in the voice of the angel:

> of the past. i have grown old
> remembering this garden,
> the hum of the great cats
> moving into language, the sweet
> fume of man's rib
> as it rose up and began to walk.

Lucifer reflects proudly on the creature's development. A beginning full of promise. Life before everything went awry. He watched the woman who grew, perhaps not as quickly as we might read, but through stages, through steps, in time. Lucifer thinks and utters aloud, "it was all glory then."

The Genesis component of the poem centers around creation, but here we are already reflecting on the Watchers. Lucifer, a term meaning "morning star," is often conflated with a fallen angel named Lucifer in Judeo-Christian tradition, due to the Vulgate's translation of "morning star" or "shining one." The theory of Lucifer and that of the Watchers overlap in history because they both represent a cosmic celestial insurrection. Clifton offers an alternative reading of Genesis 1:27 from the Priestly rendering. If humans are shaped in God's image, then, as Lucifer states directly to God: "listen, You are beyond/even Your own understanding." God seems to be omniscient; in fact, we are told that He is divinely panoptic, all-perceptive, all-knowing, and all wise beyond all comprehension. Nothing gets past or around Him. He knows all, it seems, save for one small divine detail: Himself. According to the poem, the paradox is obvious. God only knows as much about God as God allows. And maybe after perusing various assertions in the biblical text about God's jealousy, insatiable hunger for glory, and inviolable commandments, along with His irrefutable desire for monotheistic worship, it is possible to truly understand—according to the poet—that poor Adam and Eve were certainly created in His image. And this image bore characteristics that neither God nor humans were able to fathom. Lucifer, who is "less snake than angel/less angel than man," defends not only his reputation but also that of the human, and asks:

> what could i choose
> but to slide along beside them,
> they whose only sin
> was being their father's children?

Lucifer is desperately trying to understand. The early theologians' defensive argument about "free will" and human ingenuity does not fit here. If we take Genesis 1:27 as true, as "real," then how could anything but devastation and destruction occur in a world made by a deity who does not consider the worst characteristics of Himself? He then places those unobserved attributes in a creation that never asked for existence. Maybe the sides of Himself He never took seriously or even noticed were the traits in the humans that ultimately inspired their decision to disobey. The poem causes one to wonder—was the human act of defiance, the partaking of the forbidden fruit, the disobedience that sparked the fall of humanity the activity that most resembled the image of their creator?

In this poem, Lucifer, the light-bringing morning star, offers his perspective on what might have occurred in Eden. Novelists are not alone in turning to Eden for invaluable lessons for life. Poets too want answers. They want wisdom. The poem ends with Lucifer trying to communicate that he wants to hear from God but also knowing, as one of his former angels, that God's communication is usually mediated through the angels. In conclusion, Lucifer accepts that he will not hear an explanation and must accept that belief in God demands faith and silence.

Listen. The book of Genesis provides us with the foundation of the human drama. It is a tale of beginnings, of firsts, of divine inceptions. And according to countless theologians in the history of Abrahamic religions, Genesis most significantly provides the tragic myth of humanity's descent into misfortune. Theologically, I read Genesis through George Steiner's definition of tragedy:

> What I identify as "tragedy" in the radical sense is the dramatic representation or, more precisely, the dramatic testing of reality in which man is taken to be an unwelcome guest in the world. The sources of his estrangement—German *Unheimlichkeit*—conveys the actual meaning of "one who is thrust out of doors"—can be various. They can be the literal or metaphorical consequence of a "fall of man" or primal chastisement . . . But the absolute tragedy exists only where the substantive truth is assigned to Sophocles

statement that "it is best to have never been born" or where the summation of insight into the human fortunes is articulated in [King] Lear's fivefold "never."

For me, Genesis 3 is the tragic tale of the beginning of humanity's flaws, which is simultaneously the inception of human freedom. I understand Adam and Eve—in a similar vein as John Milton—as meeting *some* of Aristotle's prerequisites for proper tragic heroes. I do not read the text literally, but as an imaginative mythology of how and why evil exists in the world. The Fall of humanity, as a concept, is important because it offers a narrative among narratives to understand or imagine how and why we wreak havoc on and in the world. Genesis functions as the religious text that offers poetic insight into why human beings hurt each other, dominate each other, and ruin each other so much. I turn to the story in my own guilt to ask myself repeatedly: *Why on earth did I do that? Why do I, at times, mess up?* In other words, the story of Eden is a theodicy. A defense of God, but not of the human, and not of myself.

It is a mythological attempt to answer some fundamental questions about human existence. That is why Saint Augustine never quite let the story go. It is why Saint Paul turned to that story more times than he did to the Watchers. It is one of the richest pieces of sacred literature I have ever encountered. Its enduring presence in our consciousness is a testament to its phenomenal texture.

Black American writers have been invested in different aspects of the Garden of Eden since Phillis Wheatley's letters and poems. Whether it is invoking the serpent, Cain, or the Garden itself, the myth has been integral to the thinking and imagining necessary for these writers to hold on to notions of freedom and possibility, even against a deity who may seem to oppose their liberation.

Each writer read the Edenic tale uniquely. Each saw something different and used it for their subtle or—in Morrison's and Walker's cases—explicitly theological novels.

And despite their differences, each writer saw a chance to think about paradise, to think about love, to think about partnership, glory, pain, and tragedy. Each writer grabbed the story and made it their own. Each writer took a character and produced a version on their own page. Because we all must try to answer, at some point in our lives, all the fundamental questions of human existence. We all must, as Baldwin would say, pay the price of the ticket. And sometimes that ticket is trying to make sense of a senseless world, to gather all the pieces we are surrounded with and make something out of them. All of us must look at the fruit—whatever that fruit may be or symbolize—and decide: bite it, or leave it hanging there? Because sometimes, humanity hangs in the balance of that one dreadful decision.

ACKNOWLEDGMENTS

Words cannot properly convey the gratitude I feel toward all the people who have helped me bring this project to life. I also completely underestimated the difficulty in writing this section, because no matter how long I hold on to it, I still live in fear that I have forgotten someone. If I have, I apologize now but am also saying, please, charge it to my anxiety and not my true feelings.

I thank and acknowledge my grandmother, Loretta Fisher; my mom and dad; my stepmother; and my siblings, Brianna and Robert, for all their continued support. My godparents. My in-laws/loves, especially my sisters, Aigner, Anitra, and Ishea. Thank you.

I want to thank the bench: Joshua Bennett, Kyle Brooks, Wesley Morris, and Jeremy Scott Vinson. Thank you, JP Reynolds, for always being down to read chapters and paragraphs. For being a true support. Angela Addae, you already know. Ericka Dunbar. Nicole Diop. Amaryah Armstrong. Desiree Melonas.

This book would not be here if it were not for Farah Jasmine Griffin, who believed in it enough to vouch for it. To Josef Sorrett. Candice Love Jackson always said I should've been an

English major. And Loye Ashton changed my life in ways I can never repay. John J. Thatamanil is one of the best teachers in the world. He sat by me when I was a graduate student and taught me to listen to the rhythm of sentences. Follow the beat. Read it aloud. He also taught me so much about patience, God, grace, support, and friendship. And if you are reading this now, John, I do not send you early drafts of stuff because for some reason I just really want you to see the finished product of things and, I hope, to be proud.

Ashon Crawley read a very early draft of chapter 3. But besides that, he's remarkably supportive. Thank you.

I thank my editor and friend, Wendy K. Lochner; you're always a supportive voice. I thank Olufemi Adedoyin for her eyes and red pen.

Andre C. Willis, my forever teacher and mentor, read the entire manuscript and offered many, many criticisms and suggestions. My elder cousin, Sean, really forced me to take grades seriously when I was a child, and I'll never forget that. I want to acknowledge the warmth of the theology department at the University of San Diego (I miss you, Peter Mena), as well as the Africana studies program and the black faculty. I miss them dearly (as well as the tacos, beaches, and glorious sunsets). But let me also be specific: I want to acknowledge TJ Tallie, Channon Miller, Michele Watkins, Angela Nurse, Jillian Tullis, and Cory Gooding. During the BLM uprising, the COVID years, and the rise in numbers of black faculty in those years, we had the time of our lives. I know I did.

I thank my new home, the theology and religious studies department at Georgetown University. It's been incredible so far. I also want to acknowledge Federico Settler, Mari Hausas Engh, and my home away from home, a place I fell madly in love with, The School of Religion, Philosophy and Classics, College of

Humanities at the University of KwaZulu-Natal, South Africa (the Pietermaritzburg Campus).

Thank you, Vincent Lloyd. Thank you, Chaplain Johnson. Thank you, Pastor Anthony Bennett.

Pastor Otis Moss, III, when you didn't even know me you sent me books out the Akiba and supported me going to seminary. How do I repay kindness and generosity like that? Thank you, Pastor Claybon Lea, Jr.

Gary Dorrien, I don't know how to thank you. I'm almost scared to because if I start then I won't stop, trying to think of all that I need to thank you for. Thank you, Cornel West. I consider it an honor to have met you, to know you, and to continue doing what I have done since I was in college, and that is imitate you. You are the one who introduced me to studying theology, philosophy, and literature, and I hope this, at the very least, doesn't embarrass you. If it makes you proud, that's a blessing that is overwhelming for me.

Now, to the late Dr. James Cone. Your memory, your lessons, your gentleness, your discipline, and your guidance have meant more to me than anything. You are forever in my heart. Your voice is forever in my head. And not a single day that goes by where I don't think about you and all the times we shared. Some of those times you were laying in to me, trying to rid me of my habit of being my own worst enemy, and other times you were more than a professor—I would even cross the line and say a grandfather. I am glad and fortunate to have been your student at that moment in time. I mean, I am forever your student, but I caught you when you were older and much more concerned about your students than your own writing. And I was so blessed, and am so grateful. Thank you.

To my wife, Alexis V. Jackson, and, lastly, to *mon petite coeur*, Genevieve Loretta Calloway, please know that everything—and

I mean everything—I do is for you. Genevieve, you have my face and you have all my love. I love you more than anything, and all I want for you is to have a better life, make better decisions, and focus on your dreams and goals with all your strength. I love you and I am eternally grateful for you. Your life, your mere existence, has blessed my life more than I can adequately explain. Thank you for understanding why Daddy works so much, because again, my love, it's all for you.

NOTES

INTRODUCTION

1. Immanuel Kant, *Religion within the Boundaries of Mere Reason*, ed. and trans. Allen Wood and George Di Giovanni (Cambridge: Cambridge University Press, 1998), 38–43.
2. I want to establish a critical distance between the theory and the early interpretations of the story. Also, the Garden of Eden story was not always as authoritative as it is now in Judeo-Christian history. The story bears traces of other myths and oral stories disseminated throughout ancient Mesopotamia. In other words, the myth itself shares theological motifs with countless neighboring societies.
3. These specific texts are usually highlighted as biblical proof of Moses's authorship: Exodus 24:4: "Moses then wrote down everything the Lord had said"; Deuteronomy 31:9: "So Moses wrote down this law and gave it to the priests, the sons of Levi." And the reference in the Talmud is from Baba Bathra 14b–15a in *The Talmud: The Steinsaltz Edition*, trans. Rabbi Adin Steinsaltz (New York: Random House, 1989). Despite this historical tradition, most biblical scholars agree that the Pentateuch is not the creation of a sole author but the work of many hands, including scribes and editors, who compiled the legends and writings together. For more see John J. Collins, *A Short Introduction to the Hebrew Bible: Third Edition* (Minneapolis: Fortress Press, 2018), and Joel S. Baden, *The Composition of the Pentateuch: Renewing the Documentary Hypothesis* (New Haven, CT: Yale University Press, 2012).

4. The Yahwist account begins immediately at the fourth verse of the second chapter.
5. There is growing scholarship that offers a queer and trans reading of Genesis 1:27, stating that the sexes in the text are not strict binaries but two broad and expansive possibilities of creation. See Gerald O. West and Charlene Van Der Walt, "A Queer (Beginning to the) Bible," *Concilium Journal for Theology* 5 (2019): 583–593.
6. Giorgio Agamben, *The Kingdom and the Garden*, trans. Adam Kotsko (London: Seagull Books, 2020), 4.
7. David M. Carr, *The Erotic Word: Sexuality, Spirituality, and the Bible* (New York: Oxford University Press, 2003), 29.
8. Gregory K. Beale, The *Temple and the Church's Mission: A Biblical Theology of the Dwelling Place of God* (Downers Grove, IL: IVP Academic, 2004).
9. Carr, *The Erotic Word*, 28.
10. The proper translation in the Hebrew is "the human." Other translations add "Adam," but he is not officially named until later in Genesis. See Carol Meyers, *Rediscovering Eve: Ancient Israelite Women in Context* (New York: Oxford University Press, 2013), 59.
11. Stephen Greenblatt, *The Rise and Fall of Adam and Eve* (New York: Norton, 2017), 33.
12. The patriarchs known as Abraham, Isaac, and Jacob—and even Joseph's story—are not only placed after each other in the text but also edited into a generational storyline about the lives of fathers and sons. For more on this see Richard Elliott Friedman, *Who Wrote the Bible?* (New York: Harper & Row, 1987), and Thomas L. Thompson, *The Historicity of the Patriarchal Narratives: The Quest for the Historical Abraham* (Berlin: De Gruyter, 1974).
13. N. P. Williams, *The Ideas of the Fall and of Original Sin: A Historical and Critical Study* (London and New York: Longmans, Green, 1927), 21.
14. Williams, *The Ideas of the Fall and of Original Sin*, 21.
15. Michael A. Knibb, ed. and trans, *The Ethiopic Book of Enoch: A New Edition in the Light of the Aramaic Dead Sea Fragments* (Oxford: Clarendon Press, 1978)
16. Williams, Williams, *The Ideas of the Fall and of Original Sin*, 25.
17. Mark S. Smith, *The Genesis of Good and Evil: The Fall(out) and Original Sin in the Bible* (Louisville, KY: Westminster John Knox Press, 2019), 22.

18. James Barr, *The Garden of Eden and the Hope of Immortality* (Minneapolis: Fortress Press, 1993), 5.
19. Collins, *A Short Introduction to the Hebrew Bible*, 294.
20. In an earlier draft I made a claim that Jesus never referenced Eden; Christine Trotter pointed out that Jesus does quote from the story, though! See Matthew 19:4–5 and Mark 10:6–8, where Jesus refers to Genesis 2:24.
21. Smith, *The Genesis of Good and Evil*, 22.
22. Teresa Ann Ellis, "Is Eve the 'Woman' in Sirach 25:24?" *Catholic Biblical Quarterly* 73, no. 4 (2011): 724.

1. GIOVANNI'S EDEN

1. Jack Halberstam, *The Queer Art of Failure* (Durham, NC: Duke University Press, 2011).
2. Lisa M. Bowens, *African American Readings of Paul: Reception, Resistance, and Transformation* (Grand Rapids, MI: Wm. B. Eerdmans, 2020).
3. Howard Thurman's grandmother, Sue Bailey, famously told Thurman that she never wanted to read Paul after he was constantly read as justifying black American enslavement. Howard Thurman, *With Head and Heart: The Autobiography of Howard Thurman* (New York: Harcourt Brace Jovanovich, 1979), 30.
4. Michel Foucault, *The Confessions of the Flesh: Volume 4 of the History of Sexuality* (New York: Penguin Random House, 2022), 53.
5. Herb Boyd, *Baldwin's Harlem: A Biography of James Baldwin* (New York: Atria Books, 2008), 129.
6. James Baldwin, *Collected Essays* (New York: Library of America, 1998), 104.
7. Ashon Crawley, *The Lonely Letters* (Durham, NC: Duke University Press, 2020).
8. Crawley, *Lonely Letters*, 16.
9. David Leeming calls David's love for Giovanni a "calling." David Leeming, *James Baldwin: A Biography* (New York: Henry Holt, 1994), 123.
10. Marc Dudley, *Understanding James Baldwin* (Columbia: University of South Carolina Press, 2019), 34.

11. N. T. Wright, *Paul: A Biography* (New York: HarperCollins, 2018); Herman Ridderbos, *Paul: An Outline of His Theology* (Grand Rapids, MI: Wm. B. Eerdmans, 1975).
12. Alain Badiou, *Saint Paul: The Foundation of Universalism*, trans. Ray Brassier (Stanford, CA: Stanford University Press, 2003), 31.
13. Raymond Brown says there are seven authoritative Pauline letters in total. Raymond E. Brown, *An Introduction to the New Testament: The Abridged Edition*, ed. Marion L. Soards (New Haven, CT: Yale University Press, 2016), 419.
14. Scholars agree that 2nd Corinthians 10–13—the painful letter—more than likely belongs in the front before chapters 1–9. The other idea is that they are two different letters. E. P. Sanders, *Paul: The Apostle's Life, Letters, and Thought* (Minneapolis: Fortress Press, 2015), 232.
15. Raymond Brown states that the Church in Rome was probably in existence as early as the 40s. Brown, *Introduction to the New Testament*, 562.
16. One argument outside the purview of this project is that in Saint Paul's letter to the Galatians, notably the first chapter, he invokes ideas that stem from the possibility of an angel curse. For a more robust engagement, see Tyler A. Stewart, *The Origin and Persistence of Evil in Galatians* (Tübingen: Mohr Siebeck, 2022). This text argues compellingly that Saint Paul relies on the Enochic Watchers-Fallen Angel story to describe the origin of evil in the world, placing Paul directly in the lineage of the Second Temple Jewish writers. My argument is that both traditions are central to his messianic cosmic theodicy.
17. I make this point because the gospels, which are much later than St. Paul's materials, make very little use of the Garden of Eden, as stated by numerous New Testament and Early Christianity scholars.
18. Norman Powell Williams, *The Ideas of the Fall and of Original Sin: A Historical and Critical Study* (New York: Longmans, Green, 1927), 126.
19. Felipe de Jesús Legarreta-Castillo, *The Figure of Adam in Romans 5 and 1 Corinthians 15: The New Creation and Its Ethical and Social Reconfiguration* (Minneapolis: Fortress Press, 2014), 4.
20. Dale B. Martin writes, "My arguments here are not original; scholarship on 1 Corinthians for the past few decades has argued that a dominant minority within the Corinthian church were people of relatively

high status, when compared, that is, to the rest of the Corinthian Christians." *The Corinthian Body* (New Haven, CT: Yale University Press), 73.
21. Brown, *An Introduction to the New Testament*, 527.
22. Martin, *The Corinthian Body*, 122–123.
23. 1st Corinthians 15:17.
24. Here I am following the work of J. Christiaan Beker (*Paul's Apocalyptic Gospel* [Minneapolis: Fortress Press, 1982]) and John E. Toews (*Romans: Believers Church Bible Commentary* [Scottsdale, PA: Herald Press, 2004]), who argue that Saint Paul was an apocalyptic theologian as opposed to a narrative theologian.
25. Paula Fredriksen, *From Jesus to Christ: The Origins of the New Testament Images of Christ* (London: Yale University Press, 2000), 56.
26. Beker, *Paul's Apocalyptic Gospel*.
27. John Barton notes that Paul does not use the resurrection of Jesus to argue for the mere possibility of resurrections; for him, Jesus's resurrection from the grave simply means that the "end is near." See John Barton, *A History of the Bible: The Book and Its Faiths* (New York: Random House), 168.
28. Wisdom of Solomon 1:13–14, NRSV.
29. Herman Ridderbos, *Paul: An Outline of His Theology* (Grand Rapids, MI: Wm. B. Eerdmans, 1975), 96.
30. Tatha Wiley, *Original Sin: Origins, Developments, Contemporary Meanings* (New York: Paulist Press, 2002), 25.
31. Fredriksen, *From Jesus to Christ*, 56
32. Toews, *Romans*, 173.
33. Members across the Corinthian assemblies—like most people in the Mediterranean—struggled with Saint Paul's unique teaching of the resurrection: he taught that he was misunderstood to mean reviving corpses and stated that Jesus's resurrection serves as the beginning of the general resurrection. David Wenham writes that baptism according to Paul "represents the coming together of a Jewish and Christian understanding of baptism as initiation into the saved people of God with a distinctively Christian view of the death and resurrection of Jesus as the decisive saving event." The thought that people of "The Way" would experience resurrection because they were

baptized—connected spiritually to Jesus' resurrection—was an intervention into Jewish apocalypticism and eschatology. For more see: David Wenham, *Paul: Follower of Jesus or Founder of Christianity?* (Grand Rapids, MI: Wm. B. Eerdmans, 1995), 161.

34. Wayne A. Meeks, ed., *The Writings of St. Paul* (New York: Norton, 1972), 66; N. T. Wright, Leander E. Keck, et al., eds., *The New Interpreter's Bible: A Commentary in Twelve Volumes* (Nashville: Abingdon Press, 2002), 395.
35. Romans 5:12–14, NRSV.
36. Albert Schweitzer, *The Mysticism of Paul* (Baltimore and London: John Hopkins University Press, 1931), 167.
37. Karl Barth, *The Epistle to the Romans*, trans. Edwyn C. Hoskyns, 6th ed. (1919; reprint, New York: Oxford University Press, 1968), 174.
38. Romans 5:10–11, NRSV.
39. James Baldwin, *Giovanni's Room* (New York: Dial Press, 1956), 55.
40. *Giovanni's Room*, 54.
41. David's attitude toward Jacques mirrors St. Paul's attitude toward the other Mediterranean peoples and customs in the first chapter of Romans.
42. *Giovanni's Room*, 55–56.
43. James Baldwin, "Here Be Dragons," in *James Baldwin: Collected Essays*, ed. by Toni Morrison (New York: Library of America, 1998), 696.
44. *Giovanni's Room*, 24.
45. *Giovanni's Room*, 25.
46. *Giovanni's Room*, 39.
47. *Giovanni's Room*, 40.
48. *Giovanni's Room*, 40.
49. 1 Corinthians 7:9, NRSV.
50. Baldwin, "Here Be Dragons," 698.
51. Michel Foucault believes that in ancient Greek society there was a need for self-regulation, or self-mastery, to which the control of one's sexual patterns was intrinsic. I am saying that for Saint Paul, the only proper outlet for sexual activity is marriage, which is meant to assist with the inability to control oneself while not married. For more on Foucault's theory, see Michel Foucault, *The History of Sexuality, Volume 2: The Use of Pleasure*, trans. Robert Hurley (New York: Vintage, 1990).

52. *Giovanni's Room*, 6.
53. *Giovanni's Room*, 8.
54. *Giovanni's Room*, 8.
55. Clarence E. Hardy, III, *James Baldwin's God: Sex, Hope, and Crisis in Black Holiness Culture* (Knoxville: University of Tennessee Press, 2003), 62.
56. *Giovanni's Room*, 16.
57. *Giovanni's Room*, 17.
58. R. W. B. Lewis, *The American Adam* (Chicago: University of Chicago Press, 1959), 5.
59. Scholars of early American literature and history describe the American Adam as a symbol and archetype that emerged in the nineteenth century to describe the consciousness of American men who saw themselves as disconnected from any European or Old World ancestry. They were divorced from all prior history of the earth and ultimately imagined themselves as brand new men, new creations of modernity who were be cultivating in a new world in the United States. The United States was referenced explicitly or implicitly as a Garden of Eden, a space designated for the new men to toil and exercise dominion.
60. Baldwin, "Here Be Dragons," 686.
61. Robert Armour, " 'Deliverance': Four Variations of the American Adam," *Literature/Film Quarterly* 1, no. 3 (Summer 1973): 280–285.
62. Lee Edelman, *No Future: Queer Theory and the Death Drive* (Durham, NC: Duke University Press, 2004).
63. Lewis, *The American Adam*, 5.
64. Ernest Gibson, III, *Salvific Manhood: James Baldwin's Novelization of Male Intimacy* (Lincoln: University of Nebraska Press, 2019), 69.
65. Matt Brim, *James Baldwin and the Queer Imagination* (Ann Arbor: University of Michigan Press, 2014), 62.
66. Brim, *James Baldwin and the Queer Imagination*, 63.
67. In "Here Be Dragons" Baldwin lists "cops, football players, soldiers, sailors, Marines, or bank presidents, admen, boxers, construction workers" as the type of men he caught sexually pleasing themselves with other men or men he slept with (691).
68. Paul Tillich, *The Courage to Be* (New Haven, CT, and London: Yale University Press, 1952).

69. Leeming, *James Baldwin*, 123.
70. *Giovanni's Room*, 91.
71. Bill V. Mullen, *James Baldwin: Living in Fire* (London: Pluto Press), 65.
72. *Giovanni's Room*, 34–35.
73. Mullen, *James Baldwin*, 67.
74. *Giovanni's Room*, 24.
75. Leeming, *James Baldwin*, 124.
76. Christopher V. Hobson, *James Baldwin and the Heavenly City: Prophecy, Apocalypse, and Doubt* (East Lansing: Michigan State University Press, 2018), 89.
77. *Giovanni's Room*, 75.
78. *Giovanni's Room*, 76.
79. *Giovanni's Room*, 87.
80. *Giovanni's Room*, 88.
81. Dudley, *Understanding James Baldwin*, 34.
82. Mullen, *James Baldwin*, 66.
83. José Esteban Muñoz, *Cruising Utopia: The Then and There of Queer Futurity* (New York: New York University Press, 2009), 1.
84. Muñoz, *Cruising Utopia*, 26.
85. *Giovanni's Room*, 88.
86. *Giovanni's Room*, 168.
87. *Giovanni's Room*, 168.
88. Josiah Ulysses Young, III, *James Baldwin's Understanding of God: Overwhelming Desire and Joy* (New York: Palgrave Macmillan), 76.
89. *Giovanni's Room*, 168.
90. Hobson, *James Baldwin and the Heavenly City*.
91. Hobson, *James Baldwin and the Heavenly City*, 2.
92. James Campbell, *Talking at the Gates: A Life of James Baldwin* (New York: Viking, 1991), 108.
93. While Campbell applauds Baldwin for including an all-white ensemble of characters, I agree with David Leeming: "*Giovanni's Room* as an 'all-white' novel is not a bastard among the literary offspring of James Baldwin; it is one of the more impassioned expressions of the story he told all his life." See Leeming, *James Baldwin*, 123.
94. James Campbell, *Exiled in Paris: Richard Wright, James Baldwin, Samuel Beckett and Others on the Left Bank* (Berkeley: University of California Press, 2003), 119.

95. Hobson, *James Baldwin and the Heavenly City*, 82.
96. Hardy, III, *James Baldwin's God*, 64.
97. *Giovanni's Room*, 111.
98. Ultimately, this question goes beyond Baldwin: Are an ancient thinker's ideas always to blame for the ways those ideas traveled the history of the world?
99. James Baldwin, "Letter to the Born Again," in *James Baldwin: Collected Essays*, ed. Toni Morrison (New York: Library of America, 1998), 843–847.
100. James Baldwin, "No Name in the Street," in *James Baldwin: Collected Essays*, ed. Toni Morrison (New York: Library of America, 1998), 439.
101. Baldwin, "No Name in the Street," 443.
102. Baldwin, "No Name in the Street," 438.
103. Baldwin, "No Name in the Street," 444.

2. EVE'S PARADISE

1. Dinitia Smith, "Toni Morrison's Mix of Tragedy, Domesticity and Folklore," *New York Times*, January 8, 1998, https://www.nytimes.com/1998/01/08/books/toni-morrison-s-mix-of-tragedy-domesticity-and-folklore.html.
2. In the next chapter I will engage with Richard Wright's second novel, *The Outsider* (1953), about his reading of the Fall.
3. Toni Morrison, *The Source of Self-Regard: Selected Essays, Speeches, and Meditations* (New York: Knopf, 2019), 43.
4. Morrison explains the concept of the "master narrative" as it relates to her novel *The Bluest Eye*. Its master narrative traditionally is understood as a narrative of ugliness. According to Morrison by way of implication, the notion of Original Sin accomplishes an identical task. See "Toni Morrison," in Bill Moyers, *A World of Ideas II* (Garden City, NY: Doubleday, 1990), 5; and Justine Tally, *Paradise Reconsidered: Toni Morrison's (Hi)Stories and Truths* (Munster: Lit Verlag, 1999).
5. Original Sin is a Western idea in Christendom. The Orthodox church understands sin as inherited but creates distance from Augustine's argument. See John A. McGukin, *The Eastern Orthodox Church: A New History* (New Haven, CT, and London: Yale University Press, 2020);

Timothy Ware, *The Orthodox Church: An Introduction to Eastern Christianity* (Westminster: Penguin, 2015).

6. "Wayward" is a term used by Saidiya Hartman to describe a sense of refusing to follow social norms, especially as it relates to black women historically who have had to find ways to cultivate their own agency, sense of pleasure, and resistance to injustice. Saidiya Hartman, *Wayward Lives, Beautiful Experiments: Intimate Histories of Riotous Black Girls, Troublesome Women, and Queer Radicals* (New York: Norton 2019).

7. The term "black Atlantic" was first coined by African art scholar and historian Robert Farris Thompson in his classic text *Flash of the Spirit: African and Afro-American Art and Philosophy* (New York: Random House, 1983). Thompson used the term to articulate the visual and artistic connections between black people across the Western hemisphere. I am mostly influenced by and indebted to the rigorous work of J. Lorand Matory, whose *Black Atlantic Religion: Tradition, Transnationalism, and Matriarchy in the Afro-Brazilian Candomblé* (Princeton, NJ: Princeton University Press, 2005) opened my eyes to the complexity and nuances of Afro-Brazilian religious study.

8. I consider *Paradise* a form of eco-literature because Morrison, as always, pays attention to the life of plants and animals. See Joshua Bennett, *Being Property Once Myself: Blackness and the End of Man* (Cambridge, MA: Harvard University Press, 2020), notably chapter 2, "The Cock."

9. Nadra Nittle, *Toni Morrison's Spiritual Vision: Faith, Folktales, and Feminism in Her Life and Literature* (Minneapolis: Fortress Press, 2021), 145.

10. Charles H. Long, *Significations: Signs, Symbols, and Images in the Interpretation of Religion* (Aurora, CO: Davies Group, 1999), 101. See also Louis Benjamin Rolsky, "Charles H. Long and the Re-Orientation of American Religious History," *Journal of the American Academy of Religion* 80, no. 3 (2012): 750–774, and Juan M. Floyd-Thomas, "Towards a Religious History of the Black Atlantic: Charles H. Long's Significations and New World Slavery," *Journal of Religious History* 42, no. 1 (2018): 3–24.

11. Colorism is deftly explored in this dissertation, though it focuses mostly on Morrison's *Beloved*: Nefnouf Ahmed Seif Eddine, *Shadism and*

Female Resistance in Toni Morrison's Novels (ProQuest Dissertations Publishing, 2022).

12. The Holy Trinity was not formally mentioned as a core belief in Christendom until Constantine held the First Council of Nicaea in 325 CE Yet the belief became official church doctrine because of the declaration known as the Nicene-Constantinopolitan Creed in 381, which was developed at the First Council of Constantinople.
13. Henri Rondet, *Original Sin: The Patristic and Theological Background* (Germantown, TN: Saint Pauls/Alba House, 1972).
14. Norman P. Williams, Henri Rondet, Tatha Wiley, and Ian McFarland, among others. See Pier Franco Beatrice, *The Transmission of Sin: Augustine and the Pre-Augustinian Sources*, trans. Adam Kamesar (Oxford: Oxford University Press, 2013).
15. Rondet, *Original Sin*, 25.
16. Justo L. Gonzalez, *The Story of Christianity. Volume 1, The Early Church to the Reformation*, updated, 2nd ed. (New York:, HarperCollins, 2010).
17. Justin Martyr, "Dialogues with Trypho," in *The Ante-Nicene Fathers: The Writings of the Fathers Down to A. D. 325 Volume I—the Apostolic Fathers with Justin Martyr and Irenaeus*, ed. Alexander Roberts and James Donaldson. Revised and Chronologically arranged with brief prefaces and occasional notes by A. Cleveland Coxe (Buffalo, NY: Christian Literature Publishing Co., 1885), 455.
18. Justin Martyr, "Dialogues with Trypho," 249.
19. This aspect of Mary and Eve becomes central throughout Tertullian's writings.
20. Theophilus of Antioch, "Theophilus to Autolycus," in *Fathers of the Second Century: Hermas, Tatian, Athenagoras, Theophilus, and Clement of Alexandria*, ed. Alexander Roberts, James Donaldson, and A. Cleveland Coxe, trans. Marcus Dods, vol. 2, *The Ante-Nicene Fathers* (Buffalo, NY: Christian Literature Publishing Co., 1885), 105.
21. Augustine, *On Genesis: Two Books on Genesis Against the Manichees and on the Literal Interpretation of Genesis: an Unfinished Book* (Washington, DC: Catholic University of America Press, 1990).
22. Peter Brown, *Augustine of Hippo: A Biography*. New edition with an epilogue (Berkeley: University of California Press, 2000), 127.

23. Bruno Niederbacher, S.J., "The Human Soul: Augustine's Case for Soul-Body Dualism," *The Cambridge Companion to Augustine*, ed. David Vincent Meconi and Eleonore Stump (Cambridge: Cambridge University Press, 2014), 127.
24. Augustine and Elizabeth Ann Clark, *St. Augustine on Marriage and Sexuality*, Vol. 1 (Washington, DC: Catholic University of America Press, 1996), 39.
25. Augustine, *The City of God Against the Pagans*, trans. R. W. Dyson (Cambridge: Cambridge University Press, 1998), Book 14, Chapter 26.
26. Philip Schaff, ed., *Nicene and Post-Nicene Fathers of the Christian Church, First Series, Volume V: St. Augustine—Anti-Pelagian Writings* (Buffalo, NY: Christian Literature Publishing Co., 1887).
27. William E. Mann, "Augustine on Evil and Original Sin," *The Cambridge Companion to Augustine*, ed. David Vincent Meconi and Eleonore Stump (Cambridge: Cambridge University Press, 2014), 106.
28. Mann, "Augustine on Evil and Original Sin," 106.
29. Lenka Karfíková, *Grace and the Will According to Augustine* (Leiden: Brill, 2012), 170.
30. Pelagius, *Pelagius's Commentary on St Paul's Epistle to the Romans*, ed. and trans. Theodore de Bruyn (Oxford: Clarendon Press, 1993), 93.
31. Eugene Teselle, "The Background: Augustine and the Pelagian Controversy," in *Grace for Grace: The Debates After Augustine and Pelagius*, ed. Alexander Y. Hwang, Brian J. Matz, and Augustine Casiday (Washington, DC: Catholic University of America Press, 2014), 9.
32. Augustine, *On Nature and Grace*, trans. Peter Holmes (Münster: Cervantes Digital, 2024), 3.3.
33. Augustine, *On Merit and the Forgiveness of Sins, and the Baptism of Infants*, in *Nicene and Post-Nicene Fathers, First Series, Volume V: St. Augustine—Anti-Pelagian Writings*, ed. Philip Schaff (Buffalo, NY: Christian Literature Publishing Co., 1887), 15–88.
34. Paul B. Clayton, *The Christology of Theodoret of Cyrus: Antiochene Christology from the Council of Ephesus (431) to the Council of Chalcedon (451)* (Oxford: Oxford University Press, 2007), and Yannis Papadogiannakis, *Christianity and Hellenism in the Fifth-Century Greek East: Theodoret's Apologetics against the Greeks in Context*. Hellenic Studies Series 49 (Washington, DC: Center for Hellenic Studies, 2013).

35. James Schaefer, ed., *Advancing Mariology: The Theotokos Lectures 2008–2017* (Milwaukee, WI: Marquette University Press, 2017).
36. John A. McGukin, *The Eastern Orthodox Church: A New History* (New Haven, CT, and London: Yale University Press, 2020).
37. Augustine, *Sermons on Selected Lessons of the New Testament (1844)*, Vol. 1, ca. 392–430, trans. R. G. MacMullen, A Library of Fathers of the Holy Catholic Church, vol. 16 (Oxford: John Henry Parker, 2018).
38. Frances Young, "Theotokos: Mary and the Pattern of Fall and Redemption in the Theology of Cyril of Alexandria," in *The Theology of St. Cyril of Alexandria: A Critical Appreciation*, ed. Thomas Weinandy and Daniel A. Keating (London: T&T Clark, 2003), 70–71.
39. Lindy M. Christopher, "The Geographical Imagination in Toni Morrison's 'Paradise,'" *Rocky Mountain Review* 63, no. 1 (Spring 2009): 89–95.
40. Marni Gauthier, "The Other Side of Paradise: Toni Morrison's (Un) Making of Mythic History," *African American Review* 39, no. 3 (2005): 396. The history of black American expansion into the northwestern region of the country is the background of the story. For Morrison, black life is historically always in motion, in flight, in fugitivity.
41. Nell Irvin Painter, *Exodusters: Black Migration to Kansas After Reconstruction* (New York: Norton, 1992). That is why the Exodus story in the Pentateuch and the origin story of Ruby bear striking resemblances on the page. Ex-slaves released from bondage through war find themselves escaping states like Louisiana and Mississippi and are marching vigorously through an American wilderness trying to locate a Canaan of their own, a home safe from white Americans where they can plant their roots and live their lives within the confines of their own borders.
42. Toni Morrison, *Paradise* (New York: Knopf, 1998), 13.
43. Trina Jones, "The Case for Legal Recognition of Colorism Claims," in *Shades of Difference: Why Skin Color Matters*, ed. Evelyn Nakano Glenn (Stanford, CA: Stanford University Press, 2009).
44. Morrison, *Paradise*, 113.
45. Soane reflects on how The Oven transformed from a utility into a shrine that made the men proud. Morrison, *Paradise*, 103.

46. Morrison, *Paradise*, 14.
47. Morrison, *Paradise*, 109.
48. Ivone Gebara, "The Face of Transcendence as a Challenge to the Reading of the Bible in Latin America," *Searching the Scriptures*, Vol. 1, A Feminist Introduction, ed. Elisabeth Schüssler Fiorenza (New York: Crossroads), 172.
49. Most secondary scholarship on *Paradise* states that Connie is from Brazil; however, neither Brazil nor any other details about her original location are ever stated explicitly in the text. The only clue is that the first port the nuns reach after taking Connie on is Costa Rica.
50. Morrison, *Paradise*, 224.
51. Morrison, *Paradise*, 224.
52. Morrison, *Paradise*, 71.
53. Morrison, *Paradise*, 225.
54. Morrison, *Paradise*, 225.
55. David McLain Carr, *The Erotic Word: Sexuality, Spirituality, and the Bible* (New York; Oxford: Oxford University Press, 2005), 13.
56. Morrison, *Paradise*, 225.
57. Morrison, *Paradise*, 235.
58. Morrison, *Paradise*, 226.
59. Morrison, *Paradise*, 226.
60. Maha Marouan, *Witches, Goddesses, and Angry Spirits: The Politics of Spiritual Liberation in African Diaspora Women's Fiction* (Columbus: Ohio State University Press, 2013), 99.
61. Marouan, *Witches, Goddesses, and Angry Spirits*, 99.
62. Morrison, *Paradise*, 228.
63. Carr, *The Erotic Word*, 10.
64. M. Shawn Copeland, *Enfleshing Freedom: Body, Race, and Being* (Minneapolis: Fortress Press, 2010), 7.
65. Morrison, *Paradise*, 226.
66. Morrison, *Paradise*, 230.
67. Morrison, *Paradise*, 230.
68. Genesis 3:8, NRSV.
69. Morrison, *Paradise*, 236.
70. Jan Furman, *Toni Morrison's Fiction* (Columbia: University of South Carolina Press, 2014), 98.

71. Edward Schillebeeckx, *The Eucharist* (London; New York: Burns & Oates, 2005).
72. Morrison, *Paradise*, 240.
73. Morrison, *Paradise*, 240.
74. Morrison, *Paradise*, 241.
75. Morrison, *Paradise*, 251.
76. Morrison, *Paradise*, 73.
77. Morrison, *Paradise*, 63.
78. Morrison, *Paradise*, 66.
79. Morrison, *Paradise*, 48.
80. Morrison, *Paradise*, 70.
81. Morrison, *Paradise*, 129.
82. Morrison, *Paradise*, 176.
83. Toni Morrison, "Rootedness: The Ancestor as Foundation," in *Black Women Writers (1950–1980)*, ed. Mari Evans (Garden City, NY: Anchor Press, 1984), 342.
84. Toni Morrison, "Rootedness: The Ancestor as Foundation," 342.
85. Toni Morrison, *Conversations with Richard Wright* (Jackson: University Press of Mississippi, 1993), 17.
86. Morrison, *Paradise*, 100.
87. Morrison, *Paradise*, 115.
88. Morrison, *Paradise*, 93.
89. Morrison, *Paradise*, 155.
90. Morrison, *Paradise*, 91.
91. Morrison, *Paradise*, 190.
92. Morrison, *Paradise*, 190.
93. Morrison, *Paradise*, 272.
94. Mandrake is widely used in African American conjuring traditions.
95. Albert Raboteau, *Slave Religion: The "Invisible Institution" in the Antebellum South* (Oxford: Oxford University Press, 2004), 80.
96. Raboteau, *Slave Religion*, 80.
97. Yvonnne Chireau, *Black Magic: Religion and African American Conjuring Tradition* (Berkeley: University of California Press, 2006), 20.
98. Chireau, *Black Magic*, 20.
99. Nittle, *Toni Morrison's Spiritual Vision*, 148.

100. Jacques Derrida, "Faith and Knowledge : The Two Sources of 'Religion' at the Limits of Reason Alone," in *Religion*, ed. Jacques Derrida and Gianni Vattimo (Stanford, CA: Stanford University Press, 1998), 4.
101. Tomoko Masuzawa drives this point home in *The Invention of World Religions, or, How European Universalism Was Preserved in the Language of Pluralism* (Chicago: University of Chicago Press, 2005).
102. See Robert Conner, *Magic in the New Testament* (London: Mandrake Press, 2010).
103. Morrison, *Paradise*, 244.
104. Morrison, *Paradise*, 244.
105. Morrison, *Paradise*, 251.
106. Morrison, *Paradise*, 252.
107. Sheila S. Walker, "Everyday and Esoteric Reality in the Afro-Brazilian Candomblé," *History of Religions* 30, no. 2 (November 1990): 103–128.
108. Luis Nicolau Pares, *The Formation of Candomblé Vodun History and Ritual in Brazil* (Chapel Hill: University of North Carolina Press, 2013).
109. Manuela R. Müller, et al., "The Woman Who Chose the Terreiro. Lay Care and Medical Landscapes in Mental Health Care in Rio de Janeiro." *Anthropology & Medicine* 29, no. 4 (2022): 351–366; Vagner Gonçalves da Silva, "The 'Terreiro' and the City in Afro-Brazilian Ethnographies," *Revista de Antropologia (São Paulo)* 36 (1993): 33–79.
110. Silva, "The 'Terreiro' and the City in Afro-Brazilian Ethnographies," 33–79.
111. Morrison, *Paradise*, 262.
112. Melville J. Herskovits, "The Social Organization of the Afrobrazilian Candomble," *Phylon* 17, no. 2 (1940–1956): 150.
113. David Carrasco, Stephanie Paulsell, and Mara Williard argue that Morrison keeps an eye on excessive goodness: when a character or a community exudes a level of mercy and grace that is so rare in our world that it is "shocking." See Toni Morrison, *Toni Morrison: Goodness and the Literary Imagination: Harvard's 95th Ingersoll Lecture with Essays on Morrison's Moral and Religious Vision*, ed. David Carrasco, Stephanie Paulsell, and Mara Williard (Charlottesville: University of Virginia Press, 2019), 5.
114. Morrison, *Paradise*, 263.

2. EVE'S PARADISE ∝ 241

115. Marouan, *Witches, Goddesses, and Angry Spirits*, 97.
116. Marouan, *Witches, Goddesses, and Angry Spirits*, 97.
117. Karmen Mackendrick, *Divine Enticement: Theological Seduction* (New York: Fordham University Press, 2013), 112.
118. Mackendrick, *Divine Enticement*, 112.
119. Nittle, *Toni Morrison's Spiritual Vision*, 147.
120. Carol A. Myscofski, "Women's Initiation Rites in Afro-Brazilian Religions: A Structural Source Analysis," *Journal of Ritual Studies* 2, no. 1 (Winter 1988): 101–118.
121. Rachel E. Harding, *A Refuge in Thunder: Candomble and Alternative Spaces* (Bloomington: Indiana University Press, 2003), 98.
122. Tomoko Masuzawa, *The Invention of World Religions: Or, How European Universalism Was Preserved in the Language of Pluralism* (Chicago: University of Chicago Press, 2005).
123. Elizabeth Perez, *Religion in the Kitchen: Cooking, Talking, and the Making of Black Atlantic Traditions* (New York:, New York University Press, 2016).
124. Reginaldo Prandi, "African Gods in Contemporary Brazil: A Sociological Introduction to Candomblé Today," *Ibero-amerikanisches Archiv*, Neue Folge 24, no. 3/4 (1998): 328.
125. Nittle, *Toni Morrison's Spiritual Vision*, 149.
126. Marouan, *Witches, Goddesses, and Angry Spirits*, 101–102.
127. Ean Begg, *The Cult of the Black Virgin* (London: Arkana, 1985); Matgorzata Oleszkiewicz-Peralba, *The Black Madonna in Latin America and Europe: Tradition and Transformation* (Albuquerque: University of New Mexico Press, 2007).
128. Morrison, *Conversations with Richard Wright*, 36.
129. I take the white hegemonic imagination from Emilie M. Townes's argument in *Womanist Ethics and the Cultural Production of Evil* (New York: Palgrave Macmillan, 2006).
130. Morrison, *Source of Self-Regard*, 18.
131. Christopher, "The Geographical Imagination in Toni Morrison's 'Paradise,'" 89.
132. Morrison, *Sources of Self-Regard*, 17.
133. Nittle, *Toni Morrison's Spiritual Vision*, 148.
134. Morrison, "Foreigner's Home," *Sources of Self-Regard*, 19.

3. ADAM AS THE OUTSIDER

1. The "will to power" in Nietzsche's philosophy is how he understands human nature at its most fundamental level, with its drive for mastery, victory, and self-realization, in an amoral universe where religions are used to manipulate people with notions of beauty and the holiness of weakness. Nietzsche's idea becomes a part of the "guilty reading" that changes Wright's protagonist from gleeful to despondent, feeling without any meaning or purpose in the world. For more information see Arthur Schopenhauer, *The World as Will and Representation*, trans. E. F. J. Payne (New York: Dover, 1966); Friedrich Nietzsche, *Thus Spoke Zarathustra: A Book for All and None*, trans. Walter Kaufmann (New York: Modern Library, 1995); Friedrich Nietzsche, *The Will to Power*, ed. Walter Kaufmann and R. J. Hollingdale (New York: Vintage, 1968).
2. For more on Wright and secularism, see Christopher Cameron, *Black Freethinkers: A History of African American Secularism* (Evanston, IL: Northwestern University Press, 2020); for Wright and religion, see Tara T. Green, "'That Preacher's Going to Eat All the Chicken!': Power and Religion in Richard Wright" (PhD diss., Louisiana State University, 2000), 1–2; Jamall A. Calloway, "Wright and Religion," in *Richard Wright in Context*, ed. Michael Nowlin (Cambridge: Cambridge University Press, 2021), 150–160.
3. Richard Wright, "What Are Men to You?," drafts, typescript, corrected, n.d. Box 7, Folder 151, Beinecke Rare Book and Manuscript Library, Yale University.
4. Michael Fabre, *The Unfinished Quest of Richard Wright* (Urbana: University of Illinois Press, 1973), 316.
5. Existentialism is, according to Tommie Shelby, "less a doctrine than a philosophical tendency and literary movement." Existentialist thinkers reflect on a recurring set of themes, starting with recognizing and coming to terms with the fact that "existence comes before essence," as Sartre famously expressed it in "Existentialism Is a Humanism." Both religious and atheist writers thought through and with existentialist categories, and Wright was no stranger to (a)theological claims. Tommie Shelby, "Freedom in a Godless and Unhappy World: Wright as Outsider," in *The Cambridge Companion to Richard*

Wright, ed. Glenda R. Carpio (Cambridge: Cambridge University Press, 2019), 125.
6. In his correspondence with Dorothy Norman, Wright requested her help with Kierkegaard and existentialism overall. Norman introduced him to Paul Tillich and Hannah Arendt in 1944. Jerry W. Ward and Robert Butler, *The Richard Wright Encyclopedia* (Westport, CT: Greenwood Press, 2008), 217; Hazel Rowley, *Richard Wright: The Life and Times* (New York: Henry Holt, 2001), 299.
7. Both Zarathustra and Meursault are literary examples who appear as warnings or examples of the future. And Cross Damon is Wright's version of this template. Hazel Rowley states that Wright read Camus's *The Stranger* "slowly, weighing each sentence," under the trees in the Bois de Boulogne. See Rowley, *Richard Wright*, 362.
8. For Nietzsche, the human as we currently understand it is not the final result, and Zarathustra wishes that he could have been a bridge for man to lead them to their next evolutionary form: the overman. See Nietzsche, *Thus Spoke Zarathustra*.
9. Agreeing with Paul Tillich's lectures in his posthumous *A History of Christian Thought: From Its Judaic and Hellenistic Origins to Existentialism* (1967), where he states that this and *The Sickness unto Death* (published five years after *The Concept of Anxiety*) are the best texts to study when trying to understand Kierkegaard's central themes: sin, anxiety, dread, and despair. Paul Tillich, *A History of Christian Thought: From Its Judaic and Hellenistic Origins to Existentialism*, (New York: Simon and Schuster, 1967), 462.
10. Erik M. Hanson, "Augustine, Kierkegaard, and Evil," in *Augustine and Kierkegaard*, ed. John Doody, Kim Paffenroth, and Helene Russel (Lanham, MD: Lexington Books, 2017), 46.
11. Hanson, "Augustine, Kierkegaard, and Evil," 46.
12. Niels Jørgen Cappelørn, "The Interpretation of Hereditary Sin in 'The Concept of Anxiety' by Kierkegaard's Pseudonym Vigilius Haufniesis," *Tijdschrift voor Filosofie* 72, no. 1 (2010): 137.
13. The Kierkegaardian phrase "qualitative leap" basically means an alteration from one state of being to another: disbelief to salvation, innocence to sinfulness. It is described as a leap to avoid a connotation or connection to rational thinking. It is akin to a move without thinking

or a move that avoids thinking. The leap is made by paradoxically accepting that the leap may defy reason.

14. Gregory R. Beabout, *Freedom and Its Misuses: Kierkegaard on Anxiety and Despair* (Milwaukee, WI: Marquette University Press, 1996), 36.
15. Søren Kierkegaard, *The Concept of Anxiety: A Simple Psychologically Orienting Deliberation on the Dogmatic Issue of Hereditary Sin*, trans. Alastair Hannay (New York: Liveright Press, 2014), 40.
16. Kierkegaard, *The Concept of Anxiety*, 26.
17. Kierkegaard, *The Concept of Anxiety*, 14.
18. Following Lee C. Barrett, I do not draw a sharp distinction between Saint Augustine and Kierkegaard. Kierkegaard shares several commonalities with Augustinian (and Lutheran) theology. His approach, however, was a result of asking some different questions related to the Genesis account. For example, Barrett states that Kierkegaard—via Vigilius—"uncoupled the 'What is my identity?' question from the 'Why and how did I become a sinner?' question." See Lee C. Barrett, *Eros and Self-Emptying: The Intersections of Augustine and Kierkegaard* (Grand Rapids, MI: William B. Eerdmans, 2013), 234.
19. Kierkegaard, *The Concept of Anxiety*, 54.
20. George Pattison, *The Philosophy of Kierkegaard* (Montreal: McGill-Queen's University Press, 2005), 53.
21. Pattison, *The Philosophy of Kierkegaard*, 55
22. Pattinson, *The Philosophy of Kierkegaard*, 53.
23. Jean-Paul Sartre, *Existentialism Is Humanism*, trans. Carol Macomber (1946; reprint, New Haven, CT: Yale University Press, 2007).
24. Michael Fabre, "Richard Wright, French Existentialism, and *The Outsider*," in *The World of Richard Wright* (Jackson: University of Mississippi Press, 1985).
25. Richard Wright, *The Outsider* (New York: Harper & Brothers, 1953), 29.
26. Margaret Walker, *Richard Wright: Daemonic Genius* (New York: HarperCollins, 2000), 230–238.
27. See Lewis Gordon, "Bigger–Cross Damon: Wright's Existential Challenge," in *Philosophical Meditations on Richard Wright*, ed. James B. Haile III (Lanham, MD: Lexington Books, 2012), 3–21.

3. ADAM AS THE OUTSIDER   245

28. Richard Wright, *Black Boy: A Record of Childhood and Youth* (1945; reprint, New York: Harper, 2020), 155.
29. I delve more deeply into this topic in Jamall A. Calloway, "Wright and Religion," in *Richard Wright in Context*, ed. Michael Nowlin (Cambridge: Cambridge University Press, 2021), 150–160.
30. Wright, *The Outsider*, 389.
31. Wright, *The Outsider*, 389.
32. Wright, *The Outsider*, 389.
33. The use of memory also points to a Kierkegaardian idea because in *Either/Or* he posits that love that "lives in memory" is the only happiness there is. Søren Kierkegaard, *Either, Or* (Princeton, NJ: Princeton University Press, 1987), 55.
34. Wright, *The Outsider*, 386.
35. Wright, *The Outsider*, 389.
36. Wright, *The Outsider*, 29.
37. Nicodemus's confusion also stems from a double entendre in the original koine Greek. The Johannine writer also implies that Nicodemus is confused about whether a person is born again or born from above.
38. Claudia Tate gestures toward the gory atmosphere of this section and how it mirrors a birthing process. See Claudia C. Tate, "Christian Existentialism in The Outsider," in Henry Louis Gates, Jr., and Anthony Appiah, *Richard Wright: Critical Perspectives Past and Present* (New York: Amistad, 1983), 377.
39. Jennifer Elisa Veninga, "Richard Wright: Kierkegaard's Influence as Existentialist Outsider," in *Kierkegaard Research: Sources, Reception and Resources, Volume 14: Kierkegaard's Influence on Social-Political Thought*, ed. Jon Stewart (London: Routledge, 2016), 264.
40. LL Lawson, Lewis A. "Cross Damon: The Kierkegaardian Man of Dread," *CLA Journal* 14 (1971): 291–298.
41. Lawson, "Cross Damon."
42. Tommie Shelby, "Freedom in a Godless and Unhappy World," 130.
43. Eberhard Alsen, " 'Towards the Living Sun': Richard Wright's Change of Heart from *The Outsider* to *The Long Dream*," *CLA Journal* 38, no. 2 (1994): 215.
44. Wright, *The Outsider*, 494.
45. Wright, *The Outsider*, 494.

46. For Jean-Paul Sartre, "Bad Faith" is the existentialist crime of denying one's own freedom. A person does so to circumvent the responsibilities associated with the freedom. It is a form of self-deception that suggests believing in the lack of freedom in a given moment is easier than accepting one's freedom and facing the consequences of someone's actions and choices. Sometimes the consequences are displaying bravery, defending oneself, or saying no to one's boss. Jean-Paul Sartre, *Being and Nothingness: An Essay on Phenomenological Ontology*, trans. Sarah Richmond (New York: Washington Square Press, 2021), 86–113.
47. Wright, *The Outsider*, 494.
48. Wright, *The Outsider*, 494.
49. Richard Wright, *Black Power: Three Books from Exile: Black Power, the Color Curtain, and White Man, Listen!* (New York: Harper Perennial Modern Classics, 2008), 651.
50. Wright, *Black Power*, 661.
51. Sandra Adell, "Richard Wright's Outsider and the Kierkegaardian Concept of Dread," *Comparative Literature Studies* 28, no. 4 (1991): 386.
52. Wright, *The Outsider*, 164.
53. This representation of Eva furthers a popular feminist analysis of Wright's work, that Wright consistently presents white women characters as soft and innocent while black women in his works mostly reflect an antagonist position. Tara Green, Maria Mootry, Claudia Tate, Margaret Walker, and other critics see Wright as invested in portraying a symbolic connection between his white American and European women characters through the imagery of the Virgin Mary. I am arguing for something similar but not necessarily through Mary. In *The Outsider*, Wright presents Eva as an innocent and oblivious Eve. See Tara T. Green, "The Virgin Mary, Eve, and Mary Magdalene in Richard Wright's Novels," *CLA Journal* 46, no. 2 (2002): 168–193.
54. Wright, *The Outsider*, 589.
55. Wright, *The Outsider*, 589.
56. Wright, *The Outsider*, 589.
57. Wright, *The Outsider*, 591.
58. Jane Davis, "More Force Than Human: Richard Wright's Female Characters," *Obsidian II* 1, no. 3 (Winter 1986): 68–83.
59. Wright, *The Outsider*, 616.

3. ADAM AS THE OUTSIDER ⌘ 247

60. Wright, *The Outsider*, 616.
61. Wright, *The Outsider*, 618.
62. Wright, *The Outsider*, 822.
63. Shelby, "Freedom in a Godless and Unhappy World," 127.
64. Wright, *The Outsider*, 830.
65. Wright, *The Outsider*, 830.
66. Shelby, "Freedom in a Godless and Unhappy World," 130.
67. Shelby, "Freedom in a Godless and Unhappy World," 130.
68. Reinhold Niebuhr, *The Nature and Destiny of Man: A Christian Interpretation*, Vol. 1: Human Nature (Louisville, KY: Westminster John Knox Press, 1996), 181.
69. Wright, *The Outsider*, 830.
70. Cedric Robinson, *Black Marxism: The Making of the Black Radical Tradition* (Chapel Hill: University of North Carolina Press, 2000), 301.
71. Wright, *Black Power*, 656.
72. See James H. Cone, *The Cross and the Lynching Tree* (New York: Orbis), 2014.
73. James Baldwin, "Everybody's Protest Novel," in *Notes of a Native Son* (Boston: Beacon Press, 2012), 23.
74. Shelby, "Freedom in a Godless and Unhappy World," 125.
75. Lewis Gordon, "Bigger–Cross Damon: Wright's Existential Challenge," in *Philosophical Meditations on Richard Wright*, ed. James B. Haile, III (Lanham, MD: Lexington Books, 2012), 3–22.
76. Rowley, *Richard Wright*, 409.
77. James Campbell, *Exiled in Paris: Richard Wright, James Baldwin, Samuel Beckett, and Others on the Left Bank* (Berkeley: University of California Press, 2003), 93.
78. Rowley, *Richard Wright*, 409.
79. Shelby, "Freedom in a Godless and Unhappy World," 130.
80. James Baldwin, *Notes of a Native Son* (Boston: Beacon Press, 1955), 23.
81. *Conversations with Richard Wright*, ed. Kenneth Kinnamon and Michel Fabre (Jackson: University Press of Mississippi, 1993), 158.
82. Jane Anna Gordon and Cyrus Ernesto Zirakzadeh, eds., *The Politics of Richard Wright: Perspectives on Resistance* (Lexington: University Press of Kentucky, 2019), 330.

4. THE SERPENT/LILITH'S LIBERATION THEOLOGY

1. Tara Tuttle explores not only Morrison's *Paradise* but also Walker's *The Color Purple*. "Biting Temptation: An Examination of the Eden Myth in the Southern Fiction of William Faulkner, Alice Walker, and Toni Morrison" (PhD diss., University of Louisville, 2008).
2. While talking to Sharon Wilson about what inspired the story of the novel, Walker says that she imagined Sojourner Truth speaking directly to God about her children being sold. "A Conversation with Alice Walker," *Kalliope* 6 (1984): 44. Republished in *Alice Walker: Critical Perspectives Past and Present*, ed. Henry L. Gates, Jr. (New York: Amistad, 1993), 319–325.
3. For more on the idea of slavery persisting after emancipation see Ary Syamanad Jahir, "Gender Violence in Toni Morrison's *The Bluest Eye* and Alice Walker's *The Color Purple*," *Journal of Language and Literature Education* 11 (2014); Megan Munger, "An Aftershock of American Slavery: Violence Against Black Women in Toni Morrison's *Beloved*, Zora Neale Hurston's *Their Eyes Were Watching God*, and Alice Walker's *The Color Purple*," *Midwest Quarterly*, January 1, 2023.
4. Walker continues their story in the following novel, *The Temple of My Familiar* (1989).
5. I use this term instead of "tribes" in light of something I read from Marius Kothur, from John J. Gumperz and Dell Hymes, eds., *Directions in Sociolinguistics: The Ethnography of Communication* (New York: Holt, Rinehart and Winston, 1972).
6. Eboni Marshall Turman details wonderfully the history of how Katie Cannon, Jacqueline Grant, and Delores Williams adopted Walker's theory of womanism for womanist theology. Eboni Marshall Turman, "Black Women's Wisdom: Womanist Theology and How It Has Evolved," *The Christian Century* 136, no. 6 (2019): 30–34.
7. Gloria Steinem, "Do You Know This Woman? She Knows You," *Ms.* (June 1982): 36+.
8. Trudier Harris, "On *The Color Purple*, Stereotypes, and Silence," *Black American Literature Forum* 18, no. 4 (1984): 155–161.
9. Delores Williams, "The Color Purple," *Christianity and Crisis* 46, no. 10 (July 4, 1986): 230.

4. THE SERPENT/LILITH'S LIBERATION THEOLOGY ᛰ 249

10. Mary Daly, *Beyond God the Father: Toward a Philosophy of Women's Liberation* (Boston: Beacon Press, 1973).
11. Pamela B. June, *Solidarity with the Other Beings on the Planet: Alice Walker, Ecofeminism, and Animals in Literature* (Evanston, IL: Northwestern University Press, 2020), 118.
12. Saint Irenaeus argues in *Against Heresies* that it was the devil who used the serpent to deceive Eve. Irenaeus, *Against Heresies*, book 5, chap. 23, in *Ante-Nicene Fathers*, Vol. 1, ed. Alexander Roberts and James Donaldson, trans. A. Cleveland Coxe (Buffalo, NY: Christian Literature Publishing Co., 1885).
13. The Hebrew translation of "crafty" is *'arum* and gestures toward being wise.
14. John F.A. Sawyer, "The Image of God, the Wisdom of Serpents and the Knowledge of Good and Evil," in *A Walk in the Garden: Biblical, Iconographical and Literary Images of Eden*, ed. Paul Morris and Deborah Sawyer, (London: Bloomsbury, 1992), 66.
15. John J. Collins invokes the Greek myth of Prometheus, who steals fire from the gods, and Enkidu in the *Epic of Gilgamesh*, who kills the bull of Heaven (*A Short Introduction to the Hebrew Bible, Third Edition* [Minneapolis: Fortress Press, 2018], 72). "The idea that gods jealously guard their superiority over humanity is widespread in the ancient world."
16. Genesis 3: 14–17 (NRSV).
17. 2nd Corinthians 11:3 (NRSV).
18. Augustine, *The City of God Against the Pagans*, trans. R. W. Dyson (Cambridge: Cambridge University Press, 1998), Book 14, Chapter 11.
19. The Book of Revelations calls the serpent Satan in chapters 12:9 and 20:2 (NRSV).
20. Sawyer, "The Image of God, the Wisdom of Serpents and the Knowledge of Good and Evil," 67.
21. Ivone Gebara, "The Face of Transcendence as a Challenge to the Reading of the Bible in Latin America," in *Searching the Scriptures, Volume One: A Feminist Introduction*, ed. Elisabeth Schüssler Fiorenza (New York: Crossroad, 1993), 172–186.
22. Ivone Gebara, *Out of the Depths: Women's Experience of Evil and Salvation* (Minneapolis: Fortress Press, 2002), 8.

23. Gebara, *Out of the Depths*, 174.
24. Gebara, *Out of the Depths*, 174.
25. Gebara, *Out of the Depths*, 174.
26. Gebara, *Out of the Depths*, 174.
27. Karen Teel focuses on how five different Womanist theologians explore the image of God through theological anthropology. See Karen Teel, *Racism and the Image of God* (New York: Palgrave Macmillan US, 2010).
28. Gebara, *Out of the Depths*, 175.
29. James H. Cone, *God of the Oppressed* (Maryknoll, NY: Orbis, 1974).
30. Gebara, *Out of the Depths*, 175.
31. Gebara, *Out of the Depths*, 175.
32. Gebara, *Out of the Depths*, 175.
33. Book of Judith, *The Holy Bible, New Revised Standard Version* (New York: Oxford University Press, 1989).
34. Gebara, *Out of the Depths*, 175.
35. Gebara, *Out of the Depths*, 175.
36. Gebara, *Out of the Depths*, 178.
37. Gebara, *Out of the Depths*, 178.
38. These questions can be added to the list of questions given by James H. Charlesworth in *The Good and Evil Serpent: How a Universal Symbol Became Christianized* (New Haven, CT, and London: Yale University Press, 2010), 175.
39. Gebara, *Out of the Depths*, 179
40. Celie prays to God to smite the people who hurt Sofia.
41. Alice Walker, *The Color Purple* (New York: Penguin, 1982), 191.
42. Walker, *The Color Purple*, 191.
43. Walker, *The Color Purple*, 191.
44. Walker, *The Color Purple*, 192
45. Thomas F. Marvin, "'Preachin' the Blues': Bessie Smith's Secular Religion and Alice Walker's *The Color Purple*." *African American Review* 28, no. 3 (1994): 411–421.
46. Angela Y. Davis, *Blues Legacies and Black Feminism: Gertrude "Ma" Rainey, Bessie Smith, and Billie Holiday* (New York: Pantheon, 1998).
47. Walker, *The Color Purple*, 192.
48. Walker, *The Color Purple*, 192.

49. Alice Walker, *Anything We Love Can Be Saved: A Writer's Activism* (New York: Penguin Random House, 1997), 25.
50. Walker, *Anything We Love Can Be Saved*, 25.
51. Max Weber, *The Protestant Ethic and the Spirit of Capitalism*, trans. Talcott Parsons, intro. Anthony Giddens (New York: Routledge, 2001).
52. James 2:14–17, (NRSV).
53. James 2:14–17.
54. James 2:14–17.
55. Emilie Townes, *Womanist Ethics and the Cultural Production of Evil* (New York: Palgrave Macmillan, 2006).
56. Alice Walker, *In Search of Our Mothers' Gardens: Womanist Prose* (New York: Harcourt Brace Jovanovich, 1983), 18.
57. Ivone Gebara, *Longing for Running Water: Ecofeminism and Liberation* (New York: Fortress Press, 1999), 27.
58. Walker, *The Color Purple*, 193.
59. Walker, *The Color Purple*, 194.
60. Walker, *The Color Purple*, 194.
61. Walker, *The Color Purple*, 194.
62. Walker, *The Color Purple*, 194.
63. Karmen MacKendrick, *Divine Enticement: Theological Seductions* (New York: Fordham University Press, 2013).
64. Gebara, *Longing for Running Water*, 23.
65. Sallie McFague, *The Body of God: An Ecological Theology* (Minneapolis: Fortress Press, 1993).
66. Walker, *The Color Purple*, 195.
67. Walker, *The Color Purple*, 195.
68. Walker, *The Color Purple*, 195.
69. Walker, *The Color Purple*, 196.
70. Tuttle, "Biting Temptation," 114.
71. Walker, *The Color Purple*, preface.
72. Walker, *The Color Purple*, preface.
73. Walker, *The Color Purple*, preface.
74. Walker, *The Color Purple*, preface.
75. McFague, *The Body of God*.
76. For Coleman, Whiteheadian metaphysics and African Traditional Religions (ATR) offer noteworthy and necessary alterations to the ways

we fundamentally understand the reality in which Black women find themselves. These alterations will extend the arms of womanist thought and invite Black women whose experiences cannot and should not be enclosed in heteronormative Christian doctrines and language. To Coleman, there are several underlying issues with Womanist theology that a postmodern framework and process metaphysic could help revise. I will outline the underlying conundrums: 1) The sole reliance on a certain kind of Black woman's experience without an overarching metaphysic that can include Black women who have essentially different experiences and 2) the dominant connection of Jesus with Christ and thus with God. For Coleman, the conflation of Jesus of Nazareth, the Cosmic Christ, and God has excluded too many Black women who do not see Jesus as God or Christianity as the particular (or only) religious tradition for them.

77. Monica Coleman, *Making a Way Out of No Way: A Womanist Theology* (Minneapolis: Fortress Press, 2008), 45.
78. Samuel N. Kramer, *Gilgamesh and the Huluppu-Tree: A Reconstructed Sumerian Text* (Chicago: University of Chicago Press, 1938), 6.
79. Lilith, requested by the angels to return to Eden, passionately refuses. The angels try to drown her in the sea to prevent her from harming children, but Lilith declares that if the home has an amulet with her name, she will spare them.
80. Walker, *The Color Purple*, 120.
81. Walker, *The Color Purple*, 117.
82. Walker, *The Color Purple*, 127.
83. Walker, *The Color Purple*, 130.
84. Walker, *The Color Purple*, 131.
85. Walker, *The Color Purple*, 131.
86. Walker, *The Color Purple*, 132.
87. Walker, *The Color Purple*, 132.
88. Judith Weisenfeld, *New World A-Coming: Black Religion and Racial Identity During the Great Migration* (New York: New York University Press, 2017), 122.
89. Robbie Shilliam, " 'Ethiopia shall stretch forth her hands unto God': Garveyism, Rastafari, and Antiquity," in *African Athena: New Agendas, Classical Presences*, ed. Daniel Orrells, Gurminder K. Bhambra,

and Tessa Roynon (Oxford: Oxford University Press, 2011); Roy Kay, *The Ethiopian Prophecy in Black American Letters* (Gainesville: University Press of Florida, 2011).
90. Walker, *The Color Purple*, 139.
91. Walker, *The Color Purple*, 139.
92. Walker, *The Color Purple*, 152.
93. Walker, *The Color Purple*, 154.
94. Walker, *The Color Purple*, 170.
95. Walker, *The Color Purple*, 227–228.
96. Walker, *The Color Purple*, 257.
97. Walker, *The Color Purple*, 257.
98. Walker, *The Color Purple*, 273.
99. Genesis 3: 6–1, (NRSV).
100. Walker, *The Color Purple*, 274.
101. Walker, *The Color Purple*, 274.
102. Walker, *The Color Purple*, 275.
103. Alice Walker, *Anything We Love Can Be Saved: A Writer's Activism* (New Yor; Penguin Random House, 1997), 13.
104. Walker, *Anything We Love Can Be Saved*, 25.
105. Walker, *The Color Purple*, 195.
106. Walker, *The Color Purple*, 14.

CODA

1. Lucille Clifton, "Brothers," *The Book of Light* (Port Townsend, WA: Copper Canyon Press, 1993), 69. Clifton wrote many poems influenced by the Bible and the book of Genesis in particular. "Brothers" is one that spoke to me that I could not let go of.

WORKS CITED

Adell, Sandra. "Richard Wright's Outsider and the Kierkegaardian Concept of Dread." *Comparative Literature Studies* 28, no. 4 (1991): 379–394.
Alsen, Eberhard. "'Toward the Living Sun': Richard Wright's Change of Heart from the Outsider to the Long Dream." *CLA Journal* 38 (1992): 211–227.
Armour, Robert. "'Deliverance' Four Variations of the American Adam." *Literature/Film Quarterly* 1, no. 3 (1973): 280–285.
Ary Syamanad, Tahir. "Gender Violence in Toni Morrison's *The Bluest Eye* and Alice Walker's *The Color Purple*." *Kayseri: Journal of Language and Literature Education* 3, no. 16 (2012).
Augustine. *The City of God Against the Pagans*. Trans. R. W. Dyson. Cambridge: Cambridge University Press, 1998.
Augustine. *On Genesis: Two Books on Genesis Against the Manichees; And, On the Literal Interpretation of Genesis: An Unfinished Book*. Trans. Roland J. Teske. Washington, DC: Catholic University of America Press, 2010.
Augustine. *On Merit and the Forgiveness of Sins, and the Baptism of Infants*. In *Nicene and Post-Nicene Fathers, First Series, Volume V: St. Augustine—Anti-Pelagian Writings*, ed. Philip Schaff, 15–88. Buffalo, NY: Christian Literature Publishing Co., 1887.
Augustine. *On Nature and Grace*. Trans. Peter Holmes. Münster: Cervantes Digital, 2024.
Augustine. *Sermons on Selected Lessons of the New Testament (1844)*. Vol. 1, ca. 392–430. Trans. R. G. MacMullen. Oxford: John Henry Parker, 2018.

Augustine. *St. Augustine on Marriage and Sexuality*. Ed. Elizabeth A. Clark. Washington, DC: Catholic University of America Press, 1996.

Baden, Joel S. *The Composition of the Pentateuch*. New Haven, CT: Yale University Press, 2012.

Badiou, Alain. *Saint Paul*. Stanford, CA: Stanford University Press, 2003.

Baldwin, James. *Collected Essays*. New York: Library of America, 1998.

———. *Giovanni's Room*. New York: Dial, 1956.

Barr, James. *The Garden of Eden and the Hope of Immortality*. Eugene, OR: Wipf and Stock, 2003.

Barrett, Lee C. *Eros and Self-Emptying: The Intersections of Augustine and Kierkegaard*. Grand Rapids, MI: William B. Eerdmans, 2013.

Barth, Karl. *The Epistle to the Romans*. 2nd ed. Trans. Edwyn Clement Hoskyns 1922; reprint, London and New York: Oxford University Press, 1968.

Barton, John. *A History of the Bible: The Book and Its Faiths*. London: Penguin, 2020.

Begg, Ean. *Cult of the Black Virgin*. London: Arkana Press, 2013.

Beker, Johan Christiaan. *Paul's Apocalyptic Gospel*. Minneapolis: Fortress Press, 1982.

Bennett, Joshua. *Being Property Once Myself: Blackness and the End of Man*. Cambridge, MA: The Belknap Press of Harvard University Press, 2020.

Bowens, Lisa M. *African American Readings of Paul: Reception, Resistance, and Transformation*. Grand Rapids, MI: William B. Eerdmans,, 2020.

Boyd, Herb. *Baldwin's Harlem*. Portland, OR: Beyond Words/Atria Books, 2008.

Brim, Matt. *James Baldwin and the Queer Imagination*. Ann Arbor: University of Michigan Press, 2014.

Brown, Peter. *Augustine of Hippo: A Biography*. New edition with an epilogue. Berkeley: University of California Press, 2000.

Brown, Raymond E. *An Introduction to the New Testament: The Abridged Edition*. Ed. Marion L. Soards. New Haven, CT: Yale University Press, 2016.

Cameron, Christopher. *Black Freethinkers: A History of African American Secularism*. Evanston, IL: Northwestern University Press, 2020.

Campbell, James. *Exiled in Paris: Richard Wright, James Baldwin, Samuel Beckett and Others on the Left Bank*. Berkeley: University of California Press, 2003.

———. *Talking at the Gates: A Life of James Baldwin: With a New Afterword*. Berkeley: University of California Press, 2002.

Cappelørn, Niels Jørgen. "The Interpretation of Hereditary Sin in the Concept of Anxiety by Kierkegaard's Pseudonym Vigilius Haufniensis." *Tijdschrift Voor Filosofie* 72, no. 1 (March 31, 2010): 131–146.

Carpio, Glenda. *The Cambridge Companion to Richard Wright*. Cambridge; New York: Cambridge University Press, 2019.

Carr, David McLain. *The Erotic Word: Sexuality, Spirituality, and the Bible*. New York; Oxford: Oxford University Press, 2005.

Carrasco, David, et al. *Toni Morrison: Goodness and the Literary Imagination*. Charlottesville: University of Virginia Press, 2019.

Charlesworth, James Hamilton. *The Good and Evil Serpent: How a Universal Symbol Became Christianized*. New Haven, CT: Yale University Press, 2010.

Chireau, Yvonne Patricia. *Black Magic Religion and the African American Conjuring Tradition*. Berkeley: University of California Press, 2006.

Christopher, Lindy. "The Geographical Imagination in Toni Morrison's 'Paradise.'" *Rocky Mountain Review* 63, no. 1 (2009): 89–95.

Clayton, Paul B. *The Christology of Theodoret of Cyrus: Antiochene Christology from the Council of Ephesus (431) to the Council of Chalcedon (451)*. Oxford: Oxford University Press, 2007.

Clifton, Lucille. *The Book of Light*. Port Townsend, WA: Copper Canyon Press, 1993.

Coleman, Monica A. *Making a Way out of No Way: A Womanist Theology*. Minneapolis: Fortress Press, 2008.

Collins, John J. *A Short Introduction to the Hebrew Bible, Third Edition*. Minneapolis: Fortress Press, 2018.

Cone, James H. *The Cross and the Lynching Tree*. Maryknoll, NY: Orbis Books, 2011.

———. *God of the Oppressed*. Maryknoll, NY: Orbis Books, 1975.

Conner, Robert. *Magic in the New Testament: A Survey and Appraisal of the Evidence*. Oxford: Mandrake of Oxford, 2010.

Copeland, M. Shawn. *Enfleshing Freedom*. Minneapolis: Fortress Press, 2010.

Crawley, Ashon T. *The Lonely Letters*. Durham, NC: Duke University Press, 2020.

Daly, Mary. *Beyond God the Father: Toward a Philosophy of Women's Liberation*. Boston: Beacon Press, 1973.

Davis, Angela Y. *Blues Legacies and Black Feminism*. New York: Vintage, 2011.

Davis, Jane. "More Force than Human: Richard Wright's Female Characters." *Obsidian II* 1, no. 3 (1986): 68–83.

De, Felipe. *The Figure of Adam in Romans 5 and 1 Corinthians 15: The New Creation and Its Ethical and Social Reconfiguration*. Minneapolis: Fortress Press, 2014.

Derrida, Jacques. "Faith and Knowledge : The Two Sources of 'Religion' at the Limits of Reason Alone." In *Religion*, ed. Jacques Derrida and Gianni Vattimo, 1–78. Stanford, CA: Stanford University Press, 1998.

Edelman, Lee. *No Future: Queer Theory and the Death Drive*. Durham, NC: Duke University Press, 2004.

Ellis, Teresa Ann. "Is Eve the 'Woman' in Sirach 25:24?" *Catholic Biblical Quarterly* 4, no. 73 (2011).

Fabre, Michel. *The Unfinished Quest of Richard Wright*. Urbana: University of Illinois Press, 1993.

———. *The World of Richard Wright*. Jackson: University of Mississippi Press, 1985.

Fiorenza, Elisabeth Schüssler, and Shelly Matthews. *Searching the Scriptures: A Feminist Introduction*. New York: Crossroad, 1993.

Foucault, Michel. *Confessions of the Flesh: The History of Sexuality, Volume 4*. Trans. Robert Hurley. New York: Knopf Doubleday, 2022.

———. *The Use of Pleasure: Volume 2 of the History of Sexuality*. Trans. Robert Hurley. New York: Vintage, 1990.

Fredriksen, Paula. *From Jesus to Christ: The Origins of the New Testament Images of Christ*. New Haven, CT: Yale University Press, 2000.

Furman, Jan. *Toni Morrison's Fiction, Revised and Expanded Edition*. Columbia: University of South Carolina Press, 2014.

Gates, Henry Louis, Jr., and Anthony Appiah. *Alice Walker: Critical Perspectives Past and Present*. New York: Amistad, 1993.

———. *Richard Wright: Critical Perspectives Past and Present*. New York: Amistad, 1983.

Gauthier, Marni. "The Other Side of Paradise: Toni Morrison's (Un) Making of Mythic History." *African American Review* 39, no. 3 (2005): 395–414.

Gebara, Ivone. *Longing for Running Water*. Minneapolis: Fortress Press, 1999.

———. *Out of the Depths*. Minneapolis: Fortress Press, 2002.

Gibson, Ernest L. *Salvific Manhood: James Baldwin's Novelization of Male Intimacy*. Lincoln: University of Nebraska Press, 2019.

Gilroy, Paul. *Postcolonial Melancholia*. New York: Columbia University Press, 2005.

Giorgio Agamben. *The Kingdom and the Garden*. London, Seagull Books, 2020.

Glenn, Evelyn Nakano. *Shades of Difference: Why Skin Color Matters*. Stanford, CA: Stanford University Press, 2009.

González, Justo L. *The Story of Christianity: The Early Church to the Reformation*. Vol. 1. New York: HarperOne, 2010.

Gordon, Jane Anna, and Cyrus Ernesto Zirakzadeh. *The Politics of Richard Wright: Perspectives on Resistance*. Lexington: The University Press of Kentucky, 2018.

Green, Tara. "The Virgin Mary, Eve, and Mary Magdalene in Richard Wright's Novels." *CLA Journal* 46, no. 2 (2002): 168–193.

Green, Tara T. "'That Preacher's Going to Eat All the Chicken!': Power and Religion in Richard Wright." PhD diss., Louisiana State University (LSU Historical Dissertations and Theses 7324). 2000.

Greenblatt, Stephen. *The Rise and Fall of Adam and Eve*. New York: Norton, 2017.

Haile, James B. *Philosophical Meditations on Richard Wright*. Lanham, MD: Lexington Books, 2014.

Halberstam, Jack. *The Queer Art of Failure*. Durham, NC: Duke University Press, 2011.

Harding, Rachel E. *A Refuge in Thunder: Candomble and Alternative Spaces*. Bloomington: Indiana University Press, 2003.

Hardy, Clarence E. *James Baldwin's God: Sex, Hope, and the Crises of Black Holiness Culture*. Knoxville: University of Tennessee Press, 2003.

Harris, Trudier. "On *The Color Purple*, Stereotypes, and Silence." *Black American Literature Forum* 18, no. 4 (1984): 155–161.

Hartman, Saidiya. *Wayward Lives, Beautiful Experiments: Intimate Histories of Riotous Black Girls, Troublesome Women, and Queer Radicals*. New York: Norton, 2020.

Herskovits, Melville J. "The Social Organization of the Afrobrazilian Candomble." *Phylon (1940–1956)* 17, no. 2 (1956): 147.

Hobson, Christopher Z. *James Baldwin and the Heavenly City*. East Lansing: Michigan State University Press, 2018.

Hwang, Alexander Y., et al. *Grace for Grace: The Debates after Augustine and Pelagius*. Washington, DC: Catholic University of America Press, 2014.

June, Pamela B. *Solidarity with the Other Beings on the Planet*. Evanston, IL: Northwestern University Press, 2020.

Kay, Roy. *The Ethiopian Prophecy in Black American Letters*. Gainesville: University of Florida Press, 2011.

Kierkegaard, Søren. *The Concept of Anxiety: A Simple Psychologically Orienting Deliberation on the Dogmatic Issue of Hereditary Sin*. Trans. Alastair Hannay. New York, Liveright, 2015.

Knibb, Michael Anthony. *The Ethiopic Book of Enoch*. New York: Oxford University Press, 1978.

Kramer, Samuel. *Gilgamesh and the Huluppu-Tree: A Reconstructed Sumerian Text*. Chicago:, University of Chicago Press, 1938.

Lawson, Lewis A. "Cross Damon: Kierkegaardian Man of Dread." *CLA Journal* 14, no. 3 (1971): 298–316.

Leeming, David. *James Baldwin: A Biography*. New York:, Arcade, 2015.

Lenka, Karfíková, and Markéta Janebová. *Grace and the Will according to Augustine*. Leiden: Brill, 2012.

Lewis, Richard W. B. *The American Adam: Innocence, Tragedy and Tradition in the Nineteenth Century*. Chicago: University of Chicago Press, 2001.

Long, Charles H. *Significations: Signs, Symbols, and Images in the Interpretation of Religion*. Aurora, IL: Davies Group, 1999.

Mackendrick, Karmen. *Divine Enticement: Theological Seductions*. New York: Fordham University Press, 2013.

Marouan, Maha. *Witches, Goddesses, and Angry Spirits: The Politics of Spiritual Liberation in African Diaspora Women's Fiction*. Columbus: Ohio State University Press, 2013.

Martin, Dale B. *The Corinthian Body*. New Haven, CT: Yale University Press, 1999.

Marvin, Thomas F. "'Preachin' the Blues': Bessie Smith's Secular Religion and Alice Walker's *The Color Purple*." *African American Review* 28, no. 3 (1994): 411.

Masuzawa, Tomoko. *The Invention of World Religions: Or How European Universalism Was Preserved in the Language of Pluralism*. Chicago: University of Chicago Press, 2007.

Matory, James Lorand. *Black Atlantic Religion: Tradition, Transnationalism, and Matriarchy in the Afro-Brazilian Candomblé*. Princeton, NJ: Princeton University Press, 2005.

McGuckin, John Anthony. *The Eastern Orthodox Church*. New Haven, CT: Yale University Press, 2020.

Meconi, David Vincent, and Eleonore Stump. *The Cambridge Companion to Augustine*. Cambridge: Cambridge University Press, 2014.

Meeks, Wayne A. *The Writings of St. Paul: A Norton Critical Edition: Annotated Text Criticism*. New York: Norton, 1972.

Meyers, Carol. *Rediscovering Eve: Ancient Israelite Women in Context*. New York: Oxford University Press, 2013,

Morris, Paul, and Deborah Sawyer. *A Walk in the Garden*. Sheffield: A&C Black, 1992.

Morrison, Toni. *Paradise*. New York: Knopf, 1998.

———. *The Source of Self-Regard: Selected Essays, Speeches, and Meditations*. New York, Knopf, 2019.

———. *Toni Morrison: Goodness and the Literary Imagination: Harvard's 95th Ingersoll Lecture with Essays on Morrison's Moral and Religious Vision*. Ed. David Carrasco, Stephanie Paulsell, and Mara Williard. Charlottesville: University of Virginia Press, 2019.

Mullen, Bill. *James Baldwin: Living in Fire*. London: Pluto Press, 2019.

Müller, Manuela Rodrigues, et al. "The Woman Who Chose the Terreiro: Lay Care and Medical Landscapes in Mental Health Care in Rio de Janeiro." *Anthropology & Medicine* 29, no. 4 (December 20, 2022): 351–366.

Muñoz, José Esteban. *Cruising Utopia: The Then and There of Queer Futurity*. New York: New York University Press, 2009.

Myscofski, Carol A. "Women's Initiation Rites in Afro-Brazilian Religions: A Structural Source Analysis." *Journal of Ritual Studies* 2, no. 1 (1998): 101–118.

Niebuhr, Reinhold. *The Nature and Destiny of Man: A Christian Interpretation*. 1953. Louisville, KY: Westminster John Knox Press, 1996.

Nittle, Nadra. *Toni Morrison's Spiritual Vision: Faith, Folktales, and Feminism in Her Life and Literature*. Minneapolis: Fortress Press, 2021.

Nowlin, Michael. *Richard Wright in Context*. Cambridge: Cambridge University Press, 2021.

Oleszkiewicz-Peralba, Małgorzata. *The Black Madonna in Latin America and Europe: Tradition and Transformation*. Albuquerque: University of New Mexico Press, 2007.

Paffenroth, Kim, et al. *Augustine and Kierkegaard*. Lanham, MD: Lexington Books, 2017.

Painter, Nell Irvin. *Exodusters: Black Migration to Kansas After Reconstruction*. New York: Norton, 1992.

Papadogiannakis, Yannis. *Christianity and Hellenism in the Fifth-Century Greek East: Theodoret's Apologetics against the Greeks in Context*. Hellenic Studies Series 49. Washington, DC: Center for Hellenic Studies, 2013.

Parés, Luis Nicolau. *The Formation of Candomblé*. Chapel Hill: University of North Carolina Press, 2013.

Pattison, George. *The Philosophy of Kierkegaard*. London: Routledge, 2015.

Pelagius, and Theodore De Bruyn. *Pelagius's Commentary on St. Paul's Epistle to the Romans: Translated with Introduction and Notes*. Oxford; New York: Clarendon Press, 1998.

Plimpton, George. "Maya Angelou, the Art of Fiction No. 119." *Www.theparisreview.org*, 1990. www.theparisreview.org/interviews/2279/the-art-of-fiction-no-119-maya-angelou.

Prandi, Reginaldo. "African Gods in Contemporary Brazil." *International Sociology* 15, no. 4 (2000): 641–663.

Raboteau, Albert J. *Slave Religion: The "Invisible Institution" in the Antebellum South*. Oxford; New York: Oxford University Press, 2004.

Rahman, Fazlur. *Major Themes of the Quran*. 2nd ed. Chicago: University of Chicago Press, 2009.

Ridderbos, Herman N. *Paul: An Outline of His Theology*. Grand Rapids, MI: William B. Eerdmans, 1997.

Roberts, Alexander, et al., ed. *The Ante-Nicene Fathers: Translations of the Writings of the Fathers down to A.D. 325; Volume 2*. New York: Wipf & Stock, 2022.

Roberts, Alexander, et al. *Fathers of the Second Century: Hermas, Tatian, Athenagoras, Theophilus, and Clement of Alexandria*. Grand Rapids, MI: William B. Eerdmans, 1989.

Robinson, Cedric J. *Black Marxism: The Making of the Black Radical Tradition*. Chapel Hill; London: University of North Carolina Press, 2000.

Rondet, Henri. *Original Sin: The Patristic and Theological Background*. Germantown, TN: Saint Pauls/Alba House, 1972.

Rowley, Hazel. *Richard Wright: The Life and Times*. Chicago: University of Chicago Press, 2008.

Sanders, E. P. *Paul the Apostle's Life, Letters, and Thought*. Minneapolis: Augsburg Fortress, 2015.

Sartre, Jean-Paul. *Existentialism Is a Humanism*. 1946. Trans. Carol Macomber. New Haven, CT: Yale University Press, 2007.

Schaefer, James. *Advancing Mariology: The Theotokos Lectures 2008–2017*. Milwaukee, WI: Marquette University Press, 2017.

Schaff, Philip, ed. *Nicene and Post-Nicene Fathers of the Christian Church, First Series, Volume V: St. Augustine—Anti-Pelagian Writings*. Buffalo, NY: Christian Literature Publishing Co., 1887.

Schillebeeckx, Edward. *The Eucharist*. London; New York: Burns & Oates, 2005.

Schopenhauer, Arthur, et al. *The World as Will and Representation, Volume 2*. Cambridge; New York: Cambridge University Press, 2018.

Schweitzer, Albert. *The Mysticism of Paul the Apostle*. Baltimore, MD: Johns Hopkins University Press, 1998.

Smith, Dinitia. "Toni Morrison's Mix of Tragedy, Domesticity and Folklore." *The New York Times*, January 8, 1998. www.nytimes.com/1998/01/08/books/toni-morrison-s-mix-of-tragedy-domesticity-and-folklore.html.

Smith, Mark S. *Genesis of Good and Evil: The Fall(Out) and Original Sin in the Bible*. Louisville, KY: Westminster John Knox Press, 2019.

Stewart, Jon. *Volume 14: Kierkegaard's Influence on Social-Political Thought*. New York: Routledge, 2016.

Stewart, Tyler A. *The Origin and Persistence of Evil in Galatians*. Wissenschaftliche Untersuchungen zum Neuen Testament, 2. Reihe, vol. 566. Tübingen: Mohr Siebeck, 2022.

Steinem, Gloria. "Do You Know This Woman? She Knows You." *Ms.* (June 1982): 36+.
Tally, Justine. *Paradise Reconsidered.* Hamburg: Lit Verlag, 1999.
Tate, Claudia. *Black Women Writers at Work.* Chicago: Haymarket Books, 2023.
Teel, Karen. *Racism and the Image of God.* New York: Palgrave, 2010.
Thompson, Robert Farris. *Flash of the Spirit.* New York: Random House, 1983.
Thompson, Thomas L. *The Historicity of the Patriarchal Narratives: The Quest for the Historical Abraham.* New York and Berlin: De Gruyter, 1974.
Thurman, Howard. *With Head and Heart.* New York: Harcourt Brace, 1981.
Tillich, Paul. *The Courage to Be.* New Haven, CT: Yale University Press, 1952.
Tillich, Paul, and Carl E. Braaten. *A History of Christian Thought, from Its Judaic and Hellenistic Origins to Existentialism.* New York: Touchstone, 1972.
Toews, John E. *Romans: Believers Church Bible Commentary.* Scottsdale, PA: Herald Press, 2004.
Townes, Emilie M. *Womanist Ethics and the Cultural Production of Evil.* New York:, Palgrave Macmillan, 2007.
Turman, Eboni Marshall. "Womanist Theology and How It Has Evolved." *The Christian Century,* March 13, 2019. www.christiancentury.org/article/critical-essay/black-women-s-faith-black-women-s-flourishing.
Tuttle, Tara. *Biting Temptation: An Examination of the Eden Myth in the Southern Fiction of William Faulkner, Alice Walker, and Toni Morrison.* PhD diss., University of Louisville, 2008.
Walker, Alice. *Anything We Love Can Be Saved.* New York: Ballantine, 2012.
Walker, Margaret. *Richard Wright: Daemonic Genius.* New York: HarperCollins, 1988.
Walker, Sheila S. "Everyday and Esoteric Reality in the Afro-Brazilian Candomblé." *History of Religions* 30, no. 2 (November 1990): 103–128.
Ward, Jerry Washington, and Robert Butler. *The Richard Wright Encyclopedia.* Westport, CT: Greenwood Press, 2008.
Weber, Max. *The Protestant Ethic and the Spirit of Capitalism.* Trans. Talcott Parsons. Intro. Anthony Giddens. New York: Routledge, 2001.
Weinandy, Thomas. *The Theology of St. Cyril of Alexandria.* London: T&T Clark, 2003.

Weisenfeld, Judith. *New World A-Coming: Black Religion and Racial Identity During the Great Migration*. New York: New York University Press, 2019.

Wenham, David. *Paul: Follower of Jesus or Founder of Christianity?* Grand Rapids, MI: William B. Eerdmans, 1996.

Widmer, Kingsley, and Richard Wright. "The Existential Darkness: Richard Wright's 'The Outsider.'" *Wisconsin Studies in Contemporary Literature* 1, no. 3 (1960): 13.

Wiley, Tatha. *Original Sin: Origins, Developments, Contemporary Meanings*. New York: Paulist Press, 2002.

Williams, Delores. "The Color Purple." *Christianity and Crisis* 46, no. 10 (1986):, 230.

Williams, Norman Powell. *The Ideas of the Fall and of Original Sin*. New York: Longmans, Green, 1927.

Wood, Allen, and George Di Giovanni. *Kant: "Religion within the Boundaries of Mere Reason" And Other Writings*. Cambridge: Cambridge University Press, 1998.

Wright, N. T. *Paul*. New York: HarperCollins, 2018.

Wright, Richard. *Black Boy (American Hunger)*. New York: Harper Perennial, 1993.

———. *Black Power: Three Books from Exile: Black Power; The Color Curtain; and White Man, Listen!* New York: Harper Perennial Modern Classics, 2010.

———. *Conversations with Richard Wright*. Jackson: University Press of Mississippi, 1993.

———. *The Outsider*. New York: Harper Press, 1953.

Young, Josiah Ulysses. *James Baldwin's Understanding of God*. New York: Palgrave, 2014.

INDEX

Adam: Augustine of Hippo on, 81–90; *Giovanni's Room* (Baldwin) and, 28, 51–56, 61–62, 64–65, 71–72; Kierkegaard on, 132–40; *The Outsider* (Wright) and, 127–28, 131–32, 140–51, 155–64, 174–75; *Paradise* (Morrison) and, 101–7; Paul of Tarsus on, 34–43, 64–65; Yakub legend on, 210–11. *See also* Eden; Eve; serpent
Adell, Sandra, 150
Aesop's Fables, 3
Agamben, Giorgio, 16, 17
Alphabet of Ben Sira, 199
Amen Corner (Baldwin), 27–28
Angelou, Maya, 7
anxiety, 129, 132–40
Arendt, Hannah, 131
Aristotle, 218
Armour, Robert, 52
asceticism, 28, 29, 33, 50, 52, 71–72
Atrahasis, 19

Augustine of Hippo: on City of God, 75, 92–93; interpretation of Original Sin and Fall by, 13–14, 75–78, 80–90, 157; Kierkegaard and, 133–36, 137, 139; on Mary, 90–91; *Paradise* (Morrison) and, 6, 72–78, 92–93, 97, 120, 127; Paul of Tarsus and, 80–82, 84, 87–89; on serpent, 177; Wright and, 129, 156
Austen, Jane, 3
Autobiography of Malcolm X, The (X with Haley), 7

Badiou, Alain, 34
Bailey, Sue, 227n3
Baldwin, James: as apocalyptic writer, 63; Edenic impulse in, 5–7, 174–75, 214; on Paul of Tarsus, 13–14, 27; theological insight of, 27–28; Wright and, 164, 166. *See also Giovanni's Room* (Baldwin)

Barr, James, 23
Barrett, Lee C., 244n18
Barth, Karl, 42
Barton, John, 229n27
Beabout, Gregory R., 134
Beale, Gregory K., 17
Beauvoir, Simone de, 129, 162, 166
Beker, J. Christiaan, 63, 229n24
Beloved (Morrison), 120
black Atlantic religions, 74, 111–25
Black Boy (Wright), 3, 128, 129
Black Madonna, 123, 142–43
blues, 187–88
Bowens, Lisa M., 28
Boyd, Herb, 30
Brim, Matt, 54
"Brothers" (Clifton), 215–18
Brown, Raymond, 228n13, 228n15

Calvin, John, 67
Campbell, James, 63–64, 164
Camus, Albert, 129, 131, 140, 154, 159, 166
Candomblé, 116–20, 122–23
Cannon, Katie, 4
capitalism, 128, 160–64
Cappelørn, Niels Jorgen, 133
Carr, David, 17–18, 100, 103–4
Carrasco, David, 240n113
Catholicism: Kierkegaard and, 132–33; in *The Outsider* (Wright), 148–50; in *Paradise* (Morrison), 72, 75, 98–110, 114–15
Chireau, Yvonnne, 113
Christopher, Lindy M., 93, 124

City of God, The (Augustine of Hippo), 83–85
Clement of Alexandria, 78
Clement of Rome, 78
Clifton, Lucille, 215–18
Coleman, Monica, 196–98
Collins, John J., 23, 249n15
Color Purple, The (1985 film), 204, 210
Color Purple, The (Walker): Avery as Lilith in, 173–74, 200–201; Avery as serpent in, 6, 173–75, 178, 184–96; as black wisdom book, 7; Celie's letters and story in, 169–73; ecofeminism and, 174, 192–93, 198; *Giovanni's Room* (Baldwin) and, 171, 187, 194; grace in, 213–14; Nettie's letters and story in, 169–70, 171–72, 201–13; Olinka on serpent in, 211–13; *Paradise* (Morrison) and, 172, 173, 187, 203; process metaphysics and, 196–98; reviews of, 172–73
colorism, 75, 93–96
Concept of Anxiety, The (Kierkegaard), 6, 129, 132–40
Cone, James, 4
confession, 28, 29–34
Constantine I, 235n12
Copeland, M. Shawn, 104
Crawley, Ashon, 32
Cullen, Countee, 3
Cyril of Alexandria, 90–91, 120

Daly, Mary, 173
dancing, 122

Davis, Angela, 187
Davis, Jane, 153
Deluge, 19
Didache, 78
Douglass, Frederick, 7
drinking and drunkenness, 48, 50–51, 141–42
Du Bois, W. E. B., 7
Dudley, Marc, 33, 59

ecofeminism and eco-womanism, 174, 192–93, 198. See also Gebara, Ivone
Edelman, Lee, 52
Eden: Black American writers and, 5–7, 219–20; *Giovanni's Room* (Baldwin) and, 33, 48, 56–60; history and development of myth, 11–20, 23–25; *Paradise* (Morrison) and, 93–97; Paul of Tarsus on, 34–43. See also Adam; Augustine of Hippo; Eve; Fall; Original Sin; Paul of Tarsus; serpent
Edwards, Jonathan, 67
Ellis, Teresa, 24
Ellison, Ralph, 130, 164, 166
Emerson, Ralph Waldo, 51
Enuma Elish, 15–16, 19
Ephesus, Council of (431), 90–91, 120
Epic of Gilgamesh, 19, 20, 199
Epistle of James, 188
Epistle to the Romans, 34–36, 40–43, 89
Eve: Augustine of Hippo on, 84–85; Mary as corrective to, 79–80, 91, 108; *The Outsider* (Wright) and, 131–32, 151–56; *Paradise* (Morrison) and, 73–74, 77–78, 101–7, 120–21. See also Adam; Eden; serpent
evil, 72–73, 82–83
existentialism, 130–32, 164–66, 171. See also Kierkegaard, Søren; Nietzsche, Friedrich
Exodus, 7
Exodusters (Painter), 93
Ezekiel, 24

Fall: in *Giovanni's Room* (Baldwin), 48–51; history and development of Edenic myth and, 11–15; Paul of Tarsus on, 34–43. See also Original Sin
Fire Next Time, The (Baldwin), 7, 27–28
First Epistle to the Corinthians, 34–40, 41, 61–62
First Epistle to Timothy, 35
First Isaiah, 199
Foucault, Michel, 29–30, 230n51
Frankenstein (Shelley), 3
Fredriksen, Paula, 38
freedom: Kierkegaard on, 134, 137–39; in *The Outsider* (Wright), 128, 141, 145, 147, 158–61, 166–68
Freud, Sigmund, 152
Furman, Jan, 105

Garvey, Marcus, 206
Gauthier, Marni, 93

Gebara, Ivone, 6, 98–99, 174, 177–84, 190, 192
Genesis: "Brothers" (Clifton) and, 216–18; drunkenness in, 48, 50; as tragedy, 218–19. *See also* Eden
Gibson, Ernest L., III, 53
Giovanni's Room (Baldwin): as apocalyptic warning, 28, 43–48, 63, 68–69; asceticism in, 28, 29, 33, 50, 52, 71–72; *The Color Purple* (Walker) and, 171, 187, 194; confession in, 28, 29–34; David as "American Adam" in, 28, 51–56, 61–62, 64–65, 71–72; Fall in, 48–51; *Paradise* (Morrison) and, 71–74, 157; Paul's teaching and, 6, 28–29, 33–34, 44–48, 56, 61–69, 127; room as Eden in, 33, 48, 56–60; serpent in, 43–44
Go Tell It on the Mountain (Baldwin), 27–28, 31
"God of Justice? A" (Griffin), 5
God's Trombone (Johnson), 7–8
Gordon, Jane Anna, 167
Gordon, Lewis, 141
grace, 213–14
Grant, Jacquelyn, 4
Great Migration, 206
Greek Apocalypse of Ezra, 22
Green, Tara T., 128, 246n53
Griffin, Farah Jasmine, 5, 7

Halberstam, Jack, 28, 52
Haley, Alex, 7
Hanson, Erik M., 132–33

Harding, Rachel E., 117, 121
Hardy, Clarence E., III, 49–50, 65
Hare, John, 4
Harris, Trudier, 173
Hartman, Saidiya, 73
Heidegger, Martin, 129, 131, 138, 162, 163, 166
"Here Be Dragons" (Baldwin), 45, 52
Herskovitz, Melville J., 118
Hobson, Christopher V., 57, 62–63, 64
Hoodoo, 74, 113
Hughes, Langton, 3
Hurston, Zora Neale, 1–3, 4, 102
Husserl, Edmund, 166

Invisible Man (Ellison), 164
Irenaeus, 77, 80, 249n12
Is God a White Racist? (Jones), 144, 191

James, C. L. R., 130
James, Henry, 51
Jaspers, Karl, 166
Johnson, James Weldon, 7–8
Jones, Trina, 95
Jones, William R., 144, 162–63, 191
Jubilees, 24, 25
June, Pamela B., 174
Justin Martyr, 78, 79

Kant, Immanuel, 4
Karfíková, Lenka, 87

Kierkegaard, Søren: on anxiety and sin, 129, 132–40, 157; Wright and, 6, 128–32, 143, 147, 162–63, 166
Kramer, Samuel N., 199

Lawson, Lewis, 146–47
Leeming, David, 54, 56–57, 64, 232n93
Legarreta-Castillo, Felipe de Jesús, 35–36
Lewis, R. W. B., 51
liberation theologies, 5–7, 108, 162–63, 180–84
Lilith, 173–74, 198–201
Literal Meaning of Genesis, The (Augustine of Hippo), 83
Lonely Letters, The (Crawley), 32
Long, Charles H., 74
Lucifer, 215–18
Luther, Martin, 67
Lutheranism, 132–33

Mackendrick, Karmen, 192
magical realism, 74
Man Who Lived Underground (Wright), 128
Manichaeism, 81–82
Mann, William E., 85–86
Marouan, Maha, 103, 123
Martin, Dale B., 36–37
Marxism, 160
Mary: Augustine of Hippo on, 90–91; black Atlantic religions and, 123; as corrective to Eve, 79–80, 91, 108; *Paradise* (Morrison) and, 77–78, 120–21

massa damnata theory, 86
Masuzawa, Tomoko, 121–22
Matory, J. Lorand, 234n7
Mays, Benjamin, 4–5
McFague, Sallie, 197
Meeks, Wayne A., 40
Melville, Herman, 51
metaphysics, 196–98
Meyers, Carol, 18
Michelangelo, 200
Milton, John, 218
Mootry, Maria, 246n53
Morrison, Toni: Edenic impulse in, 5–7, 214. See also *Paradise* (Morrison); impact of, 3
Mullen, Bill V., 55, 56, 59
Muñoz, Jose, 59

Narrative of the Life of Frederick Douglass (Douglass), 7
Nation of Islam, 210–11
Native Son (Wright), 128, 129, 141, 163
Negro's God, The (Mays), 4–5
Neoplatonism, 81, 83–84
Nestorius of Constantinople, 90–91, 120
New Jerusalem, 62–63
New Testament, 12, 14–15
Newman, Dorothy, 131
Nicodemus, 145
Niebuhr, Reinhold, 76, 157–58
Niederbacher, Bruno, 84
Nietzsche, Friedrich, 26, 129, 130–32, 158–59, 162, 163, 166
Nittle, Nadra, 74, 114, 122, 125

Noah's Ark, 14–15, 20
Not Without Laughter (Hughes), 3
Notes of a Native Son (Baldwin), 27–28

On Genesis Against the Manichaeans (Augustine of Hippo), 83
On Nature (Pelagius), 86
On the Literal Interpretation of Genesis (Augustine of Hippo), 83
"Open Letter to the Born Again, An" (Baldwin), 66
Original Sin: Augustine of Hippo on, 75–78, 80–90; early theologians on, 78–79; history and development of Edenic myth and, 11–15; Kierkegaard on, 132–40; *Paradise* (Morrison) and, 72–78, 120–25, 174–75; Paul of Tarsus on, 34–43, 75–76, 78, 80–81. *See also* Fall
Orthodox Church, 233–34n5
Outsider, The (Wright): capitalism and, 128, 160–64; Cross as Adam in, 127–28, 131–32, 140–51, 155–64, 174–75; Eva as Eve in, 131–32, 151–56; freedom in, 128, 141, 145, 147, 158–61, 166–68; impact of, 4

Pagels, Elaine, 80
Painter, Nell Irvin, 93
Pandora, 24
Paradise, 16–17. *See also* Eden
Paradise (Morrison): aftermath of Original Sin and, 72–78, 120–25, 174–75; Augustine of Hippo and, 6, 72–78, 92–93, 97, 120, 127; black Atlantic religions in, 74, 111–25; Black Madonna in, 123, 142; Catholicism in, 72, 75, 98–110, 114–15; *The Color Purple* (Walker) and, 172, 173, 187, 203; ecofeminism and, 198; *Giovanni's Room* (Baldwin) and, 71–74, 157; Haven as Garden of Eden in, 93–97; process metaphysics and, 196; Ruby as City of God in, 75, 93–95, 97–98
Pattison, George, 138
Paul of Tarsus: African American hermeneutic and, 28–29; Augustine of Hippo and, 80–82, 84; Augustine of Hippo on, 87–89; Baldwin on, 13–14, 27; *Giovanni's Room* (Baldwin) and, 6, 28–29, 33–34, 44–48, 56, 61–69, 127; interpretation of Garden of Eden, Original Sin, and Fall by, 12–14, 25, 34–43, 75–76, 78, 80–81, 157; Kierkegaard and, 133–34, 136; *Paradise* (Morrison) and, 120; on "Second Adam," 161; on serpent, 177; Wright and, 129
Paulsell, Stephanie, 240n113
Pelagius, 82, 86–89, 93–94, 135
Pentateuch, 12, 14–15, 94
Perez, Elizabeth, 121–22
"Phenomenal Woman" (Angelou), 7
Pinn, Anthony, 4
Plato, 4

process metaphysics, 196–98
Pseudepigrapha, 12

Queer Art of Failure, The
(Halberstam), 28, 52
queer utopia, 59
"Question of Identity, A"
(Baldwin), 31

Raboteau, Albert J., 113
religio-racial self-making, 206
resurrection, 37–40, 42
Ridderbos, Herman, 39
Robinson, Cedric, 159
Rogers, J. A., 206
Rondet, Henri, 78
Rowley, Hazel, 164, 243n7
Russell, Leon, 4

Sartre, Jean-Paul, 129, 138, 148–49, 162, 166, 242n5
Satanail, 22
Sawyer, John F.A., 175, 178
Schweitzer, Albert, 42
Scott, Nathan A., 4
Second Book of Enoch, 22
Second Epistle to the Corinthians, 34–40
Second Temple Judaism, 14–15, 19, 24
serpent: *The Color Purple* (Walker) and, 6, 173–75, 178, 184–96, 211–13; Eve and, 79–80; Gebara on, 177–84; *Giovanni's Room* (Baldwin) and, 43–44; Jewish and Christian interpretations of, 18–19, 175–78

Shakespeare, William, 3
Shelby, Tommie, 147, 156, 162, 165, 242–43n5
Shelley, Mary, 3
Sickness Unto Death (Kierkegaard), 136–37, 157
Sirach, 24–25
slavery, 29, 129
Smith, Mark S., 22–23
Souls of Black Folk, The (Du Bois), 7
Spielberg, Steven, 204, 210
Steinem, Gloria, 172–73
Steiner, George, 218–19
Stewart, Tyler A., 228n16
"Still I Rise" (Angelou), 7
Stranger, The (Camus), 140, 154, 159
Sula (Morrison), 121

Tate, Claudia, 245n38, 246n53
Tatian, 78
Tertullian, 29
Teselle, Eugene, 86
Testaments of the Twelve Patriarchs, The, 23
Their Eyes Were Watching God (Hurston), 1–3, 4
Theodosius II, 90–91
Theophilus of Antioch, 78, 79
Thompson, Robert Farris, 234n7
Thurman, Howard, 227n3
Tillich, Paul, 4, 131, 243n9
Toews, John E., 39–40, 229n24
Townes, Emilie, 190
tragedy, 218–19
Tree of Life, 16–19
Trotter, Christine, 227n20

Truth, Sojourner, 169
Tuttle, Tara, 195

Übermensch, 130, 159
Uncle Tom's Children (Wright), 129

Veninga, Jennifer Elisa, 146

Walker, Alice: Edenic impulse in, 5–7. See also *Color Purple, The* (Walker); impact of, 3
Walker, Margaret, 140, 164, 166, 246n53
Walker, Sheila S., 117
Watchers, 13, 14–15, 20–23, 25, 34–35, 216–18, 228n16
waywardness, 73–74, 91
Weber, Max, 188
Weisenfield, Judith, 206
Wenham, David, 229–30n33
Wheatley, Phillis, 218
White Man, Listen! (Wright), 149
Whitehead, Alfred North, 197
Whitman, Walt, 51

Wiley, Tatha, 39
Williams, Delores, 173
Williams, N. P., 20–22, 35, 80
Williard, Mara, 240n113
Wilson, Sharon, 248n2
Wisdom of Solomon, 39
Wright, Ellen, 164
Wright, N. T., 40–41
Wright, Richard: disregard for religion and, 128–29, 214; Edenic impulse in, 5–7. See also *Outsider, The* (Wright); existentialism and, 130–32, 164–66, 171. *See also* Kierkegaard, Søren; Nietzsche, Friedrich; impact of, 3; on "outsiders," 72
Wynter, Sylvia, 214

X, Malcolm, 7

Yakub, 210–11
"Yet Do I Marvel" (Cullen), 3
Young, Frances, 91
Young, Josiah Ulysses, III, 61

GPSR Authorized Representative: Easy Access System Europe, Mustamäe tee 50, 10621 Tallinn, Estonia, gpsr.requests@easproject.com

www.ingramcontent.com/pod-product-compliance
Lightning Source LLC
Chambersburg PA
CBHW031236290426
44109CB00012B/320